Curmudgeing Through Paradise

Curmudgeing Through Paradise

✦

Reports from a Fractal Dung Beetle

Fred Reed

iUniverse, Inc.
New York Lincoln Shanghai

Curmudgeing Through Paradise
Reports from a Fractal Dung Beetle

iUniverse books may be ordered through booksellers or by contacting:

iUniverse
2021 Pine Lake Road, Suite 100
Lincoln, NE 68512
www.iuniverse.com
1-800-Authors (1-800-288-4677)

Because of the dynamic nature of the Internet, any Web addresses or links contained in this book may have changed since publication and may no longer be valid.

The views expressed in this work are solely those of the author and do not necessarily reflect the views of the publisher, and the publisher hereby disclaims any responsibility for them.

ISBN: 978-0-595-44374-1 (pbk)
ISBN: 978-0-595-88703-3 (ebk)

Printed in the United States of America

Contents

Forward

America has gone forever like ten-cent comic books and twenty-seven-cent gas. We're all going to be turned into numbered federal robots, and go around clicking like forlorn witless castanets with no fingers in them. I'm going to explain it all to you. That's why this book. It's more fun having leprosy if you understand why your body parts are falling off.

First, you need to know about Wunxputl. Maybe you didn't know that you needed to know about him. Well, you do. Anyway, you bought the book, so you're stuck with it. Actions have consequences.

Wunxputl was a member of the Tloxyproctl, a tribe of three pre-literate dwarf Indians in breechclouts who lived in hollow logs in the Amazon rain forest. They worshipped the Great Dung Beetle, who ruled the universe. His subordinate lesser dung beetles tirelessly pushed the planets in their orbits with their hind legs, while standing on their heads. That's what dung beetles do. Watch one.

Catholics used to figure that angels pushed the planets. Physicists think it's gravity. No. Great invisible dung beetles. In the rain forest, the Tloxyproctyls noticed, unfortunate smaller beetles did the same thing, only they pushed balls of anteater dung.

Wunxputl, captured by the Anthropology Department at Swarthmore, explained the Tloxyproctyl conception of the universe, which was that all living creatures pushed balls of dung. Many months were needed to comprehend this, since the Tloxyproctyls spoke a language consisting of only three words, none of which meant anything. They were not a complicated people.

Anyway, as they understood life, it was like fractals: At whatever level you looked, everything alive pushed dung. The Great Dung Beetle at the top, the lesser ones pushing the planets, little tiny ones on the ground following anteaters around and, in between, people who work in cubicles. Ask anybody who labors in an office. Dung. Just because you can't see it doesn't mean you're not pushing it.

Pardon me. A certain incoherency may disrupt these otherwise luminous thoughts. I am sitting on my rooftop in Jocotepec, near Guadalajara in Mexico, and comforting myself with a large bottle of Padre Kino red. Theological contemplation requires lubrication, especially when it involves dung beetles. Anyway, no one in his right mind wants to confront existence while sober.

Good stuff, Padre Kino. Seven cents a trainload. And coherency is overrated. Nothing I've ever done while sober or coherent has seemed a good idea in retrospect.

Now, not all anthropologists were quick to see the brilliance of the Tloxyproctyls. The elegant simplicity of their ideas did not appeal to the academic mind, which values complexity over understanding. Professors were more taken with gaudier savages like, say, the Mayas, who built enormous pyramids of stone, so precisely aligned that, come the summer solstice, a single ray of light shone through a certain hole and struck the left eye of the stone god Chac Mool. The absurdity of a calendar weighing four hundred thousand tons and only working for one day a year never struck the professoriate. You would have to build 365 of the damned things to know what day it was. The Tloxyproctyls didn't care what day it was. It made much more sense.

This actually does have something to do with America. Patience.

Now, the Tloxyproctyls may have had the details wrong, but they got the principle right. If you don't think we live in a world of dung, or at least that we are turning into one, look around. Especially, consider politics.

For a long time conservatives said Russia was the Dark Power, the Evil Empire. And it was, too. Uncle Joe Stalin was nobody's apple strudel. He murdered people with secret poison needles and watched everybody like he was really interested in them and stuffed people into prisons and nobody ever saw them again. Not good. Life in Russia wasn't like Saturday night in Murfreesboro, riding around the Dairy Queen in a chopped '57 Bel Air. If there is a Dairy Queen in Murfreesboro.

OK, today the only communists left are in North Korea and the Harvard faculty lounge. But … nothing much has really changed. We're doing the same thing to ourselves. Only we're going to be much better at it. Commie oppression with American efficiency. Oh God.

We used to think the problem was Marxism—all those rotten lefties, parlor pinks, the GPU, Alger Hiss (or, as we would say today, Hiss or Hearse) and the ice ax in Trotsky's head. No. The problem is greedy, pugnacious, unprincipled bastards. They're everywhere, like balls of dung. (See? It really does work.) They just call themselves commies or capitalists when it's convenient. Same people, though.

Sometimes they wave red flags and sing the Internationale and rant about the Dictatorship of the Proletariat, which the proletariat never gets. In America they wave the Stars and Stripes and holler about Democracy, which is just the dicta-torship of the proletariat by another name.

I tell you, we're back in the USSR. Might as well do it in the road. Except there's too damned much traffic.

I'm going to open another bottle of the good Padre. Somebody's got to drink this stuff. What, you want Mexico to sink under the weight of a build-up of cheap red wine, maybe throw off the gravitic balance of the earth, and cause plan-etary break-up? How smart is that? I'm saving the earth.

So America, which used to be the Boy Scout country, trustworthy, loyal, help-ful, friendly, courteous, kind, obedient, cheerful, thrifty, brave, clean, and rever-ent, now runs torture chambers just like some medieval bonehead with a horse and a pointy stick. You can't get on an airplane anymore without a public pros-tate exam by some lame-brained otherwise-unemployable second-rate Mussolini.

There is some wild shit going on, boys and girls. It's the fall of the Roman Umpire in fast-forward. Dung turns out to be a renewable resource, like Prometheus and his liver. You can't get rid of it. Push on.

There's worse. We can't fight the oncoming twilight because we've got the skitters, like after smoking dope with Paraquat on it. We've gone flat terrified of nearly about everything. We've been completely enstupidated, milquetoasted, and fearified. It isn't natural.

I mean, we get the screaming gollywoggles over second-hand smoke, for God's sake, and fill in the deep ends of swimming pools because we might drown, and take out the diving boards so we don't land on top of each other and get concus-sions. The Feddle Gummint has cameras everywhere like seven-year-olds looking under the bed for boogeymen. You gotta have a helmet to ride a freaking bicycle and probably air bags soon and a full roll-cage and Nomex suit. Wait.

This is America? Not like I knew it. Different place, same name. All this, to make the world safe for dung beetles. Us.

It's nuts. Every day on the radio you can hear a bunch of gals saying how you should always wear sun screen and not go outside between noon and four in the afternoon. See, you might get melanoma. But it's like telling Daniel Boone he can't go in the woods because he might get attacked by a rabid squirrel. Besides, he might *want* melanoma. Whose business is it? What kind of country is it when you can't decide to have melanoma?

What I figure is, we're all going to croak anyway, so we might as well not worry too much about it. Yes, I know. I'm so life-denying and self-hating or something that I'll swim in the deep end of a pool. Without a Coast-Guard

Approved flotation device, three life guards, a mobile shock-trauma unit and a certificate saying I used sunscreen. I've always had suicidal tendencies.

Fact is, I'd rather fall on my head off a bicycle than waddle around in governmental diapers all my life. (Three FBI goons will probably show up tonight, like armed Mormon missionaries, with diapers.) Anyway, it's a demographic fact that under half of eleven-year-olds who go out in the sun die of melanoma. The rest drown in the deep end. Check it out. And I don't want some lugubrious federal goober telling me I have to wear a helmet on a Harley like my head was a national treasure or something.

Anyway, like I say, this America thing is over. Done with. You might as well try to resuscitate a slide rule. There's no way we're going to avoid being safened to death. And made into politically correct automated tinkertoys. All the indicators are downward. Pretty clearly some death slug, maybe from the rain forest too, has moved into the current president's skull, which must be tight quarters. The Supreme Court is a mausoleum of octogenarians, dead but still twitching, for whom Alzheimer's would be like a remembrance of sweet sixteen. It would raise their IQ. Congress belongs to whoever pays it the most, like a Mexican sheriff but without the sense of social responsibility.

What makes it almost sure that we're going to turn into regimented hive-creatures, is that technology makes enhivement, or maybe enhivening, too easy. Almost inevitable. Think about it. It used to take work to spy on people. Now it doesn't. Cameras can read all the license numbers of passing cars. Those unpleasantly wholesome FBI agents can automatically read your email. Data bases watch us like voyeurs who have discovered a new bedroom window. It's to protect us. We need to be protected. No way we're going to stop it. Once the brain rots, it stays rotted. Or a society.

I wish the world would stop wobbling. Probably some kind of orbital problem.

Problem is, when the Foundering Fathers wrote the Constitution, they didn't take self-inflicted cerebral putrefaction into account. How could they? With the Romans, it was bread and circuses. With us, it's five hundred channels on the lobotomy box and eyes sutured to the blinking screen, porn on the net, reality TV, home theater with movies boring enough to emulsify an aquatic snail, and an SUV that would call the police if it ever saw a dirt road. If religion used to be the opiate of molasses, then Oprah is the Karo syrup of the masses. Brown and cloying. This is really good wine.

I dunno. Most likely, in a few years we'll all have chips planted in our brains and a little antenna sticking up, like those pointy spear things the Germans had on their helmets in World War I so they could head-butt the French. (No wonder they lost. They couldn't see where they were going.) I'm going to sacrifice to the Great Dung Beetle, and then get drunk. Push on, my friends, push on.

1

Death of an Alpha-Curmudgeon

When Hunter Thompson blew his brains out, a door closed somewhere and you could hear the latch click. The main man had gone. Most of us can easily be replaced. There was only one Hunter Thompson. I'll heist one tonight to a fine, fine writer, a voice of his time, the embodiment of an age the like of which there never was and which, for good or bad, will never come again.

The Sixties look drab now—unkempt Manson girls, the lost and unhappy, kids bleak and bleary-brained after waking up with too many strangers in too many sour crash pads. There was that. It was not a time for the weak-minded. But for those whose youth passed in the freak years, there was something gaudy and silly and even profound, something delightfully warped, that nobody else would ever have. Thompson caught it.

I didn't know him. Others have written better than I can of his work. But I knew the world that gave rise to him.

Starting around 1964, a restlessness came over the land, an itch. Kids trickled and later flooded onto the highways as if called by something. I can't explain it. Few had done it before. Few do it now. They—we—set forth and created the only country in which Thompson could have made sense.

It wasn't the war, at first. Nor was it only the usual impatience of youth with authority. Nor was it even that we were young and the world was wide. There was a revulsion against suburban emptiness, against the eight-to-five Ozzie and Harriet gig, a rejection of the Establishment, which meant boring jobs and sing-ing commercials.

We discovered drugs, then regarded as worse than virgin sacrifices to Moloch, and looked through a window we could never name. If the times were out of joint, we were seldom out of joints. Chemistry defined the life. You found a freak in some rotting slum and said, "Hey, man, got some shit?" You toked up. You got the munchies, the skitters, the fears. Parents really didn't understand. Dope, we said, will get you through times of no money better than money will get you through times of no dope. It did.

Thompson, a savage writer, a grand middle finger raised against the sky, essayed drugs and found them good. And said so, and we loved him. When he wrote of getting wacked out of his mind on seven illicit pharmaceuticals, and wandering in puzzled paranoia through the lobby of existence, we shrieked with laughter. We knew the same drugs. We too had tried desperately to look straight in public when the world had turned into a slow-motion movie. When it was over, everybody went into a law firm.

Our socio-political understanding was limited. After all, we were pretty much kids. I remember having a discussion in Riverside, California, of how Republicans reproduced. We didn't think it could be by sex. I figured it was by budding.

For a while though, it all worked. Apostles of the long-haul thumb, we hitchhiked in altered mental states. I don't recommend it without guidance. We stood by the western highways as the big rigs roared by, rocking in the wash and the keening of the tires, desert stretching off to clot-red hills in the distance. At night we might buy bottles of Triple Jack at some isolated gas station and dip into an arroyo, roll a fat one and swill Jack and talk and hallucinate under the stars. An insight of the times was that if you got fifty feet off the beaten track and sat down, you didn't exist. It still works if you need it.

None of it was reasonable. I've never found anything worthwhile that was.

Then there was politics, the war. Thompson was rocket smart and knew you couldn't work within the system since that meant granting it legitimacy. Peace with Honor, the Light at the End of the Tunnel, all the ashen columnists arguing about timed withdrawal and incremental pressure. He knew it was about profits for McDonnell Douglas and egotistical warts growing like malignant goiters on the neck of the country. He was Johnny Pot Seed, a Windowpane Ghandi, dangerous as Twain.

The times brought their epiphanies. I remember being gezonked on mescaline in a pad in Stafford, Virginia, and realizing that existence was the point of execution in a giant Fortran program. So it's all done in software, I thought. I was floating in the universe. In the infinite darkness of space the code stretched above and below in IBM blue letters hundreds of feet high that converged to nothingness: $N = N * 5$, Go To 43, ITEST = $4**IEXP$. For an hour I was awash in understanding. The stereo was playing Bolero, which was written by a Do-loop, so it all fitted.

Thompson savaged it all, lampooned it, creating a world of consciousness-sculpting substances and bad-ass motorcycles and absolute cynicism about the government. Today, after thirty years of journalism, I can't find the flaw in his reasoning.

The other writer of the age was Tom Wolfe, but he wasn't in Thompson's league. Wolfe was a talented outsider looking perceptively at someone else's trip. Thompson lived the life, liked big-bore handguns and big-bore bikes and had a liver analysis that read like a Merck catalog. His paranoia may be style, but you can't write what you aren't almost.

I remember standing alone in early afternoon beside some two-lane desert road in New Mexico, or somewhere else, that undulated off through rolling hills and had absolutely no traffic. I don't know that I was on anything. Of course, I don't know that I wasn't. A murky sun hung in an aluminum sky like a fried egg waiting to fall and mesquite bushes pocked the dry sand with blue mortar bursts. The silence was infinite. I lay in the middle of the road for a while just because I could. Then I followed a line of ants into the desert to see where they were going.

A grey Buick Riviera, a wheeled barge lost in the desert, slid to a stop. The trunk creaked open like a jaw. A squatty little mushroomy woman behind the wheel motioned me to get it. As we drove the cruise alarm buzzed, and she told me it was Communist radar. They were watching her from the hills.

It was a Thompson moment.

Then it was over. Everybody went into I-banking or something equally odious. We gave up drugs as boring.

You can see why he ate his gun. Everything he hated has returned. Nixon is back in the White House, Rumsnamara risen from the dead, and bombs are falling on other peoples' suburbs. The Pentagon is lying again and democracy stalks yet another helpless country. This time the young are already dead and there will be no joyous anarchy. The press, housebroken, pees where it is told. But he gave it a hell of a try.

2

Watching Maureen Dowd

It is becoming a constant, like gravity: Maureen Dowd opens her mouth, and I get email from guys saying, "Fred! Geez, man, how much do apartments go for in Guadalajara?"

Maureen is the resentment columnist for the *New York Times*. She serves as newsprint megaphone for the angry, selfish, wretchedly unhappy career woman who can't understand why she is living alone in an apartment with two cats. (I understand the alone part. I question the judgement of the cats.)

Maybe I can explain.

In a recent column, headed "Men Just Want Mommy," Maureen tells us, "A few years ago at a White House Correspondents' dinner, I met a very beautiful actress. Within moments, she blurted out: 'I can't believe I'm 46 and not married. Men only want to marry their personal assistants or P.R. women.'"

The bastards.

Here we have the eternal cry (at least it is beginning to feel eternal) of the unhappy feminist: "The whole world can't stand me. What's wrong with the whole world?" If men don't want to marry a self-absorbed menopausing ocelot, there is something wrong with men. I listen to this stuff and I want to marry someone's personal assistant, just to be sure I don't get drunk and marry a very beautiful actress.

But more of Maureen and the personal assistants. She continues observantly, "I'd been noticing a trend along these lines, as famous and powerful men took up with the young women whose job it was to tend to them and care for them in some way: their secretaries, assistants, nannies, caterers, flight attendants, researchers and fact-checkers." Men want to marry Mommy, she implies, with forty-weight passive-aggressiveness you could lube a diesel with.

Actually, what men very much do not want is to marry Mommy. The problem for Maureen is that she *is* Mommy: censorious, moralizing, self-pitying, endlessly instructive, and so achingly tedious that men find themselves thinking with longing of moldy bath sponges. I have never seen her and don't know how old she is. She may be twenty-three, radiantly gorgeous, and have seven husbands. She writes as if she were fifty, a tad overweight and, having grossly overestimated her value in the meat market, managed to miss the train. (I have a federal license to mix metaphors like that.) Since nothing can be her fault, that leaves men.

Now, why might a man want to date his secretary instead of some virile pit-viperess of a lawyer, forever coiled to strike? To start with, twenty-five is more appealing than fifty. Sorry, but there it is. Second, secretaries usually lack the misandry, vanity, and abrasiveness of the viperess. (Think Alan Dershowitz in drag, but hostile.) Which leads to, Third, the secretary is likely to be lots more fun. You don't have to spend time comparing penises with her. She won't always be looking for discrimination, like a chicken clucking after bugs in a barnyard. You won't get the throwaway snotty remarks about men.

I can't imagine doing a fast double-step jitterbug in a dirt bar in Austin with a warlike partner from Dewey, Cheatham, and Howe—you know, Little Richard shrieking *Long Tall Sally*, skirts flying in the twirls. A secretary is likely to think it is a hell of a good idea.

Maureen pretty much answers the question of why these creatures stay single. In another column she says, "When I asked a 28-year-old friend how he and his lawyer-girlfriend were going to divide the costs on a California vacation, he looked askance. 'She never offers,' he replied. 'And I like paying for her.'"

Maureen knows lots of these. "Carrie, a publicist in her late 20's from Long Island, is not unwilling to dig into her Kate Spade bag. 'He can get the jewelry, the dinners, the shoes and the vacations,' she says. 'I'll get the cab.'"

Who would marry *that*? Carrie is a parasite, like a screw-fly larva. You could find better leaning against a lamppost. Honest prostitution is preferable to dissimulated. (Incidentally, Stanford did a genetic study in which they found that a New York career woman shares ninety-five percent of her genes with the common tape worm. The remaining five percent, speculated the scientists, explains why tapeworms, though parasitic, are not uncivil.)

Maureen's women are forever nattering about sexual equality. Maureen, speaking of some movie: "Art is imitating life, turning women who seek equality into selfish narcissists and objects of rejection, rather than affection." Actually art isn't doing anything. A woman who wants a man to pay her bills is already a selfish narcissist.

I find myself wondering what parallel universe Maureen inhabits, and how she found the door. In fairness to at least some career women, maybe most of them, I dated mostly such for a decade or two in Washington, and expected them as a matter of course to split the bill. They did. It didn't seem to bother them. And—surprise—I thought of them as equals. They acted that way.

So little of what Maureen says tracks with the world I know. She thinks men don't like smart women. I know a lot of bright guys, and they all look for bright women. They just want agreeable bright women.

Further—am I alone in this?—I don't think of women I date in terms of superiority and inferiority. Sally is my date, not my competitor. Does it run through Maureen's tiny little mind that I walk along with a secretary thinking, "*Hah! Mere secretary. My inferior. Hah!*"? Actually I think, "How'd I get so lucky? Hope she doesn't think of that."

This erosion of the pecking order by mating explains why the military doesn't want officers to date enlisted women: A cute corporal is on equal terms with an admiral by virtue of going out with him. Hierarchy doesn't survive romance. But, as Maureen's status-obsessed women discover, neither does romance survive a relentless concern with hierarchy.

Thing is, the times have changed. The age-old bargain was that women exchanged sex for whatever they wanted, and men exchanged whatever they had for sex. Part of the deal was that the woman would be reasonably agreeable. A career woman today, being independent, no longer has to be agreeable, and frequently isn't. On the other hand, a man doesn't have to commit himself to anything to get sex. So the man dates his secretary, and the career woman sits in her apartment with the cats. Good.

Me, I'm going to move to Mexico. (Though come to think of it, I already have.)

3

Sour Thoughts on Slavery

In judging slavery in the United States, which we are frequently asked to do, it is useful to ask what one would oneself do if in the situation of the slave. The question brings clarity. A wide gulf lies between tolerating the wrongs inflicted on others, and suffering them oneself. We all bear up well under the misfortunes of others.

My attitude toward slavery is about as simple as things get.

If anyone tried to enslave me, or my family, I would kill him if I could. If he endeavored to make me work by wielding a whip, I would kill him. If I fled and men tracked me with dogs, I would kill them. Just put a rifle in my hands. If anyone chose to whip my children or use my daughter as a sexual toy, I would kill him. I am not given to sadistic fantasies, but in this case I would make a large exception. And if a pleasant and well-dressed family responsible for all of this lived in a nice house on a hill, I would burn it with them in it.

Some things no one should be required to endure. Slavery is one of them. Others are assault with a deadly weapon, rape, sequestration of one's children, and criminal intrusion into one's home. All of these justify killing as a remedy. A slave, again as I see things, has an inalienable right to do anything necessary to effect his escape. Whether he is enslaved in the work camps of a Stalin or a Hitler, by the Spanish conquistadors or by a cotton farmer in Mississippi, matters not at all. The right of self-defense applies absolutely, think I.

Now, you may ask, does that mean that if I had been a slave I would have killed Thomas Jefferson and George Washington? Yes. A nice prose style and enlightened ideas about other things do not justify slavery. Nothing does. Not, at any rate, if I am the slave.

If this seems excessive, ask: Would you, today, allow yourself to be made the chattel of a latter-day Jefferson, or of anyone else? Your children? Then why might you expect anyone else to view things differently?

The foregoing conveys how I would view things if I were the slave. Suppose that instead I had been born into a rich family in the countryside near Charlottesville, Virginia, in the eighteenth century. We would of course have had slaves. Slavery would have seemed natural to me, as it would have been part of the only world I had known. My childhood would have passed under the tutelage of a mammy, of whom I would have been fond.

The acceptance of accustomed evil is remarkably easy. England's poor children during the Industrial Revolution suffered horrible mistreatment, as did those of Northern sweatshops in America. Slavery has various forms. These abuses were deplored by some, excused by others, but continued because they brought advantages to those who ruled. The better classes seldom see the evils by which they live. They avert their eyes by one means or another.

Confusingly, many who owned slaves were not bad people. As the child of slave-owners in the rolling countryside of central Virginia, I might have known my mother to be kindly, my father to be a good-hearted man of principle who believed in fairness, the neighbors to be upright and civic-minded. The mind being the strange contrivance that it is, men of noble inclination can found a nation on freedom while having their farms worked by slaves. There was nothing unusual here. Hypocrisy is the natural condition of man. Today Christians insisting that God is Love bomb Moslem children. Praise Jesus.

Having come to adulthood in the circumstances of Charlottesville, what would I have then done, or thought, about slavery? I might have equivocated and had qualms, as many did. I might have had my slaves freed upon my death, as many did. This of course would have amounted to saying that slavery was a great evil, but not as great as my having to do my own work. It is the exact moral equivalent of buying goods made by sweated labor abroad while making indignant noises. (Where were your shoes made?)

A virtue of outrage is that it requires little effort. Today, the country's black children rot in wretched schools. This offends virtuous whites, who nonetheless do nothing about it. Neither do the children's parents. If indignation were petroleum, Saudi Arabia would by comparison be a minor supplier. Few, however, will suffer inconvenience to end evils they do not actually see. Ah, but we talk a good show.

A great many Southerners regarded slavery with distaste, as a moral sore, Lee and Mosby among them. I might also have. Would I have given up the wealth and comfort of my plantation, suffered the opprobrium of all around me, and cast myself adrift in life from objection to slavery? Probably not. Instead I would have treated my slaves humanely, talked of the need to find some way of eventually ending the region's peculiar institution, and enjoyed the benefits of compulsory servitude while doing nothing about it. In today's terms, I would have been a liberal.

What would you actually have done? The world is rife with evils today. What are you doing about them? Me either. At bottom, most of us are nothing but talk.

For Southern whites, the practice of slavery could have been more easily avoided than ended. It is one thing to say, "Better that I hadn't done it." Having done it, the question becomes, "How do I stop doing it?" If you are a family of ten whites on a plantation of two hundred slaves, you might well fear freeing them. The blacks of the day were ignorant beyond mere illiteracy, brutal from having been raised as brutes, and just might have turned vengeful if given the chance. People who have been whipped tend to reach for whips. In their place, would you have risked it?

Should any white reader object to my describing the blacks of the day as degraded and dangerous, I invite him to walk across, say, South Central Los Angeles or Southwest Washington at midnight. No, you say? But ... why not? I remember the hostility when Prince Edward Country, Virginia, where my familial roots are, instituted Prince Edward Academy in the Fifties to avoid integrating. How many whites reading this send their children to black urban schools? Why not?

It is remarkable how many people, put into the shoes of people doing things they deplore, perhaps more proudly than is quite necessary, would do just the same.

4

The Chinese Are Coming. I Think.

Guadalajara—

Just finished the last bag-drag back from China, jet-lagged, brain fried on caffeine, edgy groggy. Maybe I'll kill something. Or hibernate. What province am I in? Why do these Mexicans have round eyes? It's not natural. Some thoughts, barely:

I couldn't find the commies. Conservatives, the sort who preserve their minds in amber at birth, ramble on about Communist China. Their brains have parking brakes, maybe. Things are much less confusing if you have only one idea and stick with it. Anyway, if China is a communist country, I'm Julius Didianus. Who ever heard of a communist economy growing at nine percent? Or at all?

I grant you, the rascals used to be commies, but they've degenerated, and lost their touch. I could do it better. When I landed at Beijing, I got through passport control in about thirty seconds. They didn't even glance at my baggage. Grabbed a cab to my hotel. The driver tried to overcharge me. It looked like capitalism to me.

I remember going into the Soviet Union on some junket or other. Now, the Russkies could do some communism: Paranoia, thuggishness, ugly boring buildings, clothes that looked air-dropped and people walking hunched over as against a cold wind when there wasn't any wind. Nothing in the stores, and not many stores. Nothing worked. Nobody cared about anything. It was like Mexico but without the technology and consumer goods. Or the sense of urgency.

I went into St. Petersburg from Helsinki on a train, like Lenin though with less effect, because Aeroflop had lost our reservations in its central abacus. The border Nazis rolled down window shades in case we might have stashed propaganda in them. It was like going into a prison. It was going into a prison. That's how communism is supposed to work.

But China. If the government had the slightest interest in us, I didn't notice it. For two weeks we rushed about—Beijing, Xian, Chungking, Shanghai, Guilin, and such like, and spat ourselves out into Hong Kong like a cud. I don't astound easily, but this time I astounded. Sure, I knew about the vast rivers of vacuum cleaners and calculators spewing out of China into Wal-Mart. But knowing it was like knowing that the Grand Canyon is a large hole. Seeing it is different.

The joint is hopping. China has 1.3 billion people, and 1.5 billion construction cranes. I counted them. Pretty girls wander around in snug jeans and *camisetas ombligueras* so you won't wonder whether they have navels. Stores are full of things that stores are usually full of. Some of the malls could have been in Japan. China has lots of ordinary five-star hotels just like any anywhere, well-run, unpleasantly air-conditioned, and with free toothbrushes. The country is alive and shows indications of going somewhere. The shopkeepers spot a Western mark and holler. One of them successfully sold me a bottle of local booze with a cobra pickled in it.

Oh Mexico, thou of the mere little worm in thy tequila....

I suppose I was unconsciously expecting something third-worldly, maybe like Guadalajara—mildly prosperous, sidewalks crumbling, most things working most of the time, low buildings not excessively maintained, nothing happening and nothing indicating that anything ever will. No. Chungking is what New York would be if New York were a big city. We're talking forty-storey high rises that somehow don't look as dull as ours, massive highways and bridges. Every time we landed the airport turned out to have been completed four years ago, one year ago, what have you. Those cities aren't Guadalajara. They're Chicago.

The clunky Russian aircraft are gone. Now you see new stuff from Boeing and Airbus.

OK, that's the up side. The downside is lots, and smart people see real instability that could lead to an explosion. The Chinese explode well, as the Cultural Revolution of 1966–76 demonstrated. One problem is that said Revolution also left a generation of jobless ex-radicals who can't read, a bit like New Orleans. You can criticize Mousy Dung all you want, but you have to give him credit for being an unconscionable ass with no concern for his people. Anyway, those kids, no longer kids, could be trouble.

Then the policy of one child per family, combined with a preference for boy children, has left huge numbers of excess males who aren't going to find wives. They too might become disagreeable. I would. Add that the new wealth isn't reaching a whole lot of people. Corruption is rife. Poverty remains horrendous in many parts. Finally, China is said to have eighty million evangelical Christians, which means that it will likely attack Iraq, as well as a lot of Moslems.

Years ago I lived in Taiwan for a bit, studying Chinese, both the language and the young ladies, and living on fried squid bought in stalls under a bridge. At the time the island was doing a Five Year Plan. Back then every country with a patch of jungle, two colonels and a torture chamber had a Five Year Plan, efficiently doing nothing. I noticed that Taiwan was actually following its Plan: The reactors at Jin Shan were almost complete, the port at Gau Syung functioned, the steel mill made steel.

I thought: "Hmmm. These folk can obviously play big-city hardball finance and such, since that's what they are doing in Hong Kong, which is just Manhattan with slanted eyes. They can run a high-tech economy, since Taiwan is doing it. That leaves Mau, keeping China mired in darkness, as America's first line of defense."

Mau croaked. You really can't rely on communists. China now appears to be doing what Taiwan did. My take is that the Communist Party figured out that Marxism was great except that it didn't work, and anyway it could bore a tax accountant into the shrieking gollywoggles, so they decided to keep the name while doing something else. This is a novel concept for the West, which tends to eschew reason for organized imbecility, as for example liberalism and conservatism. Anyway, Katie bar the door. Better, open the bar.

Now, Beijing isn't the headwaters of compassion. I avoided staging any protests in Tien An Men Square, as the government is unprincipled and would not hesitate to use Waco-style methods to crush me. Russia, though, China isn't. Remember that when the Soviet Union was a superpower, though usually with a Guatemalan level of technology, it couldn't make a decent personal computer. Taiwan was spitting them out like aspirin tablets. Well, same people. And no Mau to paralyze them.

I'm going to go to sleep, or maybe jump off a roof. I hate airplanes.

5

Uncle Hant Ponders Eye Rack

'Tother day in the afternoon I went down the holler to ask Uncle Hant about this here Eye-rack. One of them blonde gals on TV that looks like they've been hit on the head or maybe drank Drano and didn't have her mind working right, if she had one, was talking about it. I didn't much understand. Hant, he knows everything. Hell, there's people in Wheeling even that don't know as much as he does.

Hant lives out in the woods and makes moonshine to sell to the yups from Washington. He says Yankees are dumber than retarded possums and it's the only way to make a living without working. He doesn't much like working.

I walked down the rail bed from Crumpler—that's a little place that used to be a coal camp before the mines died and the trains stopped coming. It was all peaceful and the bugs shrieking like they do so they can get laid and the sun pouring down like lit-up maple syrup and all the plants was so green you'd think they had batteries in them.

Sometimes I figure bugs got more sense than people do. All they care about is gal bugs and eating. I'll still take my girlfriend Jiffy Lube. Sometimes she gets upset and maybe smacks somebody with a tire iron, but bugs got six legs and I don't think I could get used to that.

I turned up the cut in the bank where Hant has his still and found him pouring Clorox into the moonshine. Hant's more'n six feet tall and kinda stiff, since he ain't been young since God was a pup. When he sits he sort of folds up like one of them yaller rulers that you measure things with, if you're a carpenter. He's got a face like a lantern and this hat that looks like a cow pie that the cow stepped on.

"Say, Hant," I said, by way of starting a conversation, "Tell me about this Eye-rack thing that they're always talking about on television. They say we got a war going."

His eyes lit up and he almost dropped the Clorox jug. He said, "The South done rizz again? I knew it would," and he grabbed the deer rifle that he mostly

13

keeps leaning against the cooker. Sometimes he has to shoot revenue agents. He never did like it when West Virginia joined the Feddle Gummint in the war agin cotton. He always figured West Virginia guessed wrong when the Yankees started meddling with everybody. Considering the results, I reckon he had something.

Most usually he has a jug of Beam handy. He sure ain't gonna drink that snake pizen he makes for the yups. He keeps putting stuff into his shine—brake fluid, LSD, cocaine, stove polish—to give it a kick. Mostly it kills the yups before they get back to Washington. Ain't hardly a telephone pole between Bluefield and the Yankee Capital that don't have a dent in it.

I said, "Naw, the South ain't rizz, least I don't guess so. This sort of pole-axed looking tow-headed gal said we had to drop bombs on these people in Eye-rack."

He took a hit from the Beam jug and passed it to me. His eyes got squinty and he said, "Eye-rack? Where the hell's that?"

I didn't know. That Beam sure was good. I sat down against a stump and said hello to Birdshot, that's Hant's old dog. Birdshot's only got three feet because he stuck a paw under a lawnmower once to see what was making all that noise. Sometimes it don't pay to wonder about things too much.

I said, "This ol' gal said Eye-rack blew up some buildings in New York."

"What's wrong with that?"

"That's what I hoped you'd tell me. Gimme 'nother hit off that jug."

He passed it to me, but kept an eye on it. He knows what matters to him. Then he looked into the woods the way he does when he doesn't know the answer to something.

"Too dam' many yups coming to buy shine now. Clorox seems to give it a pretty good zing, but I'm thinking about bug spray for the next batch. How's Jiffy Lube doing?"

"Pretty good, I guess. Still talks about getting married, but I figure I can hide in the next county. I still want to know about this war, Hant."

Hant don't actually exist. He's a Literary Device. He's got more sense than most people, though.

"Exactly what is a Eye-rack?" he said.

"Best I can tell, it's someone that wears a fender-cover on his head, and his wife wears a black bag."

Hant chewed on that for a moment. I could tell it moved him. "All right. I see it now. This war is to put them out of their misery … It's the Christian thing to do I reckon … Figure they'd like a little shine before they go?"

"This gal said they don't drink shine."

"Buncha dam' comminists."

Birdshot put his head on my leg and watched a squirrel that was hunting acorns in the woods. He didn't really care. He knew he was supposed to chase squirrels, but he didn't want one. He just watched from a sense of duty. I guessed it was like patriotism, that they kept talking about on TV. You didn't really want to kill whoever it was, leastways till you found some reasons maybe, or at least who they were, but you owed it to your country to do it anyway.

Hant pulled a Buck knife out of his pocket and started cutting on a stick. It's what he does if he's trying to figure out something that's too much for him.

Finally he said, "Well, if they don't drink shine, what do they do?"

"Mostly they blow up furriners, gal says."

"Then why don't the furriners go away? I would."

"That's what I'm asking you. You're supposed to know everything, ain't you?"

He pondered. "Yeah. But maybe that part slipped my mind a little. Sometimes it gets hard, knowing everything. I expect a little Beam would help." He took a three-gurgle hit and looked powerful satisfied.

"These Eye-racks planning on coming over here?" he said.

"Not that I know about. I mean, people with fender-covers on their head is hard to miss."

"Then I say leave'm there. Yankees is always meddling where they don't belong … Hoo, I'd sure like to see you tell Jiff she gotta wear a black bag." He gave this let's-you-and-him-fight chuckle he has when he wants to see someone else get in trouble.

"Not just now, Hant," I told him, thinking about that tire iron Jiffy Lube has. "Gimme that jug."

6

Sticking It to God

I find myself wondering why the ruling classes of America are so grindingly antagonistic to religion. I understand having no interest in religion. I do not understand the animosity.

One might say, "The world's religions are so many, so internally inconsistent and contradictory of each other, and so dependent on assertions that seem to me not to be factual, that I cannot believe any of them." The position is neither unreasonable nor rabid. One holding it might go about his affairs, leaving others to believe as they chose. He might respect the faith of others without sharing it, might regard religions as harmless and colorful folklore, might indeed regard them as socially beneficial.

In the Unites States, though, we see something very different: an aggressive hostility to religion, a desire to extirpate it and, though no one quite says this, to punish its practitioners. A curious witch-hunt continues in which people seem to look for any trace of religion so that they can root it out. I would call it vengeful, except that I do not know for what it might be revenge.

Why? The explanations given do not make sense. A store whose sign says "Merry Christmas" is a threat to nothing, just as a nativity scene can offend only one who is looking very hard for something to offend him. The stridency of the evolutionists seems overblown, since a mention of the theory of intelligent design would hardly lead to the closing of departments of biochemistry.

The notion that the Ten Commandments on the wall of a courthouse will lead to an established religion is palpable nonsense. Constitutional piety doesn't wash either. If nativity scenes contravene the Constitution, why was this not noticed by anyone, assuredly including the authors, until at least 1950?

(I am reminded of the joke about the high school that issued a boy a condom, and expelled him when he was discovered praying for a chance to use it.)

A common reading is that the sciences have become a sort of secular religion, with the Big Bang replacing Genesis, and evolution as a sort of deanthropomorphized god chivying humanity onward and upward. There is a large element of this, yes. The self-righteous intolerance directed by disciples of evolution against religion assuredly resembles the intolerance of religion against heresy. Does this explain the anger of the rooters-out? Is it partly that believers in America tend to be Southern or Catholic, both of which conditions are regarded as politically inappropriate?

Why have the sciences achieved such power over the popular mind? Obvious answers are that they work spectacularly within their ambit, that they produce wondrous gadgets, that they are swathed in incomprehensible runes such as triple integrals or tensors dripping with sub- and superscripts, and provide resounding incantations like "pentaerythritol tetranitrate."

I wonder whether something else is not involved. Today most of us live in profound isolation from the natural world. People in large cities can go for decades without seeing the stars. Should they drive through the countryside, it will be in a closed automobile with the air-conditioner running. On a trip to the beach, the sand will be overrun by hordes of people, half of them on whining jet skis.

We exist utterly in a manmade cocoon, as much as desert termites in their mud towers. This, I think, profoundly alters our inner landscapes. Live in the rolling hills around Austin, say, as they were before they were turned into sub-urbs, with the wind soughing through the empty expanse and low vegetation stretching into the distance, the stars hanging low and close in the night, and you get a sense of man's smallness in the scheme of nature, of the transitoriness of life, a suspicion that there may perhaps be more things in heaven and earth. It makes for reflection of a sort that throughout history has turned toward the religious.

People no longer live in large wild settings, but amid malls and freeways. The ancients believed that the earth was the center of the cosmos. We believe that we are. There is little to suggest otherwise in manicured suburbs and cities where the sirens will be howling at all hours. It is an empty world that begets philosophi-cally empty thinking.

Without the sense of being small in a large universe, and perhaps not even very important, the question arises, "Is this all there is?" and the answer appears to be "Yes." Without the awe and wonder and mystery of a larger cosmos, exist-ence reduces to blowing smog, competitive acquisition of consumer goods, and vapid television with laugh tracks. We focus on efficiency, production, and the material because they are all we have. It is not particularly satisfying, and so we are not particularly satisfied.

I suspect that the decline of religion stems less from the advance of scientific knowledge than from the difficulty of discerning the transcendent in a parking lot. Certainly the scientific has generally replaced the religious mode of thought, even in people who believe themselves to be Christians. For example, it is amusing to hear them saying that the parting of the Red Sea refers to diminution of water by a wind in what was essentially a swamp. That is, God is all-powerful, but only to the extent that he behaves consistently with the prevailing weather.

Yet note the decline of even non-religious contemplation of such matters as meaning and purpose, right and wrong, ultimate good, and so on. It is not that people behave worse without faith, but that they cannot explain why they do not. The use of the sciences as a substitute for belief in God or gods has produced a religion that cannot ask the questions central to religion. It has also made discussion of such questions a cause for eliminating the offender from the guest list for the next cocktail party.

But this does not answer the question of why the hostile stalking of religion that pervades the ranks of the educated and influential in the United States. In almost all times and places, disbelief and secularism have existed, yes. Few educated Romans actually believed in Jupiter the Lightning Chucker. There have been Cathars and Wiccans and Manicheans and innumerable agnostics. Yet, so far as I know, only communism and Americanism (is that the word, perhaps?) have tried to eradicate religion.

Mexico has separation of church and state, and yet a bus driver can hang a crucifix from the rear-view mirror without upsetting anyone. I do not know how many Thais are believing Buddhists. Certainly Buddhist symbols are visible everywhere in Thailand, and it doesn't seem to have engendered disaster. Why the angry rejection in the US? I will get email telling me that it is a Jewish plot, like everything else, but in fact it is the default attitude of the educated. Why?

7

PMS as National Policy

I begin to think that Mothers Against Drunk Drivers constitute a public nuisance, and need to be stuffed down an abandoned oil well. And indicted for fraud. We could dangle a microphone down the well on a wire so that they could testify.

These tiresome biddies aren't against drunk driving, which anyone with a possum's brains is against. Your dangerous drunks are incorrigibles who time and again blow horrific BACs and wobble around the roads like student unicyclists. The proper response is permanent revocation of driver's licenses. If they need to go to work they can buy a horse.

But the MADD girls are not against drunk driving. They are prohibitionists pretending to be something else. Their name is artfully crafted to make them seem to be no end virtuous—moral bidets squirting purest goodness. What could be more pure than motherhood? But it is like calling the Spanish Inquisition a society for the protection of orphans. It still isn't.

An example of the swindle: Texas sends undercover cops into bars to arrest drunks before they drive. A bit shaky, that. You are talking to your date over a bottle of wine and dinner when the guy at the next table pulls out a badge and a Breathalyzer. "Step this way, sir...." But never mind.

At *The Agitator* website, I find this: "Heather Hodges, an Abilene-based MADD victims advocate, said her group is working closely with the TABC on the project."

Says Heather, "We believe responsible adults should drink responsibly. And those that serve them should be responsible. A lot of people think it's OK to be drunk in a bar, but it's illegal. A bar is not intended to be a place to get fall-down drunk.... You don't have to be fall-down drunk to be considered drunk. Even after one drink, you aren't 100 percent."

Following the introductory platitude, note the logical sequence: Falling-down drunk is bad. If you aren't falling down you are still drunk. After one drink you are impaired. Therefore if you have a glass of wine at dinner, you should be arrested. This is not opposition to drunken driving. It is prohibition in drag, to be enforced by disguised police.

Let's think about this. After one drink you "are not a hundred percent." Heather believes that we must keep people from driving who are "not one hundred percent." OK. I'll buy it. Let's get impaired people off the road.

Going to the web site of *The Women's Health Channel*, I find the following listed as symptoms of PMS:

"• Mood-related ("affective") symptoms: depression, sadness, anxiety, anger, irritability, frequent and severe mood swings.

• Mental process ("cognitive") symptoms: decreased concentration, indecision."

Does that sound like one hundred percent to you? I figure it's a pretty good description of an unstable borderline psychotic. Oh good. I want to drive on the roads with someone who doesn't pay attention, couldn't decide what to do it she did, and wants to kill something. Me, probably.

We need to recognize the seriousness of PMS. People joke about it, as they do about drunkenness, but these women are public hazards. "Anger, irritability, frequent and severe mood swings"? (Now that's a revelation.) "Decreased concentration"? Sounds like a bad drunk in a pool hall, a recipe for inattentive homicidal road-rage. I think the police should send squads into supermarket parking lots to check for these impaired women. Other cops should wait outside churches. To better protect the public we should have checkpoints on highways.

How does an officer tell when a woman is irresponsibly driving while under the, er, influence? Not by asking her. The impaired lie. With drunks, the dissimulation is often obvious. ("Jush two beersh, offsher.") Those suffering from PMS can feign sanity, however briefly. Perhaps they should be required to carry a notarized letter from a gynecologist, like a hall pass. Or a governmentally issued calendar.

Ponder this from *Planet Estrogen*: "Additionally, several studies demonstrate reduced reaction time, neuromuscular coordination and manual dexterity during the pre-menstruation and menstrual phases."

Are not these the classic symptoms of a snootful? The police might reasonably carry a device to test reaction times. They might profitably lurk in nail salons. Disguised.

But there is hope in technology. Last year for a newspaper I covered a proposal in New Mexico, supported by MADD, to make it impossible to start your car if you have been drinking:

From *The Agitator*: "People across the state are upset with House Bill 126, which would require ignition interlock devices be installed on all new cars sold in New Mexico by Jan. 1, 2008, regardless of the purchaser's driving record ..." (It didn't pass.)

"... The interlock device uses a blow tube which activates sensors when one blows into the tube. If alcohol is detected, the sensors activate a mechanism which shuts down the vehicle's ignition system and the car cannot be started."

The approach illustrates the weird totalitarianism of the female. Anything, anything at all, to increase security, security, security. We are all two-year-olds in need of diapering. The Mommy State is well named.

The wisdom of the ignition-interlock is of course evident. You go camping with your daughter. While you sit around the fire heisting a brew, she falls and cuts herself on the ax. She is bleeding badly. You rush her to the car to go to the hospital and ... *it won't start*. What the hell. You can adopt.

I believe that cars should be equipped with hormone-level detectors, similar to the blood-sugar monitors used by diabetics. At the very least, to start the car the potentially impaired driver should have to insert her governmentally-issued calendar into a slot and put her hand in a fingerprint-reader.

Whatever the solution, society should not have to tolerate such threats to children. Note that women are in fact sometimes around children, when they get home from work. Further, research shows that they are habitual offenders. Drunks can sometimes be weaned off the juice, but here we are dealing with assured repeaters. At the very least perpetrators should be required to undergo therapy, perhaps in twelve-step programs. Should this not work, electronic ankle-bracelets might protect us. Institutionalization could help.

Nelson Soucasaux, gynecologist: "Psychological signs and symptoms: Increase of nervous tension, anxiety, irritability, changes in the personality, emotional instability, depression, as well as increase or reduction of the sexual desire."

Irritable sex-crazed depressives at the wheel, with bad reflexes. Alternatively, frigid nut-cases. This is the adult responsibility that Heather wants? I am going to start a group called DAMM, Dads Against Monthly Murder. We will meet in tree houses, above the roofline of an SUV.

8

Newspapers Croaking Slowly—Good Thing, Too

The drooping circulation of the paleomedia gratifies me more than bubblegum. Lord I love it. The tube-worms of the network suites have discovered that lo! Fewer of the citizenry sit nightly before the flickering propaganda modem. The readership of newspapers yet falls. This dereliction they ascribe to declining literacy, the lack of public spirit, and indeed anything but their own uselessness.

Such thunder-wumpuses as Rupert Murdoch, noting that people go to the web, frantically buy web properties. It is not the abysmal content of the media, see, that turns people away. We just want our sewage through a different pipe. If the media put the same twaddle on the web, thinks Rupert, people sick of it elsewhere will love it.

Any day now. I suggest that the reasons for the loss are otherwise and several. Permit me a few thoughts:

What are the topics of most fascination in the United States? Of most importance? Certainly among them are race, sex in the social sense, crime, and immigration. Now, let's see whether we can name four subjects about which the media speak with calculated mendacity obvious to everyone one. How about ... oh, say ... race, sex in the social sense, crime, and immigration?

Race, for example:

A story on the site of ABC News led with the lurid headline, "Young Singers Spread Racist Hate." Now, if young singers have ABC's bowels in a racial uproar, you can be sure that the singers are white. We all understand that hate is what white people do. Thus it was. A pair of very young girls, calling themselves Prussian Blue, say that they want to maintain the purity of the white race. (Why this is precisely hate eludes me.) Various authorities are quoted as to the effect that they are shocked, appalled, disappointed, and so on.

At about the same time, I found the account of a black man, one Dr. (of what, I wonder?) Kamau Kambon, who while speaking to a panel at the law school of Howard University (a black school in Washington, DC) said that the white race should be exterminated.

This is not my interpretation but rather his explicit, repeated statement. I quote: white people "have retina scans, they have what they call racial profiling, DNA banks and they're monitoring our people to try to prevent the one person from coming up with the one idea. And the one idea is, how we are going to exterminate white people because that, in my estimation, is the only conclusion I have come to. [Sic] We have to exterminate white people off the face of the planet to solve this problem." He wants to kill me, my daughters, and my friends.

This produced from the media … near silence. From Howard University … silence. From professional blacks … silence.

Now, this column is not about race relations, but about the dishonesty of the media. I do not think that many blacks want to exterminate whites, though I do think that Mr. Kambon needs to take his medication. Nor do I want to exterminate anyone, with the possible exception of lawyers and people in public relations. Nor do I know any whites who want to exterminate blacks. (You can find some very strange websites that might, though.)

We all know the pattern. When Larry Summers, president of what once was Harvard University, mentioned that men are better than women at mathematics, a fact studied to death and well settled, it was national news practically forever. Hissyfits were everywhere thrown. Summers duly whimpered and licked all feet within range. Ah, but when Mr. Kambon wants to kill most of the United States, why … ah, heh … cough.

Also about the same time, the coach of the football team of the Air Force Academy suggested that his team was faring badly because it didn't have enough black players. "It just seems to be that way, that Afro-American kids can run very, very well. That doesn't mean that Caucasian kids and other descents can't run, but it's very obvious to me they run extremely well," DeBerry said, not too articulately, in remarks first broadcast Tuesday night by KWGN-TV in Denver.

Conventional outrage gurgled tiredly forth as from a broken drain. Like Summers, DeBerry ended up squirming on the rug in apology. (Why? Whatever happened to manhood?) It is of course a fact that blacks run fast. Are they overwhelming in the running slots of the NFL because they are slow, do you think? Then why does the league not recruit me at, say, six million green ones a year? I am, I promise, far slower than any running back in football.

To point out that blacks are good athletes is virtually a firing offense, but to urge killing millions of whites is fine. Welcome to the media.

What has this to do with the circulation of newspapers? Lots. For one thing, whites who are to be killed may weary of hostility from the media, and they are most of the readership. Except I'm not any longer. For another, coverage is boring because predetermined, irritating because antagonistic and mendacious, and useless because it contributes nothing to solving, or even to understanding, the racial problems of the country. Or any problems of the country.

In fact the media aggravate racial relations. When whites think of blacks, the first two to leap to mind are (drum roll) Al and Jesse, no? Aside from driving away the audience, they give a horrible impression of blacks. But Al and Jesse are not the black race. They are just Al and Jesse. On the web you find a spectrum of black thought, much of it wildly different from that peddled by television. Try Will Powell, or LaShawn Barber.

But something else is at work here. For decades, the major media have had near-control of the news and the culture. If an event didn't appear on the networks, it hadn't happened. The paleos apparently do not realize that they have lost that control—that when they refuse to give play to a call for extermination, their refusal no longer kills the story. Kambon's call for my children's liquidation surged across the nation, copy after copy, including video clips.

Wake up, Rupert, baby. For the intelligent, the media are no longer primary. Few any longer regard them as other than advocacy lashups for certain groups. Why bother?

There is, I think, nothing the paleos can do to change this. They are irremediably ideologized, insular, and trapped by demographics into a bland editorial mass-market philosophy of one-size-fits-all. The web, far more agile, can provide focused sites about anything at any intellectual level.

The looming unknown in all of this is the circulation of the net, its influence, its clout. How important, really, is the web? How do you measure the ambit of ten thousand blogs, of thousands of personal websites like Fred On Everything, of outfits with no physical existence like LewRockwell.com and Antiwar.com? The answer I think is that you don't, really. The ghostly statistics of forwards, caches, and reposts make it difficult to determine one's own circulation, much less that of countless other sites. This makes it hard for CBS to estimate, and easy for it to underestimate, the tidal wave it faces. I'm glad that it is their problem and not mine.

9

Bush, Bushwah, and Bush's Wah

I have decided to become a drunk and live under a bench, maybe in a radiation suit. It only makes sense. The times are dire. Dark shapes twist in the international fog. The US, in the hands of puzzled children of low moral character, flaps about like a damp rag in a high wind. Anything could happen.

I figure to enjoy it since I can't stop it. It would all seem more amusing and less dark, I thought, if I weren't immoderately sober. To this end I walked to the Oxxo, which is a Mexican Seven-Eleven, and bought a bottle of Padre Kino red.

Maybe I should have bought two bottles.

There is much to cause worry. The strange little man in the White House is leering at Iran in his customary state of martial priapism. Not good. (Wild thought: Someone ought to give Iran nuclear weapons, so he won't attack it.) Anyway, wee Bush, not having enough army for his current wars, wants to start a bigger and shinier one.

Somebody explain it to me. I have limited geostrategic grasp. Perhaps he believes that by spreading unwinnability over several wars, he will reduce it in each. Victory through distributed defeat.

I keep reading that Herr Bush may use "bunker buster" nukes in Iran. To the inordinately dim, this has a comforting sound. You know, a little itsy-bitsy, teeny-weeny, perhaps yellow polka-dot nukelet goes way down in the earth and, fooomp! blows up the evil bunker, hardly rattling the windows above. Actually an earth-penetrator doesn't penetrate beyond a few feet, all of which turn into fall-out.

The Padre Kino isn't working. None of this makes any sense, even after half a bottle. I may have to go IV. The president's virtuous plan to spread democracy like bird flu goes apace. Ain't nobody heah ceptin' us missionaries. The rascal is imposing democracy right and left.

It is working. Well, it is having an effect. In Venezuela democracy brought about Hugo Chavez, who hates the United States. In Bolivia it produced Evo

Morales, who hates the United States. In Iran it empowered Ahmawhatsispelling, who hates the United States. So does the elected government in Iraq. In Palestine Mr. Bush's righteousness elected Hamas, which hates the United States, perhaps as much as does the Muslim Brotherhood, which keeps getting more elected in Egypt.

There's nothing like democracy, I say. There's nothing like brains either, but they seem to be in short supply. I mean, if you force elections in countries where everybody hates you, after doing things that make sure that everyone hates you …?

I think I'll call Oxxo and tell them to put another bottle on hold. Maybe they have a layaway plan.

See, this whole mess is a splendid contest between a Titan and a pygmy, the pygmy being very well armed and the Titan being very smart. High drama and all. Made for television. The pygmy used New York as a pretext to conquer the Middle East and get the oil. Bin Laden used New York to sucker the pygmy into a losing war that would leave the United States defanged and broken. One of them has guessed wrong. We'll know which before long.

I still don't get it. Maybe psilocybin would help. It doesn't make you understand anything, but makes everything else equally confusing so that nothing stands out. These days, it's the best you can hope for.

What jolly things are the rest of the presidential children doing? The vice president has shot someone while duck hunting, and apparently while drunk. Only wounded him, though. I grew up in a country where fifteen-year-old boys regularly hunted. Nobody ever shot anybody. I am not sure that a clown who cannot be trusted with hunting arms really ought to exert influence over intercontinental missiles. The only consolation is that he would be likely to miss.

Next I see that Mr. Rumsfeld, the secretary of alleged defense, has said "We've got Chavez in Venezuela with a lot of oil money. He's a person who was elected legally, just as Adolf Hitler was elected legally, and then consolidated power, and now is, of course, working closely with Fidel Castro and Mr. Morales and others. It concerns me."

Mr. Rumsfeld concerns me. The assertion that Hitler is working with Castro and Evo Morales does have its appeal. It implies that Adolf really did take an immortality drug and move to Argentina. Is this something NSA hasn't told us?

Maybe Mr. Rumsfeld wasn't paying attention during grade-school English classes. Hitler of course was never elected legally but appointed Chancellor by Hindenburg in 1933, never having gotten more than 37% of the vote. I knew this in high school. Why doesn't the Secretary of Defense? Reassuring, that. Pig ignorant and pugnacious.

I note that Mr. Bush was elected legally, unless of course he wasn't, and consolidates power. Fast. I do not think that he will work with Castro and Morales, though. He couldn't remember them long enough.

And of course there is Kind Of Leezer Rice, the Secretary of State. Being non-male and non-white, she is slightly more sacred than God, if only in that she is allowed on federal property.

She is said to "speak Russian fluently." Is there any evidence that she speaks it at all? Where are the publications to document her purportedly coruscating intelligence? Bookfinder.com produces only *The Soviet Union & the Czechoslovak Army 1948–1983*, noted for its poor grasp of historical fact.

I asked an academic friend about this, and he responded, "I checked a couple of computer databases for scholarly articles by Dr. Rice and couldn't find any. My suspicions were further aroused by the fact that of all the adoring articles I found about Dr. Rice (including her official curriculum vitae on the White House web site), none listed any scholarly publications apart from the aforementioned book." Oh.

The world is reeling slightly. Doubtless a gravitational anomaly. What if Bush doesn't leave when his term ends? He would say he had to remain to protect us from terror. The nation abounds in fools, as Australia does in rabbits. Who would do anything about a coup—or, pardon me, "emergency measure"? And what?

Who's in charge of this choo-choo train? A witless draft-dodger, an inept duck-hunter, an historical illiterate, and an overrated twofer. I'm going to hide.

The great fallacy of childhood is the belief that grownups must know what they are doing. There is no evidence for this in the historical record. You would do better by grabbing a government at random from the denizens of a rural high school. Democracy brings us twerps, psychopaths, ambitious ciphers, short men, and well-born drones. They are what they are. They can't change any more than a leper can change his spots. I need some really strong drugs or someone to hit me on the head with a rubber mallet. Opium is the religion of the masses. Let us pray.

10

Poverty, Whimpering, and Violeta

Repeatedly I hear that the misbehavior of the population of New Orleans sprang from the exigencies of poverty. I would offer a countering view. Permit me to start with the family of Violeta, *mi pareja* in Mexico. I know them well. Listen, and judge.

Her father was born poor 78 years ago. Poor in Mexico in the twenties meant *poor*—dirt-floor poor, village well with typhoid and no sewerage poor, no safety net, no medical care, and government by *caciques* who had unlimited power and didn't care whether you lived or died. It was hookworm, roundworm, pinworm, tapeworm poor. It was louse poor. Obesity from eating at McDonald's was not a concern. Just eating was a concern.

Her Dad learned to read from an aunt who had learned in a Catholic school. In Mexico then, as in the United States now, the Catholic schools were better than the public, when the latter existed. He then apprenticed himself to a primitive machine shop, the only kind available, and became a valve-maker.

Eventually he hired on with a company, saved hard over the years, and bought a house, now paid off, in which he still lives. Buying a house for a Mexican worker then required grim determination. After thirty-six years he retired with a pension adequate to support life. In all this time, he did not loot a single city.

Poor doesn't mean ignorant. He read whatever he could find, to include newspapers daily. He knows a lot of history and geography. If you mention, say, Ceylon, he knows where it is, and the capital. Do American college graduates?

He wasn't shiftless, you see. Poverty is a condition characterized by a lack of money. Shiftlessness involves a lack of backbone, morals, independence, self-respect, and drive. They are not the same thing. Of course, if you are shiftless, you are likely to be poor.

I note in passing that anyone who wishes can learn to read, short of the genuinely retarded. Illiteracy is a choice. So is ignorance.

Along the way he married, whence Violeta. He was an imperfect dad—strict, yelled a lot, and wasn't too tolerant, though he didn't hit her. He taught her that there are things you have to do, things you ought to do, and things you ought not to do. She learned. A thoroughgoing Catholicism reinforced these ideas.

Adolescence came, and high school. Violeta decided that she wanted to go to the University of Guadalajara. There was the little problem of no money. Mexicans do not get preferential treatment in Mexico. To her, poverty was an obstacle to be overcome, not an excuse for failure. For five years in the *Facultad de Letras y Filosofia*, she worked three jobs. And graduated.

Poor, you see, is not the same as, nor does it imply, nor justify, passive, thieving, dependent, and benighted.

At this point I am going to sacrifice literary consistency to explication. When I was nineteen a buddy of mine and I hopped the freights to New York where, listening to a Copland concert in Prospect Park, I met on the grass a little Italian girl of seventeen. We began writing, and then dating. Her father having died unexpectedly, she and her mother were living essentially on Social Security in Brooklyn. They ate, but not much more.

They were not shiftless, however.

Her mother got her into a Catholic school. Eva understood perfectly which way was out. Good grades were not optional. They were going to happen. And did. Four years of high school and a 4.0 later, she blew away the Regents and got a scholarship to NYU Washington Square. She repeated the roughly 4.0 performance. After grad school at Rochester, she is a tenured professor of mathematics in the New York system. Poor Italian kid. Never robbed Wal-Mart.

Anyway, Violeta. While in university, she became pregnant. Contraception is an imperfect art. On moral grounds she decided not to kill it. (Actually it wasn't a decision. There are things one doesn't do and, in her view, that was one of them. Today The Unkilled is fourteen, and prospering mightily.) Violeta was now a single mother as well as working three jobs and going to school.

She did it. It wasn't easy, but she had no expectation that it would be. There are things one does.

On graduating she got some wretched office job, discovered that it was a snake pit (*un nido de serpientes*) and that she couldn't give enough attention to her child, who turned out to be a girl named Natalia. So she said to hell with offices and moved to Ajijic, the American enclave on Lake Chapala, to teach Spanish to gringos.

It was a gutsy call. She had no safety net and very little money: North Americans living in half-million dollar houses object to paying an extra dollar an hour for a service that would cost ten times as much in the US. When I met Violeta, Natalia was twelve. They were living in, by American standards, a desperately tiny one-bedroom house, with one small bed and a mattress on the floor, and a total of $300 between them and destitution. Don't complain to her about the high price of running shoes.

Now in the US, social class, which we pretend doesn't exist, depends chiefly on consumer goods owned, money coming in, and credentials on paper. Two BMWs and Yale beats three Volvos and the University of Maryland. Violeta, ever wrong-headed, believed that what you are worth depends on how you behave. Again, Catholicism.

She conveyed this to Natalia, who was (and is) the best student in her school, reading constantly with the fluency of an educated adult. Principled motherhood has its virtues. If the child had been a latchkey, she would doubtless now be pushing either drugs or a stroller. Today Nata is fourteen, smart as a whip, largely over the tyrannosaur stage of hideous disagreeability that briefly afflicts teenage girls, and pretty as a flower. She very much likes boys, but has none of that unhappy—what? Lack of self-respect? Desperation for love?—that makes so many US girls easy prey to libidinous striplings.

If I may digress again, long ago on the police beat I rode in DC with a black cop from a bad section of New York. How did he get out, I asked? From my column of the time, I quote: "My father told me, 'Son, you're going to learn your lessons, or I *will* whup your ass.' He did, too. So I learned. Best thing that ever happened to me." (Boys are a little different.)

You don't have to be helpless, nor useless, nor immoral because you were born poor. If this were not true, the Irish, Italians, Jews, the Chinese of railroad coolie days, the Poles and the Czechs would still be in slums. They aren't. They made it, as Violeta made it, as Eva and lots of black cops made it, without Section Eight housing, welfare, scholarships, minority preferences with no expectations attached, medical charity, or monotonous self-pity. She has a contempt for those who could, but don't, that would peel chrome from an engine block.

11

Maribel Cuevas, A Great American. Damn Near the Only One.

Here, in the home of the free, the land of the brave, and suchlike prattle, I encounter this: "An 11-year-old girl who threw a stone at a group of boys pelting her with water balloons is being prosecuted on serious assault charges in California. Maribel Cuevas was arrested in April in a police operation which involved three police cars and a helicopter."

It seems that the rock gashed some little monster's forehead and, according to the BBC, he needed "hospital treatment." I suspect this means that he needed treatment that any general practitioner could have given him in his office, but ambulances don't take people to general practitioners.

Now, if I had a son who was ganging up with other boys to torment a girl who didn't speak English, or did (apparently Maribel barely did), I'd slap him across the room so hard that he would think he was an astronomer, and the next time the idea of doing such a thing occurred to him, he would reflect, "Maybe this isn't a good idea. Dad doesn't seem to like it." No, Dad doesn't. If he came home with a gash where she had belted him in trying to defend herself, I'd say, "Son, you go to school to learn things. You just did." Ask and ye shall receive. Actions have consequences. There are things kids need to know that you don't do, especially boys, who are pack animals.

I said, "Little monster." In fairness, this isn't fair. Kids are mean—girls as much as boys, though they go about it differently. A civilizing duty of parents, and of society, is to make clear that there are limits, and what those limits are. One of those limits is that sorry little jerks do not gang up on girls.

But … but … what leaves me gasping in wonderment is the police. First, why the police at all? Schools and parents can't manage children who haven't even reached adolescence? What is wrong with these absurd, weak, contemptible, ane-

31

mic larvae? I can be charitable to sniveling parsnips, yes. I mean, worms are people too. But not when they run the schools like Oprah grubs from under a rock.

When I was a kid in high school in rural Virginia, the principal, Larry Roller, didn't need cops to control a school full of rowdy country boys. These were kids who could hurt you. They cut cordwood in the mornings. If you don't know what that means, you need to go to a gym. My girlfriend Gloria, pretty as a flower, could pull a crab boat onto a mud flat by herself, and did. We all had guns.

No serious discipline problems. Ever. Anywhere. The concept was like presidential grammar: unheard of. Nobody bucked Chrome Dome Roller. Anyone who did would have been expelled in three seconds, and would have known better than to go home, ever. His father would be waiting.

How is it that the police department needs three squad cars, an ambulance, and a freaking helicopter to subdue an annoyed girl of eleven? In my many years of riding with the police, I knew them to be men, gutsy, hard-core, willing to go to bad places full of bad people. You might like them or you might not, and you might have reason either way. But they weren't pansies.

Real cops would be stone embarrassed to arrest little girls on assault charges. Not these cops, though.

Yet the use of police when frightened mushroomy purported teachers get upset is becoming the custom in American schools. I like this one:

"Yahoo News, Fri Apr 29: "CLOVIS, N.M.—A call about a possible weapon at a middle school prompted police to put armed officers on rooftops, close nearby streets and lock down the school. All over a giant burrito. Someone called authorities Thursday after seeing a boy carrying something long and wrapped into Marshall Junior High."

Yeah. The kid, one Michael Morrissey, had made a thirty-inch burrito for some sort of assigned project, presumably of preternatural stupidity and unrelated to the purposes of school. Anyway, jalapeños, tomatoes, things like that. Scary things.

Armed officers on rooftops? Snipers? I imagine the chief talking by radio to a swatted-out rifleman.

Chief: "You see him, sergeant?"

Sniper: "Yessir. He's got the weapon under his arm. It's wrapped in newspaper. I got a clear headshot. Do I have a green light?"

Chief: "No, not yet. If he does anything threatening...."

Sniper: "Hold on! Hold on! He's unwrapping the weapon."

Chief: "Green light! Take him out!"

Sniper. "Roger that. Wait. He's eating it...."

If I were a cop, and had to take part in something so clownish, I wouldn't admit it. Instead I'd tell my wife I'd spent the afternoon in a brothel.

These cockamamie stories are legion, like illiterate federal workers. I've followed any number of them. A little boy swats a little girl on the backside on the playground, and he is arrested by cops, charged with sexual harassment, and put into compulsory psychiatric counseling. Another kid draws a picture of a soldier with his rifle, and gets suspended. On and on.

What twisted circus of social decay is going on here? Have these people's minds, if any, been taken over by extragalactic flatworms? That is my guess. We are seeing the first step toward cocooning us. They plan to feed us to their starving wiggly populations on some croaking planet knee-deep in bloodsucking phyla unknown to science. Gurgle gurgle glop.

I'm serious.

Now, I may not know what is really going on, but I sure as hell know what is really not going on. None of this is about security. At least, it is not about security in any sane way, having some minor three-generations-back relation to reality. We are a nation frightened of our daughters of eleven? Are girl kids that dangerous? Does any other country, anywhere, fear its daughters? Give me a break.

It is truly weird. America, the most aggressive nation on the planet, the *grr, bowwow, woof* superpower, is also the most timid. Sure, I know, aggressive because frightened, the bully terrified by sock-puppets that might wait in the closet. But, my god, a kid with a burrito? In Mexico, where I live, lots of kids have burritos. You can carry one, concealed, without a permit. No helicopters and no snipers.

That's us. The country of Davy Crockett, John Singleton Mosby, Apollo Thirteen, now somehow scared of our own sprats, unable to teach them to read, absolutely absurd in the eyes of the world. Of course, the schools being what they are, lots of us have never heard of the world. It wasn't always this way. Anyway, I guess the Chinese will be merciful. Maybe they will put us in special homes, with soft walls.

12

Clueless in Baghdad

Some months ago I returned to my home in Mexico after two weeks of hard touring in Bolivia. It was the kind of travel that at my advanced age I should know better than, but never do: flying into grass strips to boat into the endless swamps of the pampas, freezing in unheated shacks in the wild high desert at 12,000 feet, mountain biking down *El Camino de la Muerte* out of La Paz next to drop-offs of half a mile. Not sensible, perhaps, but few things worth doing are.

Curiously, in South America, our backyard, my traveling-companions-by-chance were virtually never American. There were Brits, Aussies, Kiwis, yes. And German, French, and Dutch folk, but no gringos.

They weren't hippies. They ran from 22 to 40: an Irish girl of maybe 26 who had been solo on the road for six months, a French woman in the wine business in her late thirties on a two week jaunt, an English financial officer on holiday. Most carried expedition backpacks. They were friendly, gutsy, self-reliant. I liked them.

But there were no Americans.

It is a pattern. Another pattern is that almost all of the Europeans spoke at least two languages, the English-peaking peoples only one. It isn't just in Bolivia. I live in a Mexico near Guadalajara where there is a large population of American expatriates and retirees. They almost never learn Spanish and do not much mix with the Mexicans. When I covered the American military in Europe years back, the troops never learned German. Some refused to leave the base.

Why? Is it lack of intelligence? Clearly not. Laziness? If so, it is a curious, focused laziness. Americans work harder than most people at most things. The country did not achieve its position in the world by witlessness and sloth. Lack of initiative? Americans far more than most peoples start companies, take courses, invent things. If they wanted to learn languages, they would. They just do not much want to.

I think they simply do not care about other societies, do not have sufficient curiosity to make the extended effort needed to learn a language. Where I live, many hide from Mexico in gated communities and seem not really to want to be in the country. Perhaps Lauderdale was too expensive. They are ... not quite afraid, but ill at ease. They stand out by a hesitancy in their walk, in their manner of holding themselves. This is not true of all, especially not of those who take wives and go native. It is true of the majority.

They are not Ugly Americans, note. They are not discourteous toward the Mexicans. They contribute to charity and do good works. Most have led productive lives, not infrequently in demanding fields. As people go, they are good people. Yet they seem out of place.

I knew my companions in Bolivia briefly but well. When you spend nights at twenty below in unheated shacks with the wind howling outside, eight in a room in sleeping bags, an intimacy grows. One crazy night in the swamps we ran out of beer and the guides took us in boats through the night to a remote bar on stilts in the night where we drank ourselves silly. It was a splendid evening.

But there were no gringos.

The Europeans bicker among themselves a bit. "What can you expect of a German?" they will say, or "Everybody knows the Dutch are stingy," but they say it with a smile. Yet they all know each other's countries. They have been to Morocco, India, Egypt. They have a worldliness about them. It is not an air of snotty superiority. They are simply comfortable abroad.

They think Americans are idiots. By and large they aren't offensive, don't (usually) bring the subject up. I am not inclined to defend the indefensible however, and so discussions emerged. Why, they wanted to know, do Americans know nothing about the world? I never quite know what to say. Well, er, it's a big country, we don't have to speak other languages, ah, the schools are terrible (why, they ask?), we just aren't very curious or travelsome (why not, they ask?) The observable fact is that Americans display a blank, uninquiring ignorance of other cultures. Our current president is a prime example.

What effect does this have on our foreign policy? On our relations with the rest of the earth?

A lot, I think.

I remember that the White House believed that the Iraqis would welcome our invasion by strewing flowers in our path, such would be their delight with American values, etc. It slackens the jaw. Does no one in the hermetic bubble on Pennsylvania Avenue understand that other peoples have their ways of doing things? That not everybody wants to be American? Two weeks of backpacking around

Marrakech and Cairo would have disabused them—but who in the White House has done it? Who out of the White House has done it?

The American attitude implied in policy, and expressed in the bow-wow-woofish patriotism of much of my email, is that most other countries are backward if not actually aboriginal, and in need of enlightenment, perhaps armed enlightenment. Contempt is reflexive and profound. Considerable of my email tells me that Iraqis for example are dirty and flea-bitten, understand nothing but force, and deserve any treatment they get.

I find myself asking: How many of these people have spoken to an Iraqi? To any Moslem? Been to Iraq? Been anywhere? Know what countries border Iraq? Have a passport? Know why 622 may have been a year of some relevance?

The eerie parochialism leads to disaster as the country blunders into swamps it does not understand and discovers that it has underestimated the enemy.

If I mention that the rest of the world doesn't like the United States, the response usually is, "I'd rather be respected than loved." But the US is not respected. It is feared, like a muscular drunk who comes into a bar looking for a fight. If George and Condoleezza and Rumsnamara had spent a year on a shoestring on the banks of the Mekong in Vientiane, and in Rabat and Manaus and Lyon and Istanbul and Managua—we might not be the insular, puzzled country that we are today. And we might not be surprised, over and over, to find that people about whom we know nothing do not behave as we expect.

13

Diversity—Who Needs It?

Explain it to me, diversity. I don't get it. Everyone in the feddle gummint and all the news weasels and the academia nuts and assorted distasteful do-gooders with goiterous self-admiration are always honking and blowing about how we need diversity. Why? What is it good for?

I think we need homogeneity. Probably the greatest desire of humanity other than getting laid is avoiding diversity. Mostly, people can't stand each other. I respect their judgement.

Diversity causes nothing but trouble. Think about it. Do old people want to hang around young people? No. Do young people want to hang around old people? Generally they would rather take poison. Do liberals and conservatives want to get within rifle range of each other? No. Except conservatives, because they have rifles. Southerners and damyanks cordially detest each other, except after a few beers, when they stop being cordial. Urban folk and country folk loathe each other. Management and labor, Marine boneheads and army pukes, dogs and cats, on and on, don't nobody much like nobody.

So why do we spend so much sweat and money trying to force people to do what they don't want to do? It's all bass-ackwards. What if we tried … well … freedom? What if the gummint just left people the hell alone?

Naahhhh.

Especially nobody wants racial togetherness. Shoving races together just makes them mad at each other. If they had any desire to be together, you wouldn't have to shove them, would you?

In any city I've been in, blacks and whites work together because they have to by law, and then they go home and complain about each other. Blacks live in black neighborhoods because they want to, and whites do the same if allowed. As soon as black kids get to college, they want black dorms. The whites already have white dorms, and they think that's just fine. Night clubs in Washington aren't racially opposed to either race, but you find very few of one in the clubs of the other.

What happens when a gang of Chinese come to America? They go live in Chinatown because they want to be among their own. They don't hate everybody else and everybody else doesn't hate them. They just aren't comfortable mixing. The second generation moves out, but that's because they aren't really Chinese but Chinese-shaped Americans, eat Big Macs and listen to wretched music. By the third generation they'll be counting on their fingers like whites, maybe.

Fact is, men and women don't want to be together more than some. Men think that women are slightly nuts and they're certainly explosive and you always have to be careful not to set them off and they get ornery if you talk dirty around them, although they do it with each other. God knows what women think about men. Probably that we're crude and watch football and aren't in touch with our inner slug and don't care about feelings. It's all true.

When I was a kid in the South, at dinner parties everybody would eat together. Then the women went into the living room to talk, and the men stood in the kitchen and drank bourbon and told off-color jokes. It seemed to work. It was nice being around the women because they were more civilized than we were, or at least acted it. But there's such a thing as too much civilization.

Now, if you look around the world, nearly all the trouble we have is because of diversity getting stuck together with other kinds of diversity. It just isn't a good idea. In Gay Pair-Eee, (which in fact is probably less than half gay) the North Africans burn everything the French own. The French Canadians hate the rest of the country. The Hutsis and Tutus in Burundi or wherever butcher each other with abandon and machetes. Moslems and Hindus go at it in Kashmir. It isn't even a good idea to let Redskins fans and Cowboys fans get too close together if ethylated.

What do you think would happen in the United States if all the stuff 'em-together laws were dropped? I'll tell you. In about ten minutes the races would resegregate like whiskey and diesel oil. I'll bet offices and companies would get to be mostly women or mostly men before long because most of each flavor don't know how to get along with the other real well. It's more of an effort than with just one or the other.

In at least three ways, what diversity does besides irritate everybody is to Sovietize the country. One way is that the gummint has to make hundreds, nay thousands of stupid laws to intrude where it's got no business because if it doesn't, people will find a way not to mix. You got to watch them like a hawk. If you say they've got to hire twenty percent minorities, they'll hire the minorities best at whatever their business is. The others won't get hired. So the gummint has to make detailed laws and make everybody fill out brainless forms and be watched by bureaucrats, probably affirmative-action hires themselves, who bungle everything because that's what government does.

The second way compulsory mixing Russifies things is that it makes everybody worry about being informed on. Since different groups don't much like each other, at least lots of the time, the gummint, or management, has to make saying so a crime punishable by firing. Otherwise folks would get mad and say what they thought of each other. You'd have the equivalent of bar-room brawls every whichawhere. So people are very careful who they talk to at the water cooler. The OGPU is listening.

Finally, mandatory diversity gelds the press. When by law or policy a newspaper has to hire homosexuals, women, blacks, browns and what have you, it loses the ability to offend any of them. In effect this is censorship. It doesn't have to be imposed. Practically speaking, you can't point out very pointedly that eighty-five percent of some sordid behavior is committed by people like your boss. Or even the next reporter over. You have to live with them. So you write correct pabulum.

Sez me, we'd be better off if we had newspapers peopled exclusively by everything from loon commies singing the Internationale to bomb-everybody conservatives to race-based papers edited by Al Sharpton and David Duke. They could all fight with each other and keep each other straight. Fact is, with a diverse staff you don't get diverse published opinion. Homogeneous staffs would give you diverse newspapers. Then maybe readers wouldn't jump to the internet, the only diverse press we have.

14

Intelligent Design, Yet

A few thoughts regarding the recent foolishness in the courts of Pennsylvania over Intelligent Design:

A pertinent question is why the curricula of the schools should be the concern of judges, who are little more than the enforcement arm of the academic and journalistic elites, imposing on Kansas what could not be legislated in Washington. I see no evidence that judges deploy intelligence, knowledge, or any other qualification other than boundless belief in their unlimited jurisdiction.

Another question is precisely what is meant by Intelligent Design. The answer is not easily divined by reading newspapers: The press have many virtues, but facility in communication is not among them. Reporters, whose thinking is tightly templated, seem to think that Intelligent Design has something to do with Christianity. I know many people who suspect intelligent design, but are not religious. This idea is too difficult for reporters, and too dangerous for Darwinists. If one heresy may be discussed, so may others be, and the cracks in the foundations become evident.

It is interesting to put the matter in historical context. To simplify exuberantly, but not inaccurately for present purposes: People long ago saw the world in (I hate words like this one) non-mechanistic terms. They thought that events occurred because Someone or Something wanted them to occur. They believed in dryads and maenads, sylphs and salamanders, gods and demiurges. It can be debated whether they were foolish, or responding as in a fog to things real but intangible.

They thought more about death in those days, perhaps because they saw more of it, and wondered. Existence was to them more moral than physical, and more often seen as a passage from somewhere to somewhere. Come Christianity if not much earlier, they accepted Good and Evil, upper case, as things that actually existed. In the cosmic order as they understood it, mind, intention, will, and consciousness trumped the material.

Then in roughly the fifteenth century a shift began to a mechanistic view of the world. Next came Newton. There were others before him, but he, though he was himself a Christian, was the towering figure in the rise of mechanism, the view that all things occur ineluctably through mindless antecedent causes. He said (remember, I'm simplifying exuberantly) that the physical world is like a pool table: If you know the starting positions and velocities of the balls, you can calculate all future positions and velocities. No sprites, banshees, or Fates, no volition or consciousness. He invented the mathematics to make it stick, at least for pool tables.

This notion of mechanism spread to other fields. Marx said that history was a mechanical unfolding of economics, Freud that our very personalities were a deterministic result of strange sexual complexes, Darwin (or more correctly his disciples) that we were the offspring of purposeless material couplings, first of molecules and then of organisms. Skinner made us individually the will-less product of psychological conditioning. Sociology did much the same for groups, giving rise to the cult of victimhood: I am not what I am because of decisions I made, but because of social circumstances over which I have no influence. Genetics now seeks to make us the result of tinker-toy chemical mechanism.

No will, free or otherwise. No good or evil, right or wrong. Consciousness being an awkward problem for determinists, they ignore it or brush it aside. Death is harder to ignore, but accepted only as a physical termination. One says, "John is gone," but does not ask, "Where has John gone?" The world offers no mystery or wonder. All questions come down to no more than a fine tuning of our analysis of Newton's pool balls. (Again, I am exuberantly....)

These two views, which reduce to the age-old puzzle of free will and determinism, can be endlessly argued, and have been. Mechanism prevails today because, within its realm, it works, and perhaps also because it does not suffer from the internal contradictions of religion. Technology, almost the only advance made by our otherwise unimpressive civilization, produces results, such as iPods and television. It does not answer, and cannot answer, such questions as Where are we? Why? Where are we going? What should we do? So it dismisses them. Mechanists are hostile to religion in part because religion does not dismiss these questions, but harps on them.

The two conflicting schemes attract adherents because mankind always seeks overarching explanations, particularly regarding origin, destiny, and purpose. Some of us are willing to say "I don't know." Others, well denominated True Believers, have to think that they do know. The country is replete with them: Feminists, Marxists, Born-Agains, rabid anti-semites, snake handlers, Neo-Darwinists. They care deeply, brook no dissent (a sure sign of True Belief), and have infinite confidence in their rightness (or perhaps don't and pretend certainty to ward off a disturbing uncertainty).

In re Intelligent Design, the Darwinists have pretty much won. Their victory springs not so much from the strength of their ideas as from their success in preventing Intelligent Discussion. They control the zeitgeist of the somewhat educated, as for example judges. It is enough.

Evolution is one of the three sacred foundations of political correctness, along with the notions that there can be no racial and sexual difference in mental capacities, and that religion is unprogressive and should be suppressed, Yet these are delicate ideas all three, and cannot well bear scrutiny. Thus the various determinists grimly avoid examination of them.

The lacunae are nonetheless obvious. All is material? If I were to talk to a Neo-Darwinist, I might proceed as follows. "One day you will die. Where will you then be? Yes, yes, I know. We do not speak of this. Yet death does seem to be a bit of a reality. Do you never wake up at three in the morning and think, 'Where in the name of—in the name of Logical Positivism, I suppose you would think—are we?' If not, you are a great fool."

Or, "Let me put the matter differently. Either you believe that there is life after death, or you believe there isn't, or you aren't sure—which means that you believe that there may be. If there is, then there exists a realm of which we know nothing, including what if any effects it exerts on this passing world. If there is nothing beyond the grave, why do you care about anything at all? You've got only a few more years, and then—nothing."

Or I might say, "You don't mind if I boil your young daughter in oil tonight, do you? The world being purely material, the only effect would be to interrupt certain chemical reactions conjointly called 'metabolism' and to substitute others. You cannot object to such a small thing. She will not mind: Consciousness not being derivable from physics, she cannot be conscious. Boiling children cannot be Wrong, as the term has no physical meaning, and in any event all my actions follow inexorably from the Big Bang. I am only doing as blind causality instructs me."

In truth we know very little about existence, neither you nor I nor biochemists nor even federal judges. We defend our paradigms because we crave a sense of understanding this curious place in which we briefly are. We do it by ignoring the inconvenient and by punishing doubt. Thus the furor over Intelligent Design

15

New Year, Probably No Better Than the Old Year

Things are grim hereabouts. We are now deep in the Mexican winter. It is hellishly cold. You almost need a long-sleeved shirt. Instead I wore my thick tee that said "*Soy Un Autentico Hijo de la Chingada*," this constituting my formal wear. It's like truth in packaging.

Bodacious tropical flowers swarmed over Stu's balcony, all purple and orange like complex bruises. Some flamed lipstick red. They glow as if they had batteries. (I was visiting Stu on Lake Chapala, a nasty traffic-ridden gringo enclave near Guad.) The flowers had a nervous look, as if realizing that a drop of a mere forty degrees Fahrenheit would cause them to freeze. It was a near thing.

In the background some damned fool was water-skiing on Lake Chapala. If he fell in that sump of concentrated chemical offal he would mutate into something with tentacles and climb up trellises to eat children. Probably a good idea. I mean, things with tentacles have to eat too.

It being New Year's, I doubtless ought to say something profound about the passage of time, or the meaning of life, or What is Art? Or the significance if any of the last year. It's what columnists do, although we don't know any more about it than anyone else. (You didn't know that time was passing, right? You need me to tell you? OK. It is. Send money.)

All right, then. Here is Cosmic Truth: Each year is more comedic than last. We're all idiots. Life's a sitcom. There is no hope. Now you know.

Being in Mexico adds perspective, at least if you watch the great booby hatch to the north. I especially like the Warn Terr, the preferred toy of the latest Bush. Down here we read all about how the feddle gummint is keeping terrace out of the US so everyone will be safer than probably lots of them want to be. (I'd rather be in danger. Just leave me alone.)

Anyway, it's all PR. A couple of weeks back a friend drove a Mexican woman and her two kids to the airport in Guad to fly to a border town where a coyote was going to smuggle them across the border. And did. Nobody thought much about it. Coyotes are regarded hereabouts as a form of public transportation, like light rail. Only the gringos are clueless. But that's a given.

The immigration hooha (somehow I don't think this column is going to be too coherent) in the States is diverting. When the Mexicans have fiestas in Jocotepec, and high-explosive bottle-rockets swooshboom through the night and garish fireworks turn the milling crowds into a sort of leprous green-and-red cadaverish mob from some Dantean underbasement, you see floats that say, "*Nuestros Hijos Ausentes.*" It means "Our Absent Sons." These are the large number of young men who illegally cross the border to work, come back for the fiestas, and then go back across. Crossing the border illegally is as illegal as downloading illegal music.

How, I asked a Mexicana whose brother frequently crosses, do they do it? "Oh, tunnels, coyotes, people mail passports back. There are lots of ways."

Oh.

Not just wetbacks get their backs wet. When you consider the ease with which drugs go into the US, and get delivered to every small town, at prices you can't refuse, you realize that the Warn Terr couldn't keep the Queen Elizabeth II from coming across the border on wheels. With a marching band in front. Criminal enterprise is far more efficient than government. Though probably less criminal.

Think about it. The drug trade, heavily mediated through Messico, is a service industry, like delivering pizzas. After all, people *want* drugs—only the gummint doesn't want people to have them—and the narcos don't make anybody buy them, even fidgety little school boys mad with boredom. (The government forces these to take otherwise-illegal amphetamine-like substances. Pablo Escobar never did that.)

By contrast, people don't want fifth-rate schools and unpleasantly wholesome FBI heavies who look like armed accountants snooping through their library records, but government does force them to buy these unwanted services. It does force your boy children to take drugs that would land them in jail if they bought them from free enterprise, such as Colombian drug lords.

Organized crime is a better deal. I much prefer the friendly neighborhood dope dealer to any federal official. I can tell the former "no."

I'm babbling. I hope so. This has not been the classic new year, when you wake up with a hangover that feels like Godzilla trying to gnaw his way out of your skull and your eyes look like eggs fried in blood and your mouth tastes like the inside of a truck driver's glove.

No. Moderation is done struck. Last night Stu and I sat under arched brick vaulting in his living room and communed with a certain amount of tequila, yes. Actually in hindsight the amount seems rather less certain. I'll swear to nothing. Of course at five in the morning Stu *did* start bouncing up and down on his bed and playing the air guitar to Pink Floyd.

You have to understand. Stu and I are in a Twelve-Step Program. It is because we are Recovering Washingtonians. The first step is to get on an airplane to Guadalajara. The second step is to find the right relationship with your Higher Power, which I think means a really big amplifier. The third step is to find a Mexicana who does not have Ideologically Significant hairy armpits or a stupid-looking little blue blazer and a snotty attitude.

Things look strange to the North, very strange. That curious little man in the White House persists in his hobby of blowing up High Rackies, a sport which he seems to regard as a sort of video game. We should have bought him a codpiece instead. He probably couldn't have figured out the straps.

We need to think about this president thing. Teddy Roosevelt said we ought to speak softly and carry a big stick. He probably didn't have in mind speaking in tongues, or a swizzle stick. The best you can do is run. What Stu and I wondered was where to put such money as we have before the inflation hits.

After profound analysis and some air guitar, we decided that the gringos actually want a police state. (Remember, it was late at night. But I think the same thing in the morning.) Why wouldn't they? The folk who yowl about civil liberties like alley cats undergoing a hard birth are mostly writers and artists and others of the professionally disagreeable, who are always yelling, "Yo momma" at politicians. They amount to … what? Two percent of the population?

The rest want five hundred channels on the cable, beer, porn, easy sex and two weeks a year at Disney World. They don't read much, largely because of honest inability, and count on their fingers, up to maybe six. They'd be perfectly happy to have storm troopers on every corner. Uzis and flak jackets lend drama to lives that don't have any. Hitler was a consumer product.

Stu took a break to siphon the python and I ran up to the *mirador* to watch the rockets but we're running out of column and I can't tell you about, well, some really critical stuff. Later.

16

General Grumbling (As Distinct From, Say, Sergeant Grumbling)

I am persuaded that the gravest catastrophes to afflict this misguided planet were the inventions of agriculture, clean water, and antibiotics. Without these pernicious conceptions our squalid race might consist of a few millions of savages picking bananas and slaughtering the occasional bison. I do not say this in criticism of savages. Theirs was a reasonable existence. I like bananas, which contain potassium. Bison is succulent. A savage could sleep late.

We should have let well enough alone.

But no. We had to wage chemical war against the various races of bacteria, and boil them alive, and the result was Los Angeles. Three hours a day of commuting, eight more of unnatural staring at witless documents in which no one should have the slightest interest, and then several more of induced corpulence mediated by the lobotomy box. We have come down in the world. Bushmen may have poor table manners, but they don't commute.

Savagery is unjustly contemned. It is true that savages plundered, tortured, and made war mindlessly and without cease in a state of profound mental benightedness. So do we. As I write, the American president bombs some country or other; it doesn't matter which either to him or me. The Secretary of State, Kind Of Leezer Rice, runs about advocating torture. Her performance as First Iroquois puts the United States exactly on the moral level of any other Neanderthals. But then, that is the usual state of man.

The distinction is only that we butcher in volume, wholesale as it were. Ours is a brutishness made impersonal, stripped of the fun and human touch. Misbehavior that savages effortlessly wreaked with materials and implements ready to hand, we achieve with sprawling industries that make unnecessarily complicated means of destruction. Why an elaborate bomber? Why not an obsidian knife?

46

Don't misunderstand me, lest I be thought unpatriotic or subject to a balmy idealism. I believe that people should kill each other, in the greatest numbers possible, with abundance and overflow. But I say this as a matter of principle. In practice, as amusement, a bow and arrow allows a more leisurely extinction and lets all participate. It is more democratic. Sometimes it is well to sacrifice efficiency to entertainment.

Further, savages did not build shopping malls. When a primitive came out of his yurt or hogan or beaver lodge, he found nature lying about him as insouciantly appealing as a floozy in her boudoir. He presumably liked such vistas as much as we do. He did not respond to his appreciation by building a subdivision to bury what he appreciated.

Perhaps we are out of touch. Hunter-gatherism constitutes a superior form of being. Indolence beats hell out of work. It is much more pleasant to loll around the tipi, enjoying the breeze soughing over the plains and telling off-color stories than to go to some air-conditioned dismalalium and rot for thirty years as a compelled cubicle wart in an office painted federal-wall green. To any sensible being, the very idea of work is repugnant. It wastes time better spent in lazing, swimming, or the company of girls. Work usually requires effort. Effort is not a good thing. It should be essayed only in times of desperation.

I believe that modernly it was the Protestants who came up with the curious notion of the redemptive value of work. Of course, in the higher social classes the enthusiasm was usually reserved for work done by others. Like self-flagellation, enthusiasm for labor results from a perverse in-turning of the religious impulse. It gave us such horrors as Puritanism, Massachusetts, and sweatshops full of children. I see little good about it.

But it was agriculture that doomed us. Before this irreparable mistake, the females of the species spent an hour or two a day picking things to eat from trees, or finding roots and berries. The men sallied forth from time to time and killed something—food, each other, or the neighbors. It was a relaxed approach to things, and left time for admiring sunsets and raiding other tribes for women. But then.... ah, but then.

Then came farming. It required foresight, husbandry, and ploughing. None of these had much to recommend it. The practitioner had to plan, to save seed corn, to remember things; here were the awful seeds of bureaucracy. Soon he was getting up at ungodly hours of the morning to dig holes and carry great lumpish things and remonstrate with mules. By contrast the savage, replete with bananas and bison, enjoyed a gentleman's leisure.

The worst defect of agriculture was that it allowed the population to grow like over-sexed kudzu. A few people when spread over a large world are picturesque, or at least avoidable. When they can grow food, a profligate fecundity takes over and soon you have roads, malls, stoplights, and disordered people who want to ban drunk driving.

What good has come of it? Some might argue that the Cherokee in his natural habitat could not read and could not manage the rudiments of arithmetic. In this he closely resembled a modern high-school graduate. It is true that to some extent the gurgling adolescent of today can use a calculator. The Cherokee had nothing to calculate, a far better thing. Instead of spending twelve years unhappily learning nothing in a regimented ignorance-factory, he learned nothing while running through the woods and climbing trees. The choice is, as we say, a no-brainer.

The vices of the savage were precisely those of today. His virtue was that he could apply them only locally and spottily. Because he had no refrigeration, he saw no profit in killing more bison than he could immediately eat. Because he did not practice agriculture, he could not reproduce excessively, and so there were always enough bison. Incapacity has always been more a check on mankind than judgement.

The only hope may be avian influenza if the virus would only abandon its shiftless ways and mutate, although an asteroid strike would serve if I knew how to foment one. Perhaps the Black Death might return. I do not put much faith in radiation poisoning. It has not been adequately proven, though it might serve as a backup.

Those few of us remaining could live torpidly on Pacific Islands, eating mangos and crabs and only occasionally dismembering each other, intimately and with machetes. We have lost the sense of community. Bladed weapons would restore it. Between hecatombs they might lounge on white beaches and watch gorgeous red sunsets over a dark and threatening ocean. We are here for but a short time anyway. Better that we eat coconuts and rut than unduly document things.

17

Science, Perplexity, and the Unrepeatable

I wonder whether the rigidly scientific approach to the world explains quite as much as we think it does (and we seem to think it explains everything).

Everywhere and in all times people have reported sightings of apparitions and ghosts, hants and inexplicable happenings. These are dismissed by neurologists as the results of glitches in neural functioning, by psychiatrists as manifestations of schizophrenia or of heightened suggestibility, by physicists as consequent to curious refractions of light. But the explanations are usually asserted instead of substantiated. I wonder.

My impression is that a great many people have had experiences that do not fit the scientific view of the world, but do not speak of them for fear of being thought mad. A few are not so reticent. JBS Haldane, the noted geneticist, once "went into his home and saw himself sitting in his own chair smoking his favorite pipe. 'Irregular' was his word for the phenomenon, 'indigestion' his explanation. He walked across the room and sat down on his own image."* "Indigestion" of course makes not the slightest sense.

Examples abound, quietly. A woman of my acquaintance, perfectly sane, recounts having watched a window in a room at night open by itself. My father told me of driving one night with a friend in hill country, whereupon a large truck appeared suddenly over a crest, soundless, lights blazing, too close to avoid. They drove through it without effect. "Did you see what I saw?" asked my father of his friend. "Yes," replied the friend, shaken. They did not, he said, tell anyone.

Now, I can offer the usual explanations. These people all suffered from temporary insanity, there is no proof that they weren't actually making up the stories, their memories were playing tricks (whatever that means), or they were dreaming and thought they were awake—all of which seem convenient evasions.

Many people have told me of having had premonitions, as for example that someone was going to die under certain circumstances, after which it happened. Others tell of having felt a sudden, terrible fear, as though something immensely evil were nearby. Most have experienced what we call déjà vu. The plausible reason is always ready to hand: chemical imbalances, the effect of stress, fragmentary memories of similar events, what have you.

Is that really what is happening? Maybe. But saying so doesn't make it so. My father was a hard-headed mathematician, not given to the occult.

Note that the sciences are incapable of recognizing such phenomena. For the sake of discussion, let us suppose that some unscientific event actually occurred—say, that the shade of Elvis in fact appeared in my living room one night, sang Blue Moon Over Kentucky, and then vanished. Would science, or any scientist, be able to know it?

I could tell a physicist that I had seen Elvis, of course. He would assume that I was joking, lying, or deluded. I could report that the neighbors had heard Blue Moon, but the physicist would say that I had played the song on my stereo. I might show him video that I had shot of the appearance, but he would say that I had hired an Elvis impersonator, or that I had faked the footage with video-editing software.

In sum, even though it had really happened, he could never know that it had.

The difficulty is that the sciences can apprehend only the repeatable. If I could summon Elvis at will, again and again in an instrumented laboratory, physicists would eventually have to concede that something was happening, whatever it might be. While scientists defend their paradigms as fiercely as Marxists or Moslems, they can, after sufficient demonstration, be swayed by evidence. But without repeatability, they see no evidence.

Not uncommonly, those in the sciences say that they "do not accept supernatural explanations." One might observe that the world remains the same, no matter what they accept. I might choose not to accept the existence of gravity, but could nonetheless fall over a cliff.

Yet those who do not accept the supernatural never say just what they mean by "supernatural." By "nature," do we not simply mean, "that which is"? If for example genuine premonitions exist (which I do not know), how can they be supernatural, as distinct from poorly understood?

I think that by supernatural scientists mean "not deducible from physics." But of course a great many things are not so deducible—thought, consciousness, free will if any, sorrow, beauty. Scientists do not accept things which seem to have no physical cause, and of course as scientists should not accept them. If a comet were suddenly to change its path, it would hardly be useful if an astronomer said that it just happened, or that a herd of invisible unicorns had pushed it off course. He, properly, would want to find a gravitational influence.

Trouble comes when the sciences overstep their bounds. It is one thing to study physical phenomena, another to say that only physical phenomena exist. Here science blurs into ideology, an ideology being a systematic and emotionally held way of misunderstanding the world. A science is open and descriptive, an ideology closed and prescriptive. A scientist says, in principle at least, "Give me the facts and I will endeavor to derive a theory that describes them." The ideologist says, "I have the theory, and nothing that does not fit it can be a fact." Having chosen his rut, he never sees beyond it. This has not been the way of the greats of science, but of the middle ranks, adequate to swell a progress or work in a laboratory.

In the limitless confidence of this physics-is-all ideology there is a phenomenal arrogance. Perhaps we overestimate ourselves. As temporary phenomena ourselves in a strange universe we don't really understand, here for reasons we do not know, waiting to go somewhere or nowhere as may be, we might display a more becoming humility.

Long ago in a computer lab that I frequented late at night, a white mouse lived. It had escaped from the biology people. As I labored over a keypunch, the wee beastie scurried about behind the line-printer. It seemed to know where to find water, where the fragments of potato chips lay, and where it could sleep warmly.

I reflected that it probably thought it understood its world, which consisted of power supplies, magnetic-core memory, address buses, and the arcana of assembly-language programming. I'd estimate that humanity just about knows where the potato chips are.

*JBS: The Life and Work of J.B.S. Haldane, by Ronald Clark, p.111

18

Pickle Tops

On that far-off night in August of 1962, the moon floated huge and yellow over dark Virginia forests that stretched away and away to the glittering broad Potomac River. Chip Thompson and I trudged along the shoulder of US Route 301 from the Circle toward Dahlgren. We were sixteen. The county—King George County in the Tidewater—was mostly woods and creeks, less populated than now, simpler. Three-Oh-One was still two-lane, the main drag from Maine to Florida. Before us it ran like a determined snake up and down the hills to the Potomac River Bridge into Maryland.

Chip was a country boy with no sense or particular prospects but we both had the wildness of our years on us and sometimes adventured together. He was broad-shouldered and buzz-cut and had a rural economy of expression that Twain would have recognized. "Come on, Ricky," he would say (I was then called Ricky), "You're slower'n dead lice." Or, "Damn, my granny's slow, but she's dead."

I guess it was two a.m. Traffic had long since died except for the big semi rigs on the interstate hauls. The Circle, really a wide spot with a few stores, had shut down. Chip and I had gotten there in my '53 Chevy, a rounded and matronly barge, two-tone dirt brown, and in need of rings, where she had mysteriously quit.

We decided to walk the ten miles or so home to where 206 intersected the highway. He lived up the hill past Owens, I to the right toward the navy base. The distance was no problem. We were both basketball tough and spent our days on or in the creeks. The pull of the dark countryside was on us. In the spring of life the night appeals powerfully to young bucks, being a time of freedom and vague portent of you didn't know what, which was the appeal. It was a big feeling to be alone in the world, rocking in the windblast of the trucks and the singing of the tires.

We hoofed it, gravel crunching underfoot in the silence.

In those days, boys early got cars of sorts. The county was a place of distances. The nearest real town was Fredericksburg, 27 miles from my home, the Circle ten, Colonial Beach 17. The country kids lived in farms and side-roads betwixt and between. We lived in our cars too, and loved them. On a Saturday night we might drive to Freddyburg to cruise Hojo's, back to Colonial Beach just to keep moving, down to Gus's Esso to see who was working the graveyard shift. If you had a date you parked in one of various isolated spots known to all, and did much less than you let on later. Otherwise you drove endlessly through the night for the sheer independence of it, for the feeling of being alone and left alone.

We knew the roads and we knew each other's cars. We reveled in the odd comradeship of winding along the wooded narrow curves of 218 and having headlights come out of the night and it was Charlie Peyton's '57 Chev, baaaad 283, and disappear into the evening. With a two-second glimpse of grill or tail we could tell you the year, make, most probable and biggest engine, and prospects in a drag race.

But the Pluke Bucket—for so my tired Chevy was called—had expired.

On and on Chip and I walked in the silence. Bugs hollered in the trees, but bugs don't count as noise. Our talk was mostly of girls and cars, yet once he said, "Ain't it great, Ricky? Bein' so free and all?" It was. The night brooded around us, full of hunting things and lives that had nothing to do with us. We started into the hills that rise and fall before the river. Soon we could hear the eighteen-wheelers as they reached bottom, double-clutching into low gears for the up-haul, then the roaring and thudding of diesel stacks. It was a grownup sound in a grownup world which we were on the verge on entering.

Cresting a hill, we looked down the dropping highway to the valley of the next. The road at the bottom was shining. In the brilliant moonlight, the cooling asphalt lay speckled with a gleaming that made no sense, like drops of mercury or glowing dew. We had never seen anything like it. Nor would again.

Consumed by curiosity, we finally reached the outliers of the strange luminescence. I looked down and saw ... a pickle-jar top, such as you find on jars of pickles in stores. Thousands of them lay on the dark asphalt, shining in the moonlight.

Understanding came. Back in the other direction, past the Circle, was what we called the Pickle Factory. It was a bottling operation for Mount Rose Pickles, where the stronger county boys sometimes worked. Apparently a delivery truck carrying jar tops had jackknifed in the road and flipped. The truck was gone, but the pickle tops were everywhere.

It had never occurred to us that pickle tops had to come from somewhere and that whole trucks full of them might exist. In some distant state people spent their lives making pickle tops just as inhabitants of the county fished and crabbed. Here was the industrial belly of the pickle business.

For ten minutes we kicked at pickle tops, scraped them with out feet, picked them up and threw them saucerishly into the woods. No trucks came. We were alone with a thousand pickle tops glowing eerily at the moon with bugs keening in the black foliage. I think we both knew that here was a moment never to be repeated, something that maybe had never happened to anyone before.

Then we kept on down the highway. Dawn lay ahead and I wanted to be in through my window to avoid explanations. In those days you could still see the stars. They gave a sense of mystery to the great universe arching over the dark land. We could hear water trickling in low boggy spots toward Machodoc Creek and there was nobody else in the world. Just us.

19

Indians, Indians, Everywhere, and Not a Drop to Drink

I'm going to start a rickshaw factory. It's so our kids will have a way to make a living, now that America is pulling out of the First World. Maybe I'll put an iPod socket on the poles or a little tiny television, made in Japan. That way our puzzled offspring won't inadvertently start thinking. Tradition provides an anchor in the circumambient chaos.

See, what's going to happen is, all the design work and programming are going to Mumbai, except the part that already has. Manufacturing is pretty much in China already, Mexicans do all the scutwork, and blacks work for the government or not at all, or both at once. That leaves whites as midlevel bureaucrats supervising each other. Thing is, whites are getting so they can't read either, so they'll need rickshaws to pull, in case the Chinese engineers want to go somewhere.

It's over, I tell you. The United Steak has turned into a mess of pale-faced bushmen mumbling in pidgin English, the young anyway, with Orientals as missionaries trying to civilize us. Yes, friends and neighbors! Ain't it exciting? All the professors in America of anything practical are already Chinese or Indian. Or getting that way fast.

You think I exaggerate? Ha. Checking the staff of the University of Central Florida's school of Mechanical, Materials, and Aerospace Engineering, I discover that most of Mumbai has already moved to America. Shanghai too. There follows an unedited list of the staff:

Ranganathan Kumar, Linan An, Quanfang Chen, Ruey-Hung Chen, Larry Chew, Hyoung Jin "Joe" Cho, Louis C. Chow, Kevin R. Coffey, Ted Conway, Vimal Desai, Jiyu Fang, A. Henry Hagedoorn, Olusegun Illegbusi, Roger Johnson, Samar Jyoti Kalita, Jayanta Kapat, Aravinda Kar, Alain Kassab, Chris-

tine Klemenz, Alexander Leonessa, Kuo-Chi "Kurt" Lin, Antonio Minardi, Fais-
sal Moslehy, Jamal F. Nayfeh, David Nicholson, Eric L. Petersen, Sudipta Seal,
Yongho Sohn, C. "Sury" Suryanarayana, Raj Vaidyanathan, Quan Wang, Fang
Xu, Richard Zarda.

If that isn't a hotbed of Anglo-Saxon achievement, I can't imagine what might
be. It's probably just what ol' Tom Jefferson had in mind. Who can doubt it?

What we see now is backslosh from the Raj. Used to be, you had a bunch of
Brits in India and China and places, trying half-heartedly to lift the benighted
brown rascals from their slothly ways and make'm into Europeans. The White
Man's Burden, all that. Of course, you couldn't really expect the heathen Chinee
to do much more than dig holes and wash shirts. The darker races were, well, the
darker races. All right in their place but … limited. Everyone understood it.

Except, it would seem, the Indians and the heathen Chinee. Since they had
limited understanding, it figures that they didn't understand that they had limited understanding, and so acted like they didn't, and so now they're doing com-
putational fluid dynamics in their heads because they don't know any better. (A
certain logical opacity informs sociological thought.) Today we have the Empire
in reverse with Chandragupta Sahib teaching heuristic programming to the
natives. Us.

The problem is that since neither England nor the United States any longer
has a school system, the Asians will have to teach us remedial counting, probably
on our fingers, so we can work for them. (I'm from West Virginia. We'll have
base-twelve arithmetic.)

All of this is well-thought-out, like a military campaign of blitzkrieg endull-
ment. We're returning to subhuman status in a pincers movement. While the
Indians and Chinese and all are getting smarter, we're getting enstupidated at a
hell of a pace. It shows that international cooperation is possible.

There's this thing called the National Assessment of Adult Literacy, which just
came out and said that Americans not only can't read but are vigorously getting
worse. Here it is, from the *Washington* ever-loving *Post*, December 25 in the Year
of Our Decline 2005:

"Only 41 percent of graduate students tested in 2003 could be classified as
'proficient' in prose—reading and understanding information in short
texts—down 10 percentage points since 1992. Of college graduates, only 31 percent were classified as proficient—compared with 40 percent in 1992."

That's *college graduates*, brethren and sistern! They can't read simple stuff.
"See Spot run. Run, Spot…." What you think them other scoundrels can't do
that ain't graduates? Hallelujah, dearly beloved, idiots are us. Am us, I mean.

Now, sure, you can make excuses, and say, well, this dismal revelation counts all the Permanently Disadvantaged Minorities and affirmative-action nonstudents and all the other people who shouldn't be anyway in what ought to be colleges but mostly aren't. But you're supposed to be able to read when you get out of freaking high school, aren't you? If they can't read, how did they into college, much less out the other end?

You reckon the Japanese are as dim as we are? I bet a better percentage of their graduate students can read English well than ours can.

The *Post* goes on, thump, thump, thump. "Literacy experts and educators say they are stunned by the results of [the] recent adult-literacy assessment, which shows that the reading proficiency of college graduates has declined in the past decade, with no obvious explanation."

No obvious explanation? Oh no, not at all obvious—no more obvious than, say, advanced leprosy on a nekkid prom queen. How about: They can't read because our schools are in the hands of low-IQ social engineeresses with the academic inclinations of cocker spaniels? If this darkness is the result produced by "literacy experts and educators," what might we expect from them as ain't? I taught my three-year-old daughter to read phonetically in about a month of a few minutes a day. It's easy to teach kids to read (phonetically). It takes genius to waste twelve years of their lives, sixteen in the case of college graduates, and keep them from learning to read.

People deserve what they tolerate, say I, which is a frightening thought. Actually I love watching it. I'd sell tickets if I could. I've heard of countries going tits-up because they got stomped on by some other country, or got their trade cut off, but most of them don't do it unless they have to. With us, it's on purpose.

Meanwhile, you might be smart to get a wheelbarrow and fill it with cement and let your kids get a start on pulling it. Success after all goes to the economically adaptive, yet rickshaws may be trickier than we envision. Those who can't pull will clean toilets. Have your children memorize the names of the streets while they still have you to read for them—unless, that is, you aren't among the college graduates who can read.

We must look to the future.

20

Of Immigration and Chain Saws

June 21, 2005

"BOSTON, Massachusetts (AP)—On April 25, Gregory Despres arrived at the U.S.-Canadian border crossing at Calais, Maine, carrying a homemade sword, a hatchet, a knife, brass knuckles and a chain saw stained with what appeared to be blood."

American Immigrations officials, alert as pit bulls on crank, unsleepingly attentive to the security of the homeland ... let him in. And indeed, why not? Everybody has to be somewhere. It's a law of physics.

I have lived in Guadalajara, Mexico, with a splendid Mexicana, Violeta, for almost two years. She put herself through university by working three jobs, after which she lived by teaching Spanish to gringos. She has a daughter of thirteen, Natalia, who is exceedingly bright, no more than ordinarily intolerable for a teenager, and the star student in her school. The kid reads more books in a week than the public schools of Washington read in a year. Or would, if they could recognize a book.

I would like to take Vi to Washington for a couple of weeks to meet friends, see the city, and listen to Honky Tonk Confidential, a bar band which, second only to Mark Twain, constitutes America's chief contribution to world culture. I probably can't take her. She probably can't get a visa. Certainly the State Department makes it so disagreeable to try that I won't subject her to it.

But if she had a chain saw....

"Anthony [a spokesman for Immigrations] conceded it 'sounds stupid' that a man wielding what appeared to be a bloody chain saw could not be detained. But he added: 'Our people don't have a crime lab up there. They can't look at a chain saw and decide if it's blood or rust or red paint.'"

Calling it stupid is unfair. Surveys by the State Department show that over ninety-nine percent of owners of chain-saws put red paint on them. I mean, what else would they do? People who have spent time in Canada know that most owners of chain-saws also carry swords. It's just common sense. You never can tell when you may be involved in a sword fight. I can't.

Now, I understand that the United States has a problem with illegal immigration, and I understand that a country has every right to control its borders. But … might not a little common sense be desirable in matters governmental? (Of course not. But this is a theoretical column.)

Consider. I, despite my picture, am an embarrassingly respectable journalist with a record of thirty years of writing, both on staff and off, for grimly respectable organs of communication. I still do. This doubtless demonstrates poor judgement, yes. Journalism is less reputable than, say, than selling bridges in New York, though better than stealing hubcaps. Still, reporters do not import Mexican women to be table dancers in San Antonio.

It's curious. If I came in with a suitcase that said "Weaponized Ebola," and told them my name was Ahmet, they would let me in because they didn't want to profile. If Vi showed up with a gory hatchet, perhaps trailing strands of flesh, they presumably would say, "Right this way. Would you like citizenship while you're at it? A photo op with the President? Foot massage?"

Despres of the chain saw was a naturalized US citizen. Me, I might be choosier in who I naturalized. But then, I guess I don't understand security. In fact, I'm sure I don't. It may be that when you have spent years watching people come across a border, you learn to distinguish between dangerous bearers of bloody weaponry, and harmless ones.

Now, going to the Fear Box—excuse me, the Consulate—for anything at all is unpleasant. Nobody wants it to be, but it is. Used to be, you showed your passport to the Marine guard who said "Thank you, good day sir," and made you feel as if it were *your* embassy or consulate. Now you are the enemy. There's the usual terrify-the-rubes business of removing your shoes, watch, fillings, frontal lobes, prostate. Then, reportedly, you talk to someone behind bullet-proof glass. All god's chillun scared to death.

Some of these examiners, again according to common report, are friendly and courteous. Some are not. A good one may say civilly, as one did to a friend married to a Mexicana, "Look, you need to convince me that she's going to come back. What have you got?" Fair enough.

"The decapitated body of a 74-year-old country musician named Frederick Fulton was found on Fulton's kitchen floor. His head was in a pillowcase under a kitchen table. His common-law wife was discovered stabbed to death in a bedroom. Despres … was arrested April 27 after police in Mattapoisett saw him wandering down a highway in a sweatshirt with red and brown stains."

An ideal immigrant. You know, like Einstein. He would increase diversity. But for god's sale don't let a Spanish-teacher in. The consequences would be imponderable. Suppose that, in a crowded train station at rush hour, she began to explain the preterite tense? Worse, suppose that people learned it. This would set an unwholesome precedent, and constitute a threat to the teachers unions and thus to the entire educational edifice.

How could I establish that Vi wanted to come back? Well, she has an aging father she cares for. Unfortunately the poor guy can't walk. We're supposed to bring him in with a wheelbarrow? Vi has Natalia. Thing is, every Mexicana has a daughter. What's that prove? I once bumped into a State Department type who knew about such things, and said, well, how about if I put up a $20K cash bond for her return? No, can't do that. Too easy.

And so often now officials at the borders and airports are just plain unpleasant. Vi doesn't need it. She has heard the horror stories of being jerked around at the border from friends with visas. A friend of mine always has his Mexican wife taken from him at the border for aggressive questioning in separate rooms. For this we pay taxes.

Of course if Vi swam the river, she could get welfare, schooling for thirteen illegitimate offspring, a driver's license, medical care, and be eligible for a dozen consecutive amnesty programs. How sensible. Like outlawing smoking while paying farmers to grow tobacco.

Best I can come up with is to buy her a chain saw at Wal-Mart, chop a goat up with it, get her a sword, a garrote, and some anthrax, and they'll let her across, no problem. Maybe a severed head in a pillowcase, just to be sure.

21

Here Comes the Bride, or Maybe the Groom

I'm trying to figure out gay marriage. Help me. (I gave up trying to figure out heterosexual marriage long ago.)

Maybe I need to figure out gays first. Or maybe I need to figure out sex, which isn't possible. Nothing about sex makes a grain of sense. The whole idea is bizarre. If it didn't exist and you thought it up, you would end up in a struggle buggy between hefty psych orderlies.

I think it was Lord Chesterfield who said of sex, "The pleasure is fleeting, the position ridiculous, and the expense damnable." He was being charitable. Sex is probably responsible for more misery and proportionally less pleasure than anything short of hemorrhagic tuberculosis. People jump off bridges because of it. They spend hours in meat bars talking to people they don't like because of it. Its pursuit wastes unfathomable amounts of time. If the average man spent as many hours working as he did planning to get laid, the caloric output would upset the thermal balance of the earth. (Global warming. You don't suppose …?)

Now, gays. I have no idea why homosexuals want to do what they want to do, except in the case of lesbians, when it makes perfect sense, except that the average lesbian has the personality of a rat-tail file. But then, I have no idea why I want to do what I want to do. Granted, I'm not particularly at ease around homosexuals, but maybe they aren't comfortable around me. Call it a draw.

Having spent time in the undersides of cities, I know at least as much as I want to about homosexuals, crossdressers, S&M freaks, and transsexuals, as well as the odder kinks. What does one make of a six-foot-two transvestite, with an Adam's apple like a bowsprit and the jaw of a front-end loader, wearing a polka dot skirt and brandishing a monster lollipop? I'm not sure. If it happens in somebody's basement in the remote suburbs, I'm quite sure that it's not my business.

And so I decided I didn't give a damn about sexual peculiarities, provided that (a) I didn't have to watch them and (b) nobody got hurt. If you like Bactrian camels, it's fine with me, as long as the camel consents. Just do it somewhere else. Whatever it is.

So what I figure about gays is, leave'em alone, if they'll leave me alone. If the guy at the next desk is homosexual, I don't care. Gay bars? If they're reasonably discrete, leave them alone.

What's this got to do with marriage? Patience. We're getting there.

Now, Christians of the sort who do not so much love Jesus as hate everybody else will tell me that God doesn't like gays. I wonder why he made them, then? (Of course I wonder why he made hemorrhagic tuberculosis too, so this line of argument may go nowhere.) If memory serves, God (Leviticus, I think) did say we should stone homosexuals to death. While I am not antireligious, God and I are going to differ on this one. Call it jury nullification.

On the other hand, I vaguely recall that Jesus once said, "Let him among you who is without sin cast the first stone." On that basis, gays are safer than a riverboat gambler with five aces and a Derringer in his sleeve.

So why am I against marriage of gays? Which I am.

For several reasons, the first of which has precious little to do with gays. As an American in remission, I have a romantic fondness for the notion of constitutional government, which of course doesn't exist and never will again in the United States if it ever did. Face it: The constitution is deader than a doorknob. I mean a doorknob with melanoma and clogged arteries. But the memory does provide a convenient platform for launching vituperations and upsettances. That's what we in the column racket do.

The first objection is to the further extension of judicial dictatorship. Courts run the country these days. The will of the people is irrelevant.

When did you last hear of anything of lasting import being done by Congress? I can't either. But almost every week you read about some federal judge, or that ratpack of pompous drones on the Supreme Court, who has (Have? This sentence is going to hell) defunded the Boy Scouts, or invented a constitutional right to abortion, or imposed integration, or outlawed the public expression of Christianity, or made it impossible to stop immigration. They tell you who you can hire, who you can sell your house to, what your children will be taught. They serve to impose what could never be legislatively enacted. The judges are out of control.

They're at it again. Marriage doesn't mean what it has always meant. It means what some over-promoted nonentity wants it to mean. And the country will obey. Roll over. Bark. Fetch.

A second objection is that there is no logical end in sight once the courts arrogate the power to define marriage. If a man can marry a man, why can he not marry two men? I'm serious. I could argue that the bonds of affection can exist between three men as well as between two. The norm today is serial marriage. Why not parallel marriage? Who are we to discriminate in favor of couples?

Why not heterosexual polygamy? It has a long history and enjoys certain advantages. Why should a man not marry his daughter? A common argument is that it can lead to the defects peculiar to inbreeding. (As a West Virginian, I regard this as unconscionable meddling. Twelve toes are more stable than ten.) But when two people carry recessive genes for some unpleasant disease, we don't forbid them to marry. Why discriminate against members of a family?

Why should a man not marry, say, his sheep? Our current legal prejudices condemn him, and her, to a life of—I started to say "sin," but I think sin has been found to be constitutionally inexistent. The penalties for unconstitutional love are burdensome. Do you know how hard it is to get a motel room with a sheep?

Peer behind the shabby curtain of pretended principle, and you see that the government is not an impartial entity serving the public, but a means of imposing on the majority the will of any who can get their hands on the miraculous levers of the courts.

22

The Military and the Press

Much email comes my way, from military folk both current and retired, assuring me that the press consists of leftist commy anti-American liberal tree-hugging cowardly backstabbers who probably like the French and would date Jane Fonda. It is an old song. Having spent decades covering the armed forces, I have seen much of the Pentagon and the press. Things are a tad more complex. A few thoughts:

The military, particularly the officer corps, wants not reporting but cheerleading. The very idea of an uncontrolled press is repugnant to them. Thus officers try to keep reporters away from enlisted men, who are less political and tend to say things that, while true, are not policy. Thus the edgy, wary hostility in the presence of reporters. The truth of what a reporter writes doesn't matter to them, only whether it is "positive."

The reasons for this sensitivity are in part practical, given that wars cannot long be fought without the support of the public. There are deeper reasons. First, there is the military's stark with-us-or-against-us outlook. Second, there is the intense loyalty to the group that characterizes military men. Third, an authoritarian structure to which reporters seem an uncontrolled rabble. "Uncontrolled" is the key word.

The military believes that the press should be part of the team. Its job should be not to report but to support. "Are they Americans, or aren't they?" To see what the command thinks the press should be, read a base newspaper. It will be a cross between a PR handout and a *Weekly Reader*.

Reporters do not see their job as cheerleading, this being the work of PR people, whom they despise. Correspondents by nature are not team players but salaried freelances who compete with, instead of cooperating with, their colleagues. Glory hounds, they want to break the big story themselves. Instead of being loyal to any group, they are suspicious of all groups. They do not respect authority.

Frequently incompetent, they are pushy, demanding, and irritating. The military is afraid of them. You hate what you fear.

In short, they are everything the military detests. If they did their jobs perfectly, which neither they nor soldiers do, the military would still loathe them.

Further, soldiers with exceptions are insular, reporters greatly less so. Consider. A kid who goes to West Point lives for four years, in formative late adolescence, with relentless military indoctrination. This is not in all respects bad. It tends to produce a personally honest, public-spirited, responsible man who makes an admirable citizen. These same men can run a carrier battle group, as difficult and impressive a thing as I have ever seen done, and they can do it only because they obey, make sacrifices, and respect the group.

The young cadet then goes to Fort Hood, say, for three years in which he is almost exclusively in the company of other soldiers. Next, three years in an armored division in Germany (the rotations may have changed) during which he is again constantly with soldiers and, since GIs don't learn languages, unable to communicate with Germans other than bartenders. The Army is his entire existence. By the time he is thirty he is deeply imbued with a bird-politics leftwing vs. rightwing view of things. He is by no means stupid—the academies get bright students—but he is simple-minded. He believes profoundly that one is either on the team or with the enemy.

Reporters aren't on the team. They report what they see, or think they see. Many do not know what they are talking about, but the military detests even more those who do. In time of war, truthfulness makes them traitors. Soldiers often use the word, and they mean it. You are with us, or you are with the enemy.

The two groups live in sharply differing mental worlds. While reporters are more insular than they should be, they are much less so than the military. They see a broader slice of the world and rub shoulders with more kinds of people. The overseas correspondents see more wars than do soldiers. The result is a certain cosmopolitanism which, whether good or bad, is much at odds with the clarity of the military's outlook.

For example, many in Washington who actually know how the press works (the military actually doesn't) believe that the press supports the war in Iraq, has until recently given the White House a free ride, and has been adroitly controlled by the government. I agree. If newspapers had been against the war, they would have published countless photos of gut-shot soldiers who will never get a date, quadriplegics doomed to a life on a slab, and more Abu Ghraib photos (which they have). Soldiers don't know this. In any event, anything but unqualified support is treason.

The military usually regards journalists as cowards. ("Coward" and "traitor" are their gravest pejoratives.) This is questionable. When the 2000th US soldier died in Iraq, I checked the site of Reporters Without Borders and found that 72 reporters had been killed there (with two more missing), or 3.6 percent of the military total. I don't know how many troops have served in Iraq. Just now it is about 160,000. To be conservative, let's call it 130,000 on average, making 347,100 for two and two-thirds years of war. By the equation 2,000/347,000 = 72/x, one finds that there would have to have been 12,500 reporters in Iraq to have equal rates of death between reporters and soldiers. Otherwise, the press is taking casualties at a higher rate than the military. The calculation is rough, but makes the point.

Further, reporters can leave any time they choose. The government forces soldiers to fight under penalty of long jail sentences and, in many times and places, death. If you dispute this, tell the troops that they can fly home tomorrow without punishment and see how many remain. They would not leave from cowardice, but from lack of a stake in the outcome. (Would you leave your children fatherless because you wanted *democracy in Iraq?*)

More than most professions, the military lives in a world defined by idealism. Being a dentist does not carry an ideology with it. Being a soldier does. The dedicated soldier thinks in terms of honor, valor, loyalty, sacrifice, and heroism, of righting wrong and defeating evil, of proving himself in combat, of glory and exaltation and defending the fatherland. The reporter sees the dead lying in the street, the flies crawling in shattered craniums, the bombed-out cities for year after year without change. He hears this described as progress. To him it is pure bullshit.

Maybe, maybe not. But it is how he thinks.

Journalists are not idealists. Cynical, weary of being lied to, having seen the fraud and self-interest that underlie, as they come to see it, almost everything, they regard the soldiery as a riverboat gambler might regard the Boy Scouts. The soldiery regard the press as a Boy Scout might regard a riverboat gambler. Different mental worlds.

Ambiguity disturbs soldiers. Few of us can kill and die for ifs and maybes and on-the-one-hand. Thus every war is described in apocalyptic terms, whether Vietnam, Granada, Korea, or Iraq: We must defeat them there or we'll have to fight them in California. Usually this is nonsense. Journalists may suggest as much. And so, again, they become traitors.

The moral ambiguity of war is especially painful. While military men as citizens are at least as moral as the rest of the population, as warriors they are not, and can't be. Because of this conflict they therefore have to believe things about themselves that are not true. Consequently you may hear a soldier saying with perfect sincerity that the US military goes to great lengths to avoid killing civilians. Furious accusation of treason arise when reporters point out that they are in fact killing civilians.

For example, while a case can be made that the bombings of Nagasaki and Hiroshima were militarily desirable, they cannot well be described as attempts to preserve civilians. The bombings of cities in WWII were intended to kill civilians, hundreds of thousands of them, to break morale. In war utility invariably trumps decency.

Reporters, being traitorous, will write of these things. After initial cheerleading while the war goes well, they will note that it isn't going well any longer. Soldiers, who are being killed and mangled, come to hate them, seldom distinguishing between being against a war and being against the troops. After the hell of combat, who wants to hear that maybe it wasn't really a good idea after all?

On and on it goes.

23

Rednecks and the Virtues Thereof

There is a lot of snot and malice about rednecks on the internet. Most of it comes from such cornflowers and honeysuckles as college professors, other witless suburban nonentities, and assorted twits in cities. By "redneck," these bundles of intellectual lingerie seem to mean anyone without a college degree who can hang a door or lube his car.

One of them, some sort of biochemical rascal, figured that rednecks were examples of poor evolutionary fitness—compared, I guess, to him. Now, that's a stretch.

Tell you about rednecks. They're probably the only people in the whole country that *ain't* unfit. What used to be Davy Crockett's country today is full mostly of folk who can't do anything for themselves. They call someone else to fix the plumbing, shoot the burglar, gap their plugs, build their houses, get their kids off drugs. If the cat dies they need a pet-loss grief-management counselor. From a redneck's point of view, the United States is turning fast into people like those nasty white grubs that nekkid savages in New Guinea eat, only with legs.

I know the breed—rednecks, not grubs. I grew up with them, in King George County, Virginia, and in Athens, Alabama in 1957. Back then I thought I was Huck Finn. I may have been right. Certainly the evidence favored the proposition. I'd run through the woods like a Southern Mowgli with a slingshot and later got drunk with the country boys in high school and drove like three damn fools, buy one and get two free. We hunted, and crabbed in the Potomac, and such like. We called people from Massachusetts "Damyanks," or "targets."

Now, the people in KG were either farmers or fishermen. They could build a crab boat from scratch. Try it. What they were, really, was versatile. They'd snatch an old engine from a junkyard Chevy and rebuild it, convert it to marine, and mount it in the boat. They changed their own transmissions, replaced clutch plates, wired the barns they built. They could run a farm, keep old tractors going, blast a stump, raise hogs and slaughter them. They knew guns, and had them.

They could hunt, shoot, and fish. They were tough, cut cordwood and split logs and dug foundations. If they wanted a wall, they laid the brick. If something broke, they fixed it.

Maybe they came up a little short on iambic pentameter. Didn't seem to hurt'em none.

Now, if an asteroid hit Boston, which would be a good idea, and all the International Safeways and designer-cheese stores went tits-up, and the repair shops and gas stations that do things for all that human okra up there that needs someone else to water it, and if people had to take care of themselves like grownups ... how long do you think the English department at Cornell would last?

Too long, yes. Maybe minutes. Think of it: Five hundred BMWs descending on the drug stores, people squealing and clawing and snatching out eyeballs to steal the last Prozac. Why, they couldn't live without sour white wine not nearly as good as Ripple and those cheeses with names like Chartreuse. A week later they'd be eating their lawns. (I don't oppose this, understand. I'd sell tickets.)

People in the country wouldn't blink. They might wonder how to start an asteroid so they could get Washington too.

If some upscale flowerbed like Fairfax County outside DC ever had to deal with hard times, it would the best show since Aunt Sally sat on that ant nest. It isn't just that they can't do anything. They can't even think about doing anything. I mean, suppose that after the asteroid hit the cops had other things to do, like look after their families, and a larcenous parasitic lawyer encountered some Diversity with a knife in its hand and an itch for his television or daughters, what would he do? Get extra therapy? Hit him with a rubber stamp? Say, "Can't we talk about this?"

Now, in the country, people had a slightly less lenient attitude toward having their homes invaded. Nobody ever shot anybody, much anyway. People didn't think it was civilized. They did have dogs and shotguns and rifles. Further, they had the backbone to use them if the need arose. Which is why it didn't.

Now, I reckon professors are pretty smart. After all they're picked for it—except in departments whose names end in "Studies," and Departments of Education, where they're picked for being stupid. And in some other departments, if brains were oil, the inmates would be about a quart low: Anthropology, psychology, sociology, cosmetology science. The really smart ones—there must be a couple of dozen—might be able to handle an asteroid strike.

But I doubt it. The dinosaurs didn't. What happens is, most people grow up helpless in some suburb. It isn't their fault. They have to wear helmets and life-preservers to walk around the block and probably adult diapers and if they are boys they like as not get estrogen injections so they won't be. They can't wrestle or play dodge ball because it's violent. They can't play Cowboys and Engines because it's insensitive. Then they get a job in some office fiddling with forms. And that's all they do. Ever.

A redneck has a life, lots of times anyway. A buddy of mine grew up in a tough section of a Yankee city, where the deciding factor in a philosophical discussion was a good right hook. He went to Viet Nam for a couple of tours in spec ops, spent ten years in the fishing fleets of Alaska, and retired as a fireman-EMT. He knows motorcycles, scuba, and NASCAR.

A man like that has some depth to him. He knows what life is. He has seen it. You can talk to him about the street trades—cops, fire, paramedics—and he knows what happens. He knows Nana Plaza and small boats in cold oceans and Saigon in the bad times. You don't get that with a biochemist, master of aldehydes. A perfesser is like one of those polished jewels of the British upper classes, except bright, and pig-ignorant of the world. I mean, if you spend ten years in labs to get your meal ticket, you don't have time to amount to much.

Of course you might cure cancer. And I guess penicillin is pretty good stuff. Maybe everybody's got some virtue, even professors. They still can't cure an asteroid.

24

House

Ha! Vi and I just closed on a house in Jocotepec, the only remaining Mexican town on the north shore of Lake Chapala, near Guadalajara. We're going to call it The Pancho Villa. It has a big ratty-looking walled-in yard with gynormous twisted orange trees, probably planted by Methuselah's granddaddy, that drop oranges all over the place without regard to environmental piety. Flowers erupt everywhere, never asking permission. It's wonderful. I hate trimmed gardens. They remind me of the kind of over-organized desk that I associate with compulsive hand-washers.

On top is a mirador, which means a concrete place like a tennis court that lost its net. You can sit up there in the wind and sun and watch large brown mountains lolling about. Or you can fall off it. We're going to put in a railing, though. You can also watch sunsets, which are showy hereabouts, or thunderstorms and get electrocuted.

The Pancho Villa is in almost the last street of houses short of the mountains so in the mornings you hear roosters propositioning hens. Burros yell "*Eeeeeeeeeeeee*-honk!" like hairy saxophones. If you want a burro here, you just get one and put it where you think it ought to be. You don't need a rabies card, farm-animal zoning, and a federal license saying that you know how to operate a burro.

The lady from whom we bought it (and she is a lady, in the almost-forgotten sense of the word) is an Englishwoman of the generation that fought WWII. They don't make those any longer, but ought to. Since the furnishings come with the house, it was great to find that her taste was also our taste. Maybe it feels like home to me because I grew up on Kipling and Alice and suchlike British tales.

Now, I get mail saying, "What's it like to live in Mexico, Fred? Isn't it full of, you know, deadly viruses?" Well, yes, but they're optional. If you buy a little plastic bucket of yogurt, an envelope comes with it that says, "Deadly Viruses." You don't have to eat them. You can give them to a passing child.

Anyway, life in Messico. The country still works on a distributed paradiggem. That means that if you want a quart of milk, you walk a block to where there's a little Pedro-and-Maria store that probably used to be a living room and now it's a store. If you want a donut, you walk two blocks in another direction to the bread shop. You tell Conchis that you want two of those *gr-et-t* big ones with clumps of maple sugar or something on top and you chat with her a bit because that's how it's done. Then you go back home and chomp on them.

See, it's because Mexico is still primitive. Pretty soon it will get modern. Then it will have a shopping center three miles out of town with a Mall-Wart that will close down all the little shops in Joco. Then you will drive fifteen minutes, fight other angry unhappy people for a parking spot, and save seven cents on your donut. And maybe die on the way back, trying to eat a donut while using a cell phone. (Every cloud....)

We've all heard old guys talking about how great it was to live in little towns out of Norman Rockwell (or, as I guess it would be here, *Piedrapozo*). Well, it was great. Not too dynamic maybe, but especially swell for kids. A lot of Mexico is still like that. In the US the most important things are efficiency and making money, which is why it is real efficient and has lots of money and all sorts of technology. There is a definite upside to money.

Mexico isn't so hot at any of those things, but it has a certain livability to it. It's more personal. Most parents recognize their children on sight, people know each other, and towns go in for huge seething festivals for their patron saints, or because it's Easter, or maybe just Wednesday. A Mexican doesn't need much prodding to launch a fiesta. In Joco on fiesta nights the plaza is so jammed that it takes twenty minutes to cross it. You've got three bands going at once and kids on dad's shoulders and fireworks fizzing and whirling on tall wicker *castillos*. Most of it would be illegal up north. So would everything else, though. Consistency is a Nordic virtue, much overrated. There has to be a reason why intelligent people want to live with so many rules, but I don't know what it is.

There's a relaxed feel to things here. If you want to ingest a brew, you can sit on the sidewalk (in a chair) at the beer joint on the plaza and watch Mexico go by, mostly on motor-scooters or *cuatrimotos*, those four-wheeled things that roll over and crush you. Kids of about nine drive them, but not where they can roll over. The girl-watching is excellent, the women not given to scatological demonstrations of morbid virility. Joco reminds me of Athens, Alabama, in 1957.

Not everybody would like it. If you are the kind of pedestrianly lordly (can you be that?) and meddlesome retiree who really wants to live in suburban Lauderdale but can't afford it, don't come here. Go to Lauderdale. Live under a bush. Better yet, play in traffic. You wouldn't like Joco.

A lot of the streets aren't paved. There's burro traffic, and horses. They would probably give you germs. There aren't any anti-smoking regulations. The second-hand smoke would make you crump from cancer before you could whip out your EPA-approved mini-oxygen set, and probably dissolve the paint from your car.

Actually, there aren't many regulations of any kind. Everything is disordered, and people take care of themselves. If you want a beer, you go to the beer store, where the owner's kids will be playing inside, and no one will arrest the owner. Not nearly enough things are illegal here to suit the emerging North American taste. Try Canada.

We move in on the 28th. There will be a most disreputable party. People will dance on the mirador and fall on their heads. There will be ribs and tequila (which sounds unnatural, but we'll do it anyway). I'm going to get a shack and put a serf in it so we can be authentic hacendados. (What do serfs eat, I wonder?) What with barbecue and ruckus juice and socially deviant behavior, no one will make it to work the next day. But no one would have anyway.

25

Will Somebody for God's Sake Marry Maureen?

I read with ashen resignation that Maureen Dowd, the professional spinster of the *New York Times,* will soon birth a book, no doubt parthenogenetically, called *Are Men Necessary?* The problem apparently is that men have not found Maureen necessary. (Hell hath....) Clearly there is something wrong with men. I weary of the self-absorbed clucking of aging poultry.

Why is Maureen hermetically single? For starters, she is not just now your classic hot ticket. She's not just over the hill, but into the mountains, to Grandmother's house we go. She probably gets more daily maintenance than a 747, but she still looks as though a vocational school held an injection-molding contest and everyone lost. That leaves her with only her personality as bait. The prognosis is grim.

Was that ungentlemanly? She makes a career of being disagreeable about men. What's sauce for the gander is sauce for the goose, say I.

Reading her unending plaints, one concludes that she is deeply in love—with herself, and too loyal ever to cheat with a man. Behind her writing you always hear the little voice, "I'm so wonderful, so elite ... why doesn't somebody marry me?" (Well, Maureen, I can give you a few ideas. You're a pain in the ass....) "I'm so smart, I'm so powerful, I'm so, *sooo* elite, so talented, so ... special." As, in their way, are ingrown toenails. "I'm successful, shriek. Men hate me because I'm smart. They feel threatened because I'm so wonderful."

Actually, Maureen, you are no more threatening, or appealing, than somebody else's gym socks. I suspect that men don't like you because you aren't likeable.

Now, precisely why are you so wonderful? Clearly you aren't stupid. You are a competent if sophomoric writer. Dummies can't do that. But I'll tell you what, Sweet Potato: I don't think I know anyone who would want to go out with you.

As best I can tell, should you have an original thought, it would need counseling, for depression and loneliness.

Smart women are an attraction of Washington, at least the parts off the cocktail circuit. They made fifteen years in that wretched city bearable for me. I knew women with serious brains, golden-girl biochemists at NIH, a gal who ran a federal positron-emission tomography lab, weirded-out computer techs, startlingly good writers and chicks who had popped scores you wouldn't believe on tests at NSA that aren't supposed to exist. They'd eat you for lunch, Maureen.

Now, I know that people at the *New York Times* have ample self-esteem, and indeed come coated with it to a depth of inches. How about we have a little understanding here. In journalism as in politics, advancement has little to do with merit. Have you checked the contents of the White House lately? Are Dan Rather and Connie Chung pinnacles of anything at all? I've been around this game as long as you have, Maureen, and I know how the scam works. Getting to the upper ranks of journalism is a matter of luck, sexual sharing, brown-nosing, and staying carefully within the bounds of the regnant politics of the newsroom.

You are journalistic glitter, Maureen—Reporter Barbie, a literary Streisand. While working for the *Times* is perhaps nothing to be ashamed of, I'd keep quiet about it.

Maureen's agonizing does however provide exegesis of the American female mind at a curious moment. Again and again their question seems to be, what form of pretense is needed to achieve marriage? Must I feign sex-kittenhood? Be a calculated suck-up who always laughs at his jokes? Hide my brains? The underlying idea is that they must commit some fraud to attract a man. This of course implies that they aren't attractive without committing fraud.

I'll give them that.

Those of us who have wives from Mexico, Thailand, the Philippines, Chile, or China view Maureen as being a very strange creature indeed, perhaps expelled from a geothermal vent. ("Hi! I'm Fred. What's your phylum?") Like Maureen, so many gringas don't seem to know who they are, what they are, what they want to be, or how to get there. I think of a tinkertoy construction made by an insane two-year-old: a lot of protruding parts that don't fit together.

By contrast foreign women are psychologically coherent. They are sexy because they are women and like being sexy, not as a Vaudeville act or marketing tool. Resentment is not their primary emotion. They love their children and regard raising them as a pleasure, not an imposition of which they are ashamed.

If you read Maureen and her littermates, you realize that they are those most uncomfortable of women, heterosexual man-haters. For example, Maureen, from her new book:

"Men, apparently, learn early to protect their eggshell egos from high-achieving women. The girls said they hid the fact that they went to Harvard from guys they met because it was the kiss of death."

Who would marry that? Yet it is classic Maureen, snotty, catty, hostile. As for her own Kevlar ego, there's this, from her interview with Howard Kurtz:

"Even after a decade of writing a *New York Times* column, she admits to being 'very thin-skinned' about criticism. 'I'm just not temperamentally suited to it,' Dowd says. 'The first couple of years I spent curled up on the floor and crying.'"

I frequently curl up on the floor and cry when criticized. It's my eggshell ego.

The drumbeat of animosity is never missing from her hetero-anguished feminism. Men are vain, frightened, immature, unreliable, treacherous, fascinated by gewgaws, obsessed with sex, and unfaithful. Several questions arise. If men are so bad, why does Maureen want one? What kind of men has she been running around with? Those closely resembling herself, it sounds as if. Most to the point, why would any man want anything to do with such a woman?

This confusion and hostility has made the American woman into an internationally acclaimed shrew. Yes, there are degrees, and perhaps more exceptions than examples, but talk to white men from Washington to Hong Kong and you see the same shudder.

These gals are wound too tight. Recently I was aboard a highway bus in an American enclave in Mexico. A gringa wanted to get off where there was no stop. The driver didn't understand her. In Mexico they speak Spanish, a point which apparently had eluded her. She began yelling at him abusively. (Verbatim quote: "You're the worst! You suck! You're the worst!")

They do this. People notice. A friend somehow found himself talking with a gringa who had one of those puffy little white dogs you could buff a truck with. He said, "Cute little thing. I've got a real dog." This mild witticism set her into yelling.

Par.

*(Howard Kurtz, Washington Post, Saturday, November 5, 2005)

26

The Peasantariat

The other day I found myself trapped next to the idiot box in the house of a friend. The show was one of those dismal productions based on sexual innuendo, the sort that I would have found titillating when I was eleven. The format was not complex. Neither, I suspect, was the audience.

Several shapeless young couples sat together. The host asked them seriatim such questions as, "Other than your wife, who did you last take a shower with?" or "What part of your anatomy does your husband most like to kiss?" The studio audience invariably moaned, "*Ooooooooooooooooooh!*" like third-graders who have heard a bad word. The couples themselves giggled with delicious embarrassment, also in the manner of dimwitted children.

I happily imagined sending them to some barely heard-of tribe in the Amazon Basin for use in human sacrifice. Almost human. Something involving army ants would have done nicely.

The sexual reference didn't offend me. I have misspent more hours in third-world skin bars than those people had aggregate brain cells, which means at least three skin bars. I've seen raunchy sex shows to the point of boredom. I am not real shockable. Pornography doesn't upset me. If I had to choose whether my kids watched Dory Duz Dallas, or Oprah, I might go with Dory.

No, it was the infantilism, the snickering, low-IQ tastelessness of a class of people who belong in a bus station. These, with their childish prurience and slum-dweller's aversion to civilized behavior, now dominate American culture. Anyone who points out that they are crass finds himself attacked as elitist—which, since elitism simply means the view that the better is preferable to the worse, all people should be.

We are not supposed to use phrases like "the lower orders," which is the best of reasons for using them. Yet the lower orders exist. Its members are not necessarily poor, and the poor are not necessarily members. Nor is the level of schooling a reliable indicator of loutdom. Nor is intelligence or race a particularly good marker. One may be a moral moron without being unable to tie one's shoes. The lower orders consist of people who think fart jokes uproarious.

How did we get here? Probably Henry Ford bears responsibility. He paid workers on his assembly lines a good wage. This was as culturally deplorable as it was economically admirable. Before, the unwashed had lacked the money to impose their tastes, or lack of them, on the society. The moneyed classes of the time may have been reprehensible or contemptible in various ways, but they minded their manners—if only because it set them apart from the lower orders, perhaps, yet it worked. The middle class likewise eschewed bathroom humor except in such venues as locker rooms, probably for the same reasons. They knew what "distasteful" meant.

But as the peasantry and proletariat gained economic power, inevitably they also asserted dominance over the arts, or entertainment as the arts became under their sway, as well as schooling and the nature of acceptable discourse. If millions of people who can afford SUVs want scatological humor, television will accommodate them. Since all watch the same television, no class of people will escape the sex-and-sewage format. This happened. Today the cultivated can no longer insulate themselves from the rabble.

The fear of social inferiority always concerns the peasantariat: "You ain't no gooder'n me." Until the sudden florescence of pay packets occurred, the lower orders had either accepted that they were the lower orders, however resentfully, or tried to rise. They might learn to speak good English, read widely, and cultivate good manners. Or they might not. If they did, it was likely to work, since in America those who behave and speak like gentlefolk (another inadmissible word) will usually be accepted as such. In either case, they did not impose their barbarousness on others.

Ah, but with their new-found and enormous purchasing power, they discovered that they could do more than compel the production of skateboards, trashy television, and awful music. They could make boorish childishness and ignorance into actual virtues. And did. Thus wretched grammar is now a sign of "authenticity," whatever that might mean, rather than of defective studies. Thus the solemnity with which rap "music" is taken. Briefly the sound of the black ghetto, it is now around the world the heraldic emblem of the angry lower orders. Thus the degradation of the schools: It is easier to declare oneself educated than to actually become so, and the half-literate now had the power to have themselves so declared.

With the debasement of society came a simultaneous, though not necessarily related, extension of childhood and adolescence. In the remote prehistorical past, which for most today means anything before 1940, the young assumed responsibility early. It wasn't a moral question, but a practical one. If the plowing didn't get done, the family didn't eat. By the age of eighteen, a boy was likely to carry a man's burdens.

Today, no. Today a combination of the enstupidation of the schools, the inflation of grades, and the threat of class-action suits by the parents of failing students means that an adolescent can graduate without assuming any burden whatsoever. Indeed escaping schooling is easier than finding it. Countless colleges will accept almost anyone and graduate almost anyone. Chores do not exist. Sex and drugs are everywhere available. Few things have obvious consequences.

The result is a cocoon of childhood that stretches on almost as long as one wants it to. I encounter adults in their mid-twenties who cannot be relied upon to show up at an appointed time, who judge a professor by whether he makes the material "fun," who have no idea where they want to go in life. It is not grownup behavior.

I wonder whether a democracy can ever prosper without declining fast into tasteless decadence. Half of the population is of intelligence below the average, this being the nature of a symmetric distribution. Another goodly number aren't much better. Once they discover that together they can both sanctify and very nearly require bad behavior and low tastes, will they not do so? With control of the media goes control of the culture. Such is the power of the market.

Thus the staged television shows in which fat couples shriek obscenities at each other over discovered infidelities, adipose couplings of no significance yet so absorbing to an audience both puerile and uncouth—but authentic.

"Ooooooooooooooooooooooh!"

27

Reinventing the Bushman

I imagine taking a bushman from some hitherto undiscovered Pacific isle and setting him down in front of a television in, say, Washington. The fellow would be astounded. He might say, "*Whoa*, boss! Heap magic! Spirits inside, talk talk. Bad juju." He would have no idea how the babbling box worked, or of the civilization that produced it—where it came from, why it was as it was, what its literature might be, what its thoughts had been.

What would distinguish him from the graduate of today's high schools or, latterly, the universities? Only that the bushman would have sense enough to be astonished. I do not see why being complacently ignorant is preferable to being honestly amazed.

It is hardly necessary to recite the endless polls showing that even the graduates of what once were universities cannot give the dates of the Civil War, do not know who fought in WWI, have never read Shakespeare, cannot name the first five books of the Old Testament, believe that Martin Luther had something to do with civil rights in Mississippi, and cannot write a coherent paragraph in their own language.

They are pitiable without knowing it. Being innocent of history, they live in temporal isolation. Knowing nothing of painting, literature, or music, they are aesthetically crippled. Never having acquired a taste for reading, they are incorrigible. This is remarkable. The society has managed in a generation to overcome everything that civilization has strived for, replacing it with—nothing.

Now, the one thing that one must never do today is to express other than profound respect for our gilded bushmen. But is it possible to respect the contemptible? Have we not made a society in which the educated very few must quietly regard the enstupidated many with disdain? I for one cannot listen to anchors on the news without thinking of arboreal primates swinging from tree to tree.

Benightedness need not be the fate of so many. I studied long ago in a small Southern college for boys (Hampden-Sydney) with modest entrance standards. I believe the average SATs were something like 1100. The prevailing philosophy at H-S was, first, that the reasonably intelligent could be cultivated; second, that adults knew better than school boys what school boys should study; and third, that a liberal education produced a civilized citizenry.

It was assumed, incidentally, that freshmen read fluently and knew algebra cold. There were no remedial courses. A college was a college, it was held, and not a repair shop for the academically hopeless who had no business on campus.

The studentry were largely told what they would study. We could choose our majors of course, though even within a major most courses were required. If memory serves, the student of arts could choose which of two ancient languages he would study, the choices being Latin or Greek. The student of the sciences could take three years of a modern language, or two years each of two languages. The candidate for the degree of bachelor of arts could choose which two basic science courses he would take. They were demanding courses, the same ones taken by those with majors in the sciences.

And so the student left college having, with some variation, a grasp of history ancient and modern, languages including his own, literature, philosophy, the sciences, and the Old and New Testaments. (It was a Presbyterian college. The civilization being Christian, one can grasp neither the arts, music, nor literature without knowledge of the Bible.)

We were civilized, to the extent that young males can be civilized. We knew where we were in place and time, and where we came from. We knew what we knew and what we did not know, and how to learn anything else that interested us. (Go to a library.)

So much has changed. Then as now, many in the nation had neither the intellectual wherewithal nor the interest to acquire much of an education. Yet until at least the midpoint of the last century, it was thought that those who went to college, and therefore would end in positions of responsibility, should be schooled. Today we craft a society in which a very few are truly educated, though many have the trappings. One may issue a diploma to a bushman, or to a log. The recipient remains a bushman or a log.

We become bushmen and do not know it. And it is getting late. Afternoon comes. Twenty years ago the observant wrote that those of the rising generation of the time were the first in America to be less schooled than their parents. Those students are now in midlife and have their own intellectually bedraggled children, the second generation of complacently unwashed.

Lest it be thought that I exaggerate: Perhaps five years ago I went to a middle school in Arlington County, just outside of Washington, D.C. Arlington is not the ghetto. On the wall I saw a student's project, intended no doubt to celebrate diversity. In large orange letters it spoke of Enrico Fermi's contributions to, so help me, "Nucler Physicts." In the schools of small town Alabama in 1957, where I was a student, such invertebracy would not have been tolerated in an exercise, much less put on the wall. We have come a long way.

The schools remain a cultural slum, a dark night of the mind. As my daughters passed through these dismal moors, I saw misspelled handouts from teachers, heard of a teacher being reprimanded for correcting a student's grammar, saw endless propaganda disguised as history. How does one recognize the onset of a dark age?

What have we done? And what now? Once the chain is broken, once no one any longer remembers how to write a sentence, much less the uses of the subjunctive, once Coleridge is forgotten and Milton and indeed everything beyond the mall, how can we recover what has been lost? I do not think we can.

This comes with a price. The effects of the degradation are twofold. One is to deprive the bright and curious of a wonderful heritage that would enrich their lives. This is a high crime, and brings to mind the forgotten virtues of drawing and quartering, or throwing from the Tarpeian rock. Another effect is to separate the country into two classes, an invisible aristocracy enjoying things the rest have never heard of; and the rest, with 500 channels on the cable, watching Oprah, and having not the foggiest idea who, or what, or where they are. This is very, very bad juju.

28

Buckshot and Designer Water

I have received thousands of letters (all right, three letters, but I'm rounding up) asking me to explain the election of Mr. Bush to a second term. Bending to the public will, I'll try.

The way it looks to me is coastal snots against the heartland. The wine-and-cheese folk against pickups with gun racks. Texas against Massachusetts. Maybe that's too simple, but I'm not going to admit it. I don't have to. I'm writing the column.

Put it this way: If Kerry had worn a cowboy hat, he'd be president. Yep, he was a hat away from the brass ring. About size three, I'd guess.

It was the cultural divide. The coastal snots have enormous contempt for Texas, Oklahoma, the South, and any other place where people can change a flat tire. Along the Northeast Corridor the snots talk of rednecks, express wonderment that some of them can read, and regard them as barbarians inhabiting blank spaces on the map with dragons drawn in them. For snots in Massachusetts, most of the country is just an inconvenience in getting to the other coast. Flyover Land. They think that people in Alabama live naked in the forest and eat grubs they dig out of stumps.

The pickup people are tired of it. And the cheese people just found out. Whether we will like the results remains to be seen, but the mechanism is clear.

A lot of columnists and talking heads on the coasts thought that the election was going to be a referendum on the war in Iraq. I doubt it was. Few in the middle of the country know, or care, anything about the world outside the United States. Nobody in Massachusetts knows anything, or cares much, about the world inside the United States. The Bush people have never heard of the Crimea. The Kerry people have barely heard of Texas.

This is why I'd like Texas to make my domestic policy, and Massachusetts my foreign policy. Or maybe have both of them just go away.

People in Oklahoma, I'll bet you, are tired to the eyeballs of coastal, septic, hypersexual sludge forced on their children by Hollyork, of music so foul that you wouldn't clean a toilet with it, of galloping repression of a religion that matters to them, of abortion without representation, of the constant pressure to give up their guns, which they enjoy, because subhuman inner-city savages back East kill everybody who goes into a Seven-Eleven; of the Latinization of America, and of schools run by federal fools so meddlesome and perverted that they would defile a landfill.

It's as obvious as warts on a Playboy Bunny (sez me, anyway) that a whole lot of people are sick of having their lives controlled by people they can't stand, sick of being messed with from afar, sick of affirmative action and racial preferences and partial-birth abortion—the old Sandy Day O'Connor Brain Suck. Well, they just said so.

Me too, by the way. If Bush had campaigned on a promise to toss the Supreme Court into an industrial grinder, I would have voted. For him. And I can't stand him.

Which brings us to the Feddle Gummint. Between the coasts it's seen as the enforcement arm of the coastal snots—a gray, repressive, stupid, intrusive, and alien force, as degrading as having your leg humped by the dog in somebody else's living room. To a lot of people, Washington isn't the capital of their country. It's The Enemy. It pushes on them everything they loathe. They hate it. Me too.

To many in the middle of the country, Bush somehow feels as if he were with the people against Washington's inroads, though he isn't. In fact he favors bigger and more intrusive government, and spends as Hillary could only dream. He's in favor of most of what his constituency hates. But he's against gun control and abortion, the emotional hot issues. That's enough.

When you have seen a thousand impassioned sheep waving witless placards at a political rally, you realize that facts don't matter. Look and feel are everything. Bush and Kerry are both pampered ineffectual rich brats, one a drunk, the other a gigolo. Kerry comes from Massachusetts, though, and you just know he eats curious salads with strange names. By contrast, Bush has a certain ferret-like pugnacity to him and a low-wattage mind that people between the coasts are comfortable with. He isn't going to use any of them high-falutin' words, because he honestly doesn't know them. He won't confuse anyone.

People in Kansas aren't stupid—not given the admittedly sorry baseline for humanity. They are intensely local, though, and use their minds for practical things. When it comes to foreign policy they are better on principle than detail. I keep reading that sixty-some percent of Republicans believe that Iraq did New York. (Given what Republicans generally think of New York, I'm not sure why they aren't grateful.) They know that somebody did something bad to us, and they want to smack the bejesus out of someone for it. That's principle. "Smack who" is a detail.

Bush looks like (and is) a Texan who isn't going to take any crap. For people who have taken an awful lot of it from Washington for awfully long, that's appealing. Whether he has the slightest idea what he's doing doesn't matter. He sounds conservative and patriotic if you don't pay too much attention to what he is saying. Or doing. He is against ter and terrace. He wants to protect America and smack them infiddles upside the head. It's the spirit of the thing.

There is horror on the coasts over the influence of evangelical Christians. How much evangelical Christianity has to do with Christianity, I don't know. Sometimes it looks to me more like an assertion of independence from federal intrusiveness than a religious awakening. However spiritual it may or may not be, it is an organized, satisfying way of hating the bastards on the coasts.

Hallelujah.

Rational people, always at a disadvantage in American politics, wonder how Christians can favor bombing cities. Jesus, they say in puzzlement, didn't seem to be persuasively bloodthirsty. True, but irrelevant.

You have to understand that Christians have never regarded the teachings of Christ as authoritative. Christians are as savage a clan as can be found, matched only by Moslems, Jews, and Shintoists. And probably everybody else. Check the headlines.

Exactly as the Kerry people believe in separation of church and state, evangelicals believe in separation of church and behavior. What you do isn't the point. It's whose side you are on. In a country where everybody hates everybody else, that matters. And, as we just discovered, it did matter.

That's me on the elections. Air Mexico may give a discount to lynch mobs, but I'll be outa here before you can find your rope.

29

Memin Penguin

Guadalajara, Mexico—

A few thoughts regarding the clownish performance apparently ongoing in the US over Mexico's issuance of the now-famous stamps of Memin Penguin, a *negrito* hero of Mexican comic books of decades back.

Let's see. How many of those throwing fits had ever heard of Memin Penguin before this week? How many of them have seen a Memin Penguin comic book? How many can read Spanish? How many read English? Have been to Mexico? Have the foggiest idea what they are talking about? How many are not spoiled, puerile, self-admiring twits?

Just checking.

Blacks are not making themselves friends in this part of the world. (More correctly, American blacks are not. Hispanic blacks behave normally, speak Spanish instead of Hisbonics, and seem to be pretty good people.) The Mexican reaction, certainly as I find it among people I know, and in the media, is one of annoyance, or something stronger than annoyance. "What business do American blacks have telling us what stamps we can issue? Who the hell do they think they are?"

Good question.

This may, or may not, be fair. I don't know what proportion of American blacks are part of this absurd holding of breath and turning blue. Yet Mexicans do not stop to think, "Maybe not *all* blacks...." They just know what they see. Jesse Jackson is making faces and throwing food from his high chair and, from here, he seems to represent all blacks in the US. Maybe he doesn't. I don't know.

Remember that a while back, Vicente Fox, president of Mexico, ignited another international incident when he spoke of Mexican immigrants to the US as being willing to "take jobs that not even Negroes would do." This is of course exactly true. Go the parking lot of the Seven-Eleven, or wherever Mexican illegals gather at five a.m. to take any job at all, and see how many black laborers are there. From here it looks as if the United States is trying to force an apology on Fox for having stated the obvious.

Mexicans do not react well to seeing their country forced to knuckle under to silly gringo demands. Jesse may not know this, or care. Yet there are reasons. Remember that Latin America has a long history of being invaded or politically controlled by America: Panama, Chile, Colombia, United Fruit, Cuba, Haiti, and so on. Mexicans remember that Texas and California were taken from their country by force of arms. A main avenue in Guadalajara is *Niños Heroes*, Heroic Children, who fought the Americans in 1847. How many Americans have even heard of that war?

Whatever the rights and wrongs, or possible historic inevitabilities, the result is that locals resent interference, but do not greatly upset themselves over the plight of blacks who, after all, live in America. From their point of view, American blacks have all the privileges and opportunities of gringos. What are they sniveling about?

Good question.

In re the stamps again: Radio Mujer ("Woman's Radio") in Guadalajara would in the US be called a liberal station, being very opposed to discrimination against racial minorities, homosexuals, and such. A medical commentator I listened to for an hour on the station or so was scathing in his criticism of American blacks because of the Memin Penguin business. He was funny about it, but angry. He pointed out that Speedy Gonzales is a rat and a caricature Mexican, but nobody gets upset.

Mexicans, Jesse, don't buy into this crap. As you will soon find out in the Southwest.

I asked my lady, Violeta, to go to the post office to buy me several sets of the stamps. She came back to report that the post office had told her that the stamp had been repealed. She looked not too happy. Once again, the gringos had gotten their way. Later I told her that I'd found several news stories saying that Vicente Fox wasn't going to back down, and her eyes lit up like stars. Wow! For once her country had not licked the feet of Bush, who was licking the feet of Jesse.

"By Friday afternoon, people were bidding more than $125 on the Internet auction site eBay for the complete set of five stamps—each of which has a face value of 60 cents. Hundreds lined up at the capital's main post office to buy the stamps, and Mexicans snapped them up at such a rate that all 750,000 sold out." (*The Guardian*, July 1, 2005) Friends emailed me, saying, "Fred! I *gotta* have a set of those things!"

Why do Americans want them? Because, methinks, whites (and Asians) are seriously fed up with the special privilege, the affirmative action, the blisterish sensitivity and racial hucksterism of … Who? I hesitate to say "of blacks" because I don't know how many blacks support it. But the blacks one hears of do. Anytime anyone says or does anything that displeases—again, do I mean "blacks" or "Jesse"?—it becomes a national or international incident, whites cringe and cower and apologize desperately in hopes of keeping their jobs or offices. And so they delight when someone actually stands up, however briefly, to the hucksters.

This brings me to my belief that the intense racial discord that quietly underlies American life is largely the product of the policies of special privilege and lack of responsibility. As I've said before, when I was twenty I believed that policy should be determined without regard to race, creed, color, sex, or national origin. I was called the merest liberal and perhaps a communist. Now, forty years later, I believe that policy should be determined without regard to race, creed, color, sex, or national origin. This makes me a racist, a racist being one who does not believe that blacks should automatically get everything they want.

How smart is this?

We have trained our blacks, or a great many blacks, to believe that they should get anything—jobs, promotions, acceptance into college, and immunity from criticism—just by being black. A comic book upsets them? The world should stand on its head in apology. A Latin American president states a truth that they would prefer not to have stated? Why, it's an international incident. Should we send the Marines?

And of course they are trained from birth, as best I can tell, to regard anything they do not like as racism. It isn't true, but what has truth got to do with anything?

I'm sick of it. I don't see the world as having been created to pamper me. Why do they? If blacks want to advance on their merits, I'm for them. But this self-absorbed diaperism is more than I can handle. *Viva* Vicente Fox.

30

Therapy

The remnants of the national character ferment like a jar of mayonnaise in August, bubble, bubble, bubble. Let's hear it for bacteria. It is good to see that at least something is working. Better a robust rot than a pallid decline, I say.

Symptoms of moral putrefaction seem normal to us because we have nothing but symptoms. Does a toad notice warts? Still, some stand out. A friend involved in municipal government in a medium-sized city in California tells me that 63% of the city's employees take anti-depressants. Yeah. An official secret figure.

Two-thirds? My god. Either life is depressing or the United States is squirreling out big-time. Is the number a national average? Two of three Americans can't get through the day without rejiggering their neurotransmitters? We are mostly chemical train wrecks?

It may in fact be a national average. Maybe we aren't designed to spend half our lives in isolated bedroom cities and the other half in rooms full of sound-absorbent cubicles, like inmates in a cross-word puzzle. I dunno. But something ain't right.

A few jack-leg observations. Over half of the single women over thirty-five that I knew in Washington took Zoloft, Prozac, Welbutrin, Paxil, Xanax, or lithium. My daughters, then in high school, told me of depressed girlfriends of seventeen gobbling psychoactive pellets, or in and out of drunk tanks and drug rehab.

This is nuts. It would be so nice to live in a comparatively normal place. Weimar Berlin, maybe.

Therapy. If I hear that word again, I'm going to kill something. I'd rather have plague, but it isn't a choice. (There should be a check box on medical forms. "You may elect either (a) Plague, or (b) Therapy.") This witchcraft mind-mindery is out of control. It's everywhere, like boredom, like air, a church for people running on empty, for the unhappy peering into the inner vacuum.

And it's pretty much compulsory. Around Washington, when some poor kid was miserable because her parents, or more likely parent, weren't bothering to raise her, the guidance counselor always urged ... therapy. The therapist always suggested ... drugs. It wasn't easy to say no. Expulsion might follow. The girls ended up on nut-adjustors. The boys said the hell with it, dropped out, and smoked dope.

Now that's a recipe for a successful economy.

I have sat in on therapy. It is something to see. For starters, the whole routine is a vaguely sadomasochistic power trip. The Therapist is the domme, the patient a humble supplicant who must bare her soul, confess her psychic sins, embarrass herself, and obey. (A few New Age males go in for this stuff. It is overwhelmingly a woman's racket.)

Therapy reminds me of nothing so much as a castrated religious order. There is the same proselytizing, the same zeal. Therapists see only two classes of people, those who are in therapy and those who ought to be. ("Are you saved?") They exhibit the smug assurance of those who have seen the light, and have Truth in a half-Nelson. The difference is that, whereas religions usually say that you are responsible for your bad behavior and you ought to stop it, therapy tells you that you are never responsible for anything. No. It was your childhood. Or some chemical imbalance. The Church of Avoided Guilt.

The cult wants to get everybody. Repeatedly therapists assert that ninety-five percent of people suffer from "codependency," and must go into counseling. See? We are all in a state of sin. The humiliation of baring one's inmost thoughts to a condescending estrogenated Hitleress is a mix of self-flagellation and the rite of confession. It is the religious impulse de-Godded.

You can't hide. Where I live, in Mexico near Guadalajara, the *Ojo del Lago* is the gringo fishwrapper for bored Americans who shelter in gated communities because they don't like Mexico. It specializes in low-IQ political correctness that seems to have been written by a high-school class in Creative Writing.

In it I discover the following by Ilse Hoffman, the very voice of therapeuticity: "A large percentage of the human population has some kind of mental disorder: major depression, schizophrenia, bipolar, obsessive compulsive disorder or panic disorders...." Yes. We are all crazy. We can't make it without drugs, support groups, and drumming circles. It isn't just Ilse. The women's programs on the radio in Guad peddle the same recipes. See a counselor. Go early and often.

Ilse wants to propagate the faith—and expand the market. Never forget that salvation goes for $125 an hour. The church of pointless introspection shares the financial disinterestedness of a televangelist pitching for Aunt Nelly's social security check.

Self-help books are a boom market. ("The Horror of Vague Dissatisfaction on Dull Afternoons, A Survivor's Guide.") Uncle Sucker passes out other people's money in the form of grants. The courts, wanting to appear to do something without stuffing more people into jail space that doesn't exist, sentence criminals to "counseling." This mildly annoys the criminal, gets the judge off the hook, and—the crucial point—puts public money in the counselor's pocket.

Compulsory therapy isn't limited to junkies who just want to score in peace. Get a DWI ticket and, depending on the jurisdiction, you are likely to have to attend a dozen or two sessions of alcohol therapy at $35 a pop. These accomplish nothing, except presumably that you come out wanting a drink. The alleged drunks invariably think that the therapeutress is an idiot. However, it does put lots of money in therapeutic pockets.

And there is the seminal discovery of therapy, that insurance will cough up the green if the purported malady is medicalized and published in the DSM-4. Consequently everything is now a diagnosable disorder. Borderline personality disorder, narcissistic personality disorder, can't-get-a-date disorder, disorder, datorder, dotherorder. (I would like to suggest the addition of barely-got-a-personality disorder. Then therapists could treat each other.)

All of this ties subtly into an American strength, vindictiveness applied in the name of virtue. Examples abound. Read the laws against smoking and you will see that they make sense only as means of humiliating smokers. Therapy's contribution to predatory goodness is the drugging of schoolboys who refuse to become passive psychic transvestites. To understate, the psychotrades are not branches of conservative rationalism. Feminism is getting even.

We buy into this stuff. Which is probably to say that we deserve it. There must be an awful lot of emptiness out there.

31

Wastrelsy in Mexico

Guadalajara—

The yearmeter hit 2005 coupla months back, I just hit fifty-nine, and I'm deciding what to do with my life. (Inexplicably you may not care what I do with my life, but I'm writing the column.) I'm going to screw off. You may ask how you could tell the difference. Dunno. I don't do fine distinctions after lots of red wine. (Keep reading. There's probably some kind of deep philosophical import in here somewhere.) Lupita my ace travel agent just got me tickets for the Galapagos and some other wacked-out parts of Ecuador. Big-ass turtles.

I'm going to be explosively useless, take inutility to a higher plane. My daughters arrive in shifts to help me. They have a talent for adventuresome uselessness. Can't imagine where they got it. My old man once told me that they were the only thing I had ever really done right. It's enough, though.

You may be thinking, "Fred doesn't sound mentally organized today. Some underlying pathology is breaking through." Herewith a revelation: The key to a philosophical existence is cheap Mexican wine. Violeta and I stayed home this evening, jitterbugged again in the living room like soda-shop teenagers in 1950, and split a large bottle of Padre Kino red. It's like Mexican Ripple except you wouldn't want to put ice-cream in it. I wondered what else I might ask from the world. Outside rockets boomed down toward the Expiatorio, idiots honked, and drunks ran into each other and over unwary innocents. (Sky rockets, I mean. The US is not bombing Mexico into democracy. Yet. But the locals worry.) 'Nother Saturday night.

This has been a good year for a curmudgeon. Things go badly everywhere, lending a comforting continuity to existence. A tidal wave ate most of Asia. Slugs and ferrets rule the world with low cunning. There is an expectation of cholera in Indonesia. NASA or somebody says that there is hope that an asteroid may hit the earth in 2010.

Instead of working, I'm going to cultivate a talent for quietly disliking a great many people and things. To hell with Marcus Aurelius, Churchill, Pericles, Popsicles, what have you. I'm going to pattern myself on Eeyore, a great thinker and less of an ass than most.

I figure I'll continue hiding in Messico. I recommend it to all. Actually no, I don't, as there are already entirely too many gringos here. Try the Philippines. But I'd like to offer to all the little sensible advice I have accreted in most of a lifetime. Bail while you can. You can both run and hide, at least for a while. When you are sixty, are you going to think, "Gosh, I wish I had another thirty years to do whatever depressing and deleterious thing I'm doing now"?

Flee.

I can't flee. I already have. I'm in Mexico for the long haul, having inexplicably acquired a splendorous lady that I'm not about to throw over for anything this world offers. (When something good happens, you gotta figure that you're being set up. Look over your shoulder.)

Up north vast swarms of people with maxed-out credit cards wobble in ethylated pre-suicidal fugue states engendered by uneasy contemplation of the mortgage on some prestigious McMansion in Brookmill Estates or Dalebrook Mews or Meadow Brook Dales. (No mews is good mews. I can't brook those mews.) (Sorry. Blame Padre Kino.) Outside of these badly constructed shoeboxes creeping across the landscape like mold sit two Volvos with massive payments. A Volvo is a beautifully engineered, well-built statement that the owner has the soul of a dung beetle. Twenty or thirty years roll pointlessly off into the future because they are trapped in the retirement program. It's like sharecropping, but without a crop.

Pasado manana my other lunatic daughter arrives. The Reed family sloshes in and out of Guad like barrels from a shipwreck.

I tell my kids, never get into a retirement program. Save your own money. Steal. Set up a business, found a cult. Learn credit-card fraud. Retirement programs are indentured servitude with a better address, the financial equivalent of a lobster trap: You can get in but you can't get out. Half the US is running at $6500 on the Visa and counting the last fifteen years until life begins.

Don't do it.

Thank god most people can't distinguish between what they want and what they think they want. It keeps them up north. A buddy of mine lives in Jocotopec in a $130 a month house, small but nice enough, better than a cardboard box in Brooklyn. Fast internet is $50, his wife is a peach, the ghetto blaster plays music stolen online. He sits on the roof and watches the storm clouds roll in over the lake as if they had a grudge to settle, and gobbles chops and beer under gaudy sunsets like fluorescent oriental rugs.

People pay too much for vanity. Who are we kidding? We all scratch, belch, pick our noses one leg at a time. Are you a partner at some swinish law firm in New York? I'm awe-struck. A tee shirt and shorts constitute adequate cover for anyone who doesn't need props to respect himself. Owning more house than you can live in is a sure sign of insecurity. Suits are what you wear when doing things you shouldn't want to do anyway.

They say clothes make the man, a frightening thought but one that seems to hold true. You wear a coat and tie to the drone farm every day, worry whether the knot is tied right, feel humiliated if you get a ketchup stain, and pretty soon you turn into a very worried creature. I did that for a year once at a mausoleum of the spirit called *Federal Computer Week*, a trade journal of the governmental dead in the remote suburbs of the Yankee Capital. Just walking in the door made my cojones retract into my abdominal cavity. I'd sit there, looking like an Executive Ken Barbie, with my fingers autonomously seeking something to throttle. I know why boys take their guns to school and kill six teachers. It's because rifles have small magazines.

Switch to a Harley tee-shirt and cutoffs, take up knocking over Seven-Eleven instead of sucking up to some tedious editor with a mind you wouldn't use to blow your nose, and the world changes. In Mexico you never feel as if you needed a hall pass. It's like being a grownup. Or in the Philippines, Thailand, Argentina.

Guadalajara ain't bad, but I want to get up in the mountains around Mazamïtla, get a place with a big interior garden and a burro that says "*Eeeeeeeeeeeeeeeeeeeeeeee*honk!" and a guacamayo that shrieks obscenities in Spanish. Chilly mornings, not too much oxygen.

I didn't tell you that this was going to make sense.

32

Weathering the Fears in Soviet Washington

Washington, DC—

It's getting stranger, I tell you. Riding the subway from Vienna Station to Franconia-Springfield, at every stop the woman driving the train said in an over-elocuted voice, "A-ten-tion, customers. This is a Metro Safety Tip. Pay attention to your surroundings. Look up from your newspapers and blackbirds [it sounded like, though nobody seemed to be carrying any sort of bird at all] every now and then. Report suspicious activity to Metro employees immediately."

Then—I can't stand it: "Let's be prepared, not scared."

Nobody paid the slightest attention to these motherish admonitions. I was glad, picturing the whole car of us peering at each other furtively, ready to rat each other out to some bored kiosk worker who wanted to go home and would regard the reporting party as an irritating lunatic. Report suspicious activity on an urban subway at one in the morning?

Apparently the intercom is the only chance the drivers will ever have to be publicly noticed, and they make the most of it. "Let's be prepared, not scared." The phrase had the cutesy fatuity of a fifty-thousand dollar bumper-sticker slogan bought from an ad agency. Don't run with scissors.

I wondered how much safer Metro Safety Tips made us. Obviously any terrorist with the brains of a pencil eraser would be sure not to look suspicious, and if he did nobody would notice. At rush hour, the trains are packed with people carrying briefcases and large bags. When the bars close, the cars swarm with drunks, people in turbans and dashikis and with dots on their foreheads, swarthy men with mustaches chattering in Spanish or languages unknown, transvestites, schizos conversing with God or their little voices or the wall, and lots of people who look like revolutionaries.

There is something unconvincing about so many of these terrorism preventives. Yet they are everywhere. The papers carried stories about New York's random searches of passengers on the subway, for example. Washington's subway was pondering the same idea.

Random searches? If you randomly search every fiftieth passenger in rush hour, you have a two percent chance of catching a terrorist. Now that makes me feel safe. "Random"? Who are they kidding? The searches won't be random. They will be searches of whoever the searchers feel like searching. Quite irrationally, officials said that anyone who didn't consent to being searched could simply leave. This obviously would include terrorists, who would walk out and go the next station. That is, we will search everybody except those we are looking for, who are free to leave.

When I was on the police beat, cops had to have probable cause to search anyone. This was defined as "an articulable reason for believing that a specific person was committing a specific crime." Carrying a bolo knife and a severed head meets that standard. I'm not sure that riding a subway is adequately suspicious. New York's searches seem to establish the principle that local jurisdictions can search, with no reason at all, anyone aboard public transit—buses, subway, trains, ferries. Why not people within fifty feet of governmental buildings, in crowded places thought attractive to terrorists, or on sidewalks?

And of course if they find illegal paraphernalia of a non-terrorist persuasion, such as drugs, or cigarettes without a tax stamp, they will arrest the bearer. Soon it will be pirated CDs. The police will naturally use "random" searches to conduct fishing expeditions.

It is curious that an entire system of constitutional protections can be dismantled just by ignoring it. I would have thought it more difficult, but it isn't.

How much of this drama is actually intended to reduce the prospect of terrorism? Some of it, perhaps. Yes, it is a practical proposition to try to keep explosives off airplanes. People can occasionally sneak by with knives and whatnot, but the likelihood of being caught is very high, and presumably discourages the bomb-prone. Since the Israelis began taking security seriously, they haven't lost an airplane.

But why do terrorists need to blow up airplanes? Everybody I talk to immediately thinks of multitudinous ways of getting a car bomb or a backpack into a crowd. Are terrorists thought to be blind to the obvious? Towing vehicles parked in public places does nothing to stop suicide bombers, who seem to be trendy. The urgings on the web site of Homeland Security, such as that we lay in plastic sheeting and duct tape and compile terrorism kits of food and water—does anybody do this?

The papers say that the mayors of both Washington and Baltimore want more cameras installed. Some such official, I forget which, wants more of the sort of camera that automatically reads license plates. Oh good. A permanent record of your every move. I don't do pub-crawls with these mayors, so I don't know whether they have the foggiest idea in their tiny little minds of the downstream implications. I doubt it, though.

Which brings up an interesting point. Many view this largely pointless circus as a deliberate attempt to impose—the phrase is getting wearisome—a police state. I don't know, not being privy to the councils of the mighty. You know the theory: Tell the rubes that they're in danger of some dread thing, tell them that they need to give up civil liberties in order to be protected, and then tell them that nothing happened because of the protections and now the danger has grown again so that....

If so, it works. The papers quote subway riders in New York as saying what a good thing searches are because they feel *soooo* much safer. That seems to be as far as their thinking gets. I forget whether it was Goebbels or Goring who I first saw endorsing the effectiveness of this useful principle.

But much of it to me looks to be the anti-boredom efforts of officious dim-witted bureaucrats who desperately want meaning in their lives. A little terrorism is at least exciting, gets the juices running.

A friend in California puts it this way: "Fred, people like being searched. They spend their lives in meaningless jobs they hate and then watch stupid sit-coms on the box. Getting searched makes them feel important. It means someone thinks they might actually be dangerous. Swatted-out cops with submachine guns give them their only sense of adventure. It's like being in a video game."

Dunno. My suspicion is that if bin Laden manages another major attack, or anyone else does, we will see something very close to martial law. It will be welcomed by all but a noisy few because it will be to make them secure and to take care of them, and give a wonderful sense of living through parlous times, just like Sergeant Rock, and all.

33

Fredwin on Evolution

I was about fifteen when I began to think about evolution. I was then just discovering the sciences systematically, and took them as what they offered themselves to be, a realm of reason and dispassionate regard for truth. There was a hard-edged clarity to them that I liked. You got real answers. Since evolution depended on such sciences as chemistry, I regarded it as also being a science.

The question of the origin of life interested me. The evolutionary explanations that I encountered in textbooks of biology seemed a trifle weak, however. They ran to, "In primeval seas, evaporation concentrated dissolved compounds in a pore in a rock, a skim formed a membrane, and life began its immense journey." I saw no reason to doubt this. If it hadn't been true, scientists would not have said that it was.

Remember, I was fifteen.

In those days I read *Scientific American* and *New Scientist*, the latter then still being thoughtfully written in good English. I noticed that not infrequently they offered differing speculations as to the origin of life. The belief in the instrumentality of chemical accident was constant, but the nature of the primeval soup changed to fit varying attempts at explanation.

For a while, life was thought to have come about on clay in shallow water in seas of a particular composition, later in tidal pools with another chemical solution, then in the open ocean in another solution. This continues. Recently, geothermal vents have been offered as the home of the first life. Today (Feb 24, 2005) on the BBC website, I learn that life evolved below the oceanic floor. ("There is evidence that life evolved in the deep sediments," co-author John Parkes, of Cardiff University, UK, told the BBC News website.")

The frequent shifting of ground bothered me. If we knew how life began, why did we have so many prospective mechanisms, none of which really worked? Evolution began to look like a theory in search of a soup. Forty-five years later, it still does.

Questions Arise

I was probably in college when I found myself asking what seemed to me straight-forward questions about the chemical origin of life. In particular:

(1) Life was said to have begun by chemical inadvertence in the early seas. Did we, I wondered, really know of what those early seas consisted? *Know*, not sus-pect, hope, theorize, divine, speculate, or really, really wish.

The answer was, and is, "no." We have no dried residue, no remaining pools, and the science of planetogenesis isn't nearly good enough to provide a quantita-tive analysis.

(2) Had the creation of a living cell been replicated in the laboratory? No, it hadn't, and hasn't. (Note 1, at end)

(3) Did we know what conditions were necessary for a cell to come about? No, we didn't, and don't.

(4) Could it be shown to be mathematically probable that a cell would form, given any soup whatever? No, it couldn't, and can't. (At least not without cook-ing the assumptions.) (Note 2)

Well, I thought, sophomore chemistry major that I then was: If we don't know what conditions existed, or what conditions are necessary, and can't repro-duce the event in the laboratory, and can't show it to be statistically proba-ble—why are we so very sure that it happened? Would you hang a man on such evidence?

My point was not that evolutionists were necessarily wrong. I simply didn't see the evidence. While they couldn't demonstrate that life had begun by chemi-cal accident, I couldn't show that it hadn't. An inability to prove that something is statistically possible is not the same as proving that it is not possible. Not being able to reproduce an event in the laboratory does not establish that it didn't hap-pen in nature. Etc.

I just didn't know how life came about. I still don't. Neither do evolutionists.

What Distinguishes Evolution from Other Sciences

Early on, I noticed three things about evolution that differentiated it from other sciences (or, I could almost say, from science). First, plausibility was accepted as being equivalent to evidence. And of course the less you know, the greater the number of things that are plausible, because there are fewer facts to get in the way. Again and again evolutionists assumed that suggesting how something *might* have happened was equivalent to establishing how it *had* happened. Asking them for evidence usually aroused annoyance and sometimes, if persisted in, hostility.

As an example, it seems plausible to evolutionists that life arose by chemical misadventure. By this they mean, I think, that they cannot imagine how else it might have come about. (Neither can I. Does one accept a poor explanation because unable to think of a good one?) This accidental-life theory, being somewhat plausible, is therefore accepted without the usual standards of science, such as reproducibility or rigorous demonstration of mathematical feasibility. Putting it otherwise, evolutionists are too attached to their ideas to be able to question them.

Or to notice that others do. They defend furiously the evolution of life in earth's seas as the most certain of certainties. Yet in the November, 2005 *Scientific American*, an article argues that life may have begun elsewhere, perhaps on Mars, and arrived here on meteorites. May have, perhaps, might. Somewhere, somewhere else, anywhere. Onward into the fog.

Consequently, discussion often turns to vague and murky assertion. Starlings are said to have evolved to be the color of dirt so that hawks can't see them to eat them. This is plausible. But guacamayos and cockatoos are gaudy enough to be seen from low-earth orbit. Is there a contradiction here? No, say evolutionists. Guacamayos are gaudy so they can find each other to mate. Always there is the pat explanation. But starlings seem to mate with great success, though invisible. If you have heard a guacamayo shriek, you can hardly doubt that another one could easily find it. Enthusiasts of evolution then told me that guacamayos were at the top of their food chain, and didn't have predators. Or else that the predators were colorblind. On and on it goes. But ... is any of this established?

Second, evolution seemed more a metaphysics or ideology than a science. The sciences, as I knew them, gave clear answers. Evolution involved intense faith in fuzzy principles. You demonstrated chemistry, but believed evolution. If you have ever debated a Marxist, or a serious liberal or conservative, or a feminist or Christian, you will have noticed that, although they can be exceedingly bright and well informed, they display a maddening imprecision. You never get a straight answer if it is one they do not want to give. Nothing is ever firmly established. Crucial assertions do not tie to observable reality. Invariably the Marxist (or evolutionist) assumes that a detailed knowledge of economic conditions under the reign of Nicholas II or whatever substitutes for being able to answer simple questions, such as why Marxism has never worked. This is the Fallacy of Irrelevant Knowledge. And of course almost anything can be made believable by considering only favorable evidence and interpreting hard.

Third, evolutionists are obsessed by Christianity and Creationism, with which they imagine themselves to be in mortal combat. This is peculiar to them. Note that other sciences, such as astronomy and geology, even archaeology, are equally threatened by the notion that the world was created in 4004 BC. Astronomers pay not the slightest attention to creationist ideas. Nobody does—except evolutionists. We are dealing with competing religions—overarching explanations of origin and destiny. Thus the fury of their response to skepticism.

I found it pointless to tell them that I wasn't a Creationist. They refused to believe it. If they had, they would have had to answer questions that they would rather avoid. Like any zealots, they cannot recognize their own zealotry. Thus their constant classification of skeptics as *enemies* (a word they often use)—of truth, of science, of Darwin, of progress.

This tactical demonization is not unique to evolution. "Creationist" is to evolution what "racist" is to politics: A way of preventing discussion of what you do not want to discuss. Evolution is the political correctness of science.

The Lair of the Beast

I have been on several lists on the internet that deal with matters such as evolution, have written on the subject, and have discussed evolution with various of its adherents. These men (almost all of them are) have frequently been very bright indeed, often Ivy League professors, some of them with names you would recognize. They are not amateurs of evolution or high-school principals in Kansas eager to prove their modernity. I asked them the questions in the foregoing (about whether we really know what the primeval seas consisted of, etc.) I knew the answers; I wanted to see how serious proponents of evolutionary biology would respond to awkward questions.

It was like giving a bobcat a prostate exam. I got everything *but* answers. They told me I was a crank, implied over and over that I was a Creationist, said that I was an enemy of science (someone who asks for evidence is an enemy of science). They said that I was trying to pull down modern biology (if you ask questions about an aspect of biology, you want to pull down biology). They told me I didn't know anything (that's why I was asking questions), and that I was a mere journalist (the validity of a question depends on its source rather than its content).

But they didn't answer the questions. They ducked and dodged and evaded. After thirty years in journalism, I know ducking and dodging when I see it. It was like cross-examining hostile witnesses. I tried to force the issue, pointing out that the available answers were "Yes," "No," "I don't know," or "The question is not legitimate," followed by any desired discussion. Still no straight answer. They would neither tell me of what the early oceans consisted, nor admit that they didn't know.

This is the behavior not of scientists, but of advocates, of True Believers. I used to think that science was about asking questions, not about defending things you didn't really know. Religion, I thought, was the other way around. I guess I was wrong.

Practical Questions

A few things that worry those who are not doctrinaire evolutionists. (Incidentally, it is worth noting that by no means all involved in the life sciences are doctrinaire. A friend of mine, a (Jewish, atheist) biochemist, says "It doesn't make sense." He may be wrong, but a Creationist he isn't.)

To work, a theory presumably must (a) be internally consistent and (b) map onto reality. You have to have both. Classical mechanics for example is (so far as I know) internally consistent, but is not at all points congruent with reality. Evolution has a great deal of elaborate, Protean, and often fuzzy theory. How closely does it correspond to what we actually see? Do the sweeping principles fit the grubby details?

For example, how did a giraffe get a long neck? One reads as a matter of vague philosophical principle that a proto-giraffe by chance happened to be taller than its herdmates, could eat more altitudinous leaves than its confreres, was therefore better fed, consequently rutted with abandon, and produced more child giraffes of height. This felicitous adaptation therefore spread and we ended up ... well, up—with taller giraffes. It sounds reasonable. In evolution that is enough.

But what are the practical details? Do we have an unambiguous record of giraffes with longer and longer necks? (Maybe we do. I'm just asking.)

Evolution is said to proceed by the accretion of successful point mutations. Does a random point mutation cause the appearance of longer vertebrae? If so, which mutation? If not one, then how many random point mutations? What virtue did these have that they were conserved until all were present? Have we isolated the gene(s) that today control the length of the beast's neck? How can you tell what happened in the distant past, given that we have no DNA from proto-giraffes?

There may be perfectly good, clear, demonstrable answers to a few of these questions. I'm not a paleontological giraffologist. But if evolutionists want people to accept evolution, they need to provide answers—clear, concrete, non-metaphysical answers without gaping logical lacunae. They do not. When passionate believers do not provide answers that would substantiate their assertions, a reasonable presumption is that they do not have them.

The matter of the giraffe is a simple example of a question that inevitably occurs to the independently thoughtful: How do you get evolutionarily from A to B? Can you get from A to B by the mechanisms assumed? Without practical details, evolution looks like an assertion that the better survives the worse; throw in ionizing radiation and such to provide things to do the surviving, and we're off to the races. But ... can we get there from here? Do we actually know the intermediate steps and the associated genetic mechanics? If we don't know what the steps were, can we at least show unambiguously a series of steps that would work?

Lots of evolutionary changes just don't look manageable by random mutation. Some orchestrated jump seems necessary. Consider caterpillars. A caterpillar has no obvious resemblance to a butterfly. The disparity in engineering is huge. The caterpillar has no legs, properly speaking, certainly no wings, no proboscis. How did a species that did not undergo metamorphosis evolve into one that did? Pupating looks like something you do well or not at all: If you don't turn into something practical at the end, you don't get another chance.

Think about this. The ancestor of a modern caterpillar necessarily was something that could reproduce already. To get to be a butterfly-producing sort of organism, it would have to evolve silk-extruding organs, since they are what you make a cocoon with. OK, maybe it did this to tie leaves together, or maybe the beast resembled a tent-caterpillar. (Again, plausibility over evidence.) Then some mutation caused it to wrap itself experimentally in silk. (What mutation? Are we serious?) It then died, wrapped, because it had no machinery to cause it to undergo the fantastically complex transformation into a butterfly. Death is almost always a discouragement to reproduction.

Tell me how the beast can gradually acquire, by accident, the capacity gradually to undergo all the formidably elaborate changes from worm to butterfly, so that each intermediate form is a practical organism that survives. If evolutionists cannot answer such questions, the theory fails.

Here the evolutionist will say, "Fred, caterpillars are soft, squashy things and don't leave good fossils, so it's unreasonable to expect us to find proof." I see the problem. But it is unreasonable to expect me to accept something on the grounds that it can't be proved. Yes, it is possible that an explanation exists and that we just haven't found it. But you can say that of anything whatever. Is it good science to assume that evidence will be forthcoming because we sure would like it to be? I'll gladly give you evidence Wednesday for a theory today?

Note that I am not asking evolutionists to give detailed mechanics for the evolution of everything that lives. If they gave convincing evidence for a few of the hard cases—proof of principle, so to speak—I would be inclined to believe that equally good evidence existed for the others. But they haven't.

Evolution, Like Gaul, Is Divided Into Three Parts

Evolution breaks down into at least three logically separable components: First, that life arose by chemical accident; second, that it then evolved into the life we see today; and third, that the mechanism was the accretion of chance mutations. Evolutionists, not particularly logical, refuse to see this separability.

The first, chance formation of life, simply hasn't been established. It isn't science, but faith.

The second proposition, that life, having arisen by unknown means, then evolved into the life of today, is more solid. In very old rocks you find fish, then things, like coelacanth and the ichthyostega and later archaeopteryx, that look like transitional forms, and finally us. They seem to have somehow gotten from A to B. A process of evolution, however driven, looks reasonable. It is hard to imagine that these animals appeared magically from nowhere, one after the other.

The third proposition, that the mechanism of evolutions is chance mutation, though sacrosanct among its proponents, is shaky. If it cannot account for the simultaneous appearance of complex, functionally interdependent characteristics, as in the case of caterpillars, it fails. Thus far, it hasn't accounted for them.

It is interesting to note that evolutionists switch stories regarding the mechanism of transformation. The standard Neo-Darwinian view is that evolution proceeds very slowly. But when it proves impossible to find evidence of gradual evolution, as for example when sudden changes appear in the fossil record, some evolutionists turn to "punctuated equilibrium," which says that evolution happens by sudden undetectable spurts in small populations. The idea isn't foolish, just unestablished. Then there are the evolutionists who, in opposition to those who maintain that point-mutations continue to account for human evolution, say that now cultural evolution has taken over.

Finally, when things do not happen according to script—when, for example, human intelligence appears too rapidly—then we have the theory of "privileged genes," which evolved at breakneck speed because of assumed but unestablished selective pressures. That is, the existence of the pressures is inferred from the changes, and then the changes are attributed to the pressures. Oh.

When you have patched a tire too many times, you start thinking about getting a new tire.

The Theory of Improbability

As previously mentioned, evolutionists depend heavily on plausibility unabetted by evidence. There is also the matter of implausibility. Suppose that I showed you two tiny gear wheels, such as one might find in an old watch, and said, "See? I turn this little wheel, and the other little wheel turns too. Isn't that cute?" You would not find this surprising. Suppose I then showed you a whole mechanical watch, with thirty little gear wheels and a little lever that said tickticktick. You would have no trouble accepting that they all worked together.

If I then told you of a mechanism consisting of a hundred billion little wheels that worked for seventy years, repairing itself, wouldn't you suspect either that I was smoking something really good—or that something beyond simple mechanics must be involved?

If something looks implausible, it probably is. Evolution writ large is the belief that a cloud of hydrogen will spontaneously invent extreme-ultraviolet lithography, perform Swan Lake, and write all the books in the British Museum.

More Questions on the Fit with Reality

Does the theory, however reasonable and plausible (or not), in fact map onto what we actually see? A principle of evolution is that traits conferring fitness become general within a population. Do they?

Again, consider intelligence. Presumably it increases fitness. (Or maybe it does. An obvious question is why, if intelligence is adaptive—i.e., promotes survival—it didn't evolve earlier; and if it is not adaptive, why did it evolve at all? You get various unsubstantiated answers, such as that intelligence is of no use without an opposable thumb, or speech, or something.)

Those who deal in human evolution usually hold *The Bell Curve* in high regard. (So do I. It's almost as good as *Shotgun News* or, more appropriate in this context, the *Journal of Irreproducible Results*.) A point the book makes is that in the United States the highly intelligent tend to go into fields requiring intelligence, as for example the sciences, computing, and law. They live together, work together, and marry each other, thus tending to concentrate intelligence instead of making it general in the population. They also produce children at below the level of replacement. (Perhaps fitness leads to extinction.)

Black sub-Saharan Africans (say many evolutionists) have a mean IQ somewhere near 70, live in wretched poverty, and breed enthusiastically. White Europeans, reasonably bright at IQ 100 and quite prosperous, are losing population. Jews, very bright indeed at a mean IQ of 115 and very prosperous, are positively scarce, always have been, and seem to be losing ground. From this I conclude either that (a) intelligence does not increase fitness or (b) reproduction is inversely proportional to fitness.

I'm being a bit of a smart-ass here, but … the facts really don't seem to match the theory.

In human populations, short of concentration of the bright in the professions, do the fit really reproduce with each other? It is a matter of daily observation that men prefer cute, sexy women. It then becomes crucial for evolutionists to show that cute and sexy are more fit than strong, smart, and ugly. Thus large breasts are said to produce more milk (Evidence? Chimpanzees have no breasts yet produce ample milk.) and that broad hips imply a large birth canal. (But men are not attracted to broad hips, but to broad hips in conjunction with a narrow waist.) Curvaceous legs are said to be curvaceous because of underlying muscle, important for fitness.

Of course Chinese women do not have muscular legs or buttocks, wide hips, or large breasts, and seem to reproduce satisfactorily. (White and Asian women are more physically delicate than African women, as witness the lower rates of training injuries among black women in the American army. Thus European women, said to have emigrated from Africa and evolved to be Caucasians, lost sturdiness. Why?)

Then it is said that ugly woman are hypertestosteronal, and therefore have more spontaneous abortions. A sophomore logic student with a hangover could point out the problems and unsaid things in this argument.

There is an air of desperation about all of it. Transparently they begin with their conclusion and craft their reasoning to reach it.

Fast and Faster

To the evolutionarily unbaptised, it seems that evolution might occur slowly, by the gradual accretion of random point-mutations over millions of years, but certainly could occur rapidly by the spread of genes already available in the population. For example, genes presumably exist among us for the eyes of Ted Williams, the endurance of marathon runners, the general physical plant of Mohammed Ali, the intelligence of Gauss, and so on. (This of course assumes genetic determinism, which not all geneticists buy.) Are, or were, these becoming general? Perhaps. Show me. If not, one must conclude either that these qualities do not confer fitness, or that fitness does not become general. It seems odd to believe that massive structural changes can occur slowly through the accumulation of accidental changes, but much more rapid increases in fitness do not occur through existent genes. Can we get answers, please? Concrete, non-metaphysical, demonstrable answers?

Consciousness

With evolution the sciences run into the problem of consciousness, which they are poorly equipped to handle. This is important. You don't need to consider consciousness in, say, physical chemistry, which gives the correct answers without it. But evolution is a study of living things, of which consciousness is at least sometimes a quality. Evolutionists know this, and so write unwittingly fatuous articles on the evolution of consciousness. They believe that they are being scientific. But ... are they?

Obvious questions: What is consciousness? Does it have a derived definition, like f = ma? Or is it an undefined primitive, like "line" or "point"? With what instrument do you detect it? Is something either conscious or not, or do you have shades and degrees? Is a tree conscious, or a rock? How do you know? Evolution means a continuous change over time. How do you document such changes? Do we have fossilized consciousness, consciousness preserved in amber? Does consciousness have physical existence? If it does, is it electromagnetic, gravitational, or what? If it doesn't have physical existence, what kind of existence does it have?

If you cannot define it, detect it, or measure it, how do you study its evolution, if any? Indeed, how do the sciences, based on physics, handle anything that is physically undetectable?

Speculation disguised as science never ends. For example, some say that consciousness is just a side-effect of complexity. How do they know? Complexity defined how? If a man is conscious because he's complex, then a whole room full of people must be even more conscious, because the total complexity would have to be more than any one fellow's complexity. The universe has got to be more complex than anything in it, so it must be motingator conscious.

Ah, but the crucial questions, though: (Again, the possible answers are, "Yes," "No," "I don't know," or "The question doesn't make sense.")

First, does consciousness interact with matter? It seems to. When I drop a cinder block on my foot, it certainly interacts with my consciousness. And if I consciously tell my hand to move, it does.

Second, if consciousness interacts with matter, then don't you have to take it into account in describing physical systems?

Vague Plausibility Revisited

Humans are said to have a poor sense of smell because they evolved to stand upright in the savanna where you can see forever and don't need to smell things. This makes no sense: Anyone can see that the better your senses of smell and hearing, especially at night but even in daytime if you have lions that look like dirt and know how to sneak up on things, you are better off. I note that horses have good vision and eyes at about the same altitude as ours, but they have great noses.

Then the evolutionist says, well, people's noses retracted into their faces, and there wasn't room for good olfaction. How much olfactory tissue does a house cat have? They can sure smell things better than we can. Oh, then says the Evolutionist, a large olfactory center in the brain would impose too much metabolic strain and require that people eat more, and so they would die of starvation in bad times. Evidence? Demonstration?

My favorite example, which does not reach the level of plausibility, is such artifacts as the tail of a peacock which obviously makes the bird easier to see and eat. So help me, I have several times seen the assertion that females figure that any male who can survive such a horrendous disadvantage must really be tough, and therefore good mating material. The tail increases fitness by decreasing fitness. A Boy Named Sue.

Traits That Ought To Be Dead, But Don't Seem To Be

Supposedly traits that kill off an animal die out of the population, and things that help the beast survive spread till they all have them. That makes sense. But does it happen?

That it does is certainly an article of faith. I once asked a doctor why Rh negative people stayed in the population. Fifteen percent of white women are negative, so they are usually going to mate with positive men, with the consequent possibility that children will suffer from hemolytic disease. Well, said the doctor, being Rh negative obviously must have some survival value, or it wouldn't exist. (Then why hasn't it become general? Or is it doing so?) She simply believed.

She then rolled out sickle-cell anemia, the poster child of evolution, which is caused by a point mutation on the beta chain of hemoglobin and, when heterozygous, helps people survive malaria.

Maybe Rh negativity does have some survival value, which can be shown to be greater than its non-survival value. Maybe asthma does too, and fatal allergies to bee stings, and migraines, schizophrenia, panic, cluster headaches, masochism, anaphylactic shock in general, homosexuality in males, allergies, a thousand genetic diseases, suicide, and so on. (I suppose you could argue that being a suicide bomber ensures wide dispersal of one's genetic material.)

For that matter, why are there so many traits that have no obvious value? For example, kidneys have well developed nerves. Kidney stones are agonizing. Yet there is absolutely nothing an animal can do about a kidney stone. How do those nerves increase fitness? Traits that do not increase fitness, remember, die out.

Evolutionists don't ask. Always the question is How does this fit in with evolution, instead of, Does this fit in with evolution?

Intelligent Design

An interesting thought that drives evolutionists mad is called Intelligent Design, or ID. It is the view that things that appear to have been done deliberately may have been. Some look at, say, the human eye and think, "This looks like really good engineering. Elaborate retina of twelve layers, marvelously transparent cornea, pump system to keep the whole thing inflated, suspensory ligaments, really slick lens, the underlying cell biology. Very clever."

I gather that a lot of ID folk are in fact Christian apologists trying to drape Genesis in scientific respectability. That is, things looked to have been designed, therefore there must be a designer, now will Yahweh step forward. Yet an idea is not intellectually disreputable because some of the people who hold it are. The genuine defects of ID are the lack of a detectible designer, and that evolution appears to have occurred. This leads some to the thought that consciousness is involved and evolution may be shaping itself. I can think of no easy way to test the idea.

In any event, to anyone of modest rationality, the evolutionist's hostility to Intelligent Design is amusing. Many evolutionists argue, perhaps correctly, that Any Day Now we will create life in the laboratory, which would be intelligent design. Believing that life arose by chemical accident, they will argue (reasonably, given their assumptions) that life must have evolved countless times throughout the universe. It follows then that, if we will soon be able to design life, someone else might have designed us.

In Conclusion

To evolutionists I say, "I am perfectly willing to believe what you can actually establish. Reproducibly create life in a test tube, and I will accept that it can be done. Do it under conditions that reasonably may have existed long ago, and I will accept as likely the proposition that such conditions existed and gave rise to life. I bear no animus against the theory, and champion no competing creed. But don't expect me to accept fluid speculation, sloppy logic, and secular theology."

I once told my daughters, "Whatever you most ardently believe, remember that there is another side. Try, however hard it may be, to put yourself in the shoes of those whose views you most dislike. Force yourself to make a reasoned argument for their position. Do that, think long and hard, and conclude as you will. You can do no better, and you may be surprised."

Notes

* An example, for anyone interested, of the sort of unlogic to which I was exposed by evolutionists: Some simple viruses are strings of nucleotides in a particular order. In 2002 Eckhard Wimmer, at the University of New York at Stony Brook, downloaded the sequence for polio from the internet, bought the necessary nucleotides from a biological supply house, strung them together, and got a functioning virus that caused polio in mice. It was a slick piece of work.

When I ask evolutionists whether the chance creation of life has been demonstrated in the laboratory, I get email offering Wimmer's work as evidence that it has been done. But (even stipulating that viruses are alive) what Wimmer did was to put OTS nucleotides together according to a *known pattern* in a well-equipped laboratory. This is intelligent design, or at least intelligent plagiarism. It is not chance anything. At least some of the men who offered Wimmer's work as what it wasn't are far too intelligent not to see the illogic—except when they are defending the faith.

** Many Evolutionists respond to skepticism about life's starting by chance by appealing to the vastness of time. "Fred, there were *billions and billions* of gallons of ocean, for billions of years, or billions of generations of spiders or bugs or little funny things with too many legs, so the odds are that in all that time...." Give something long enough and it has to happen, they say. Maybe. But probabilities don't always work the way they look like they ought.

Someone is said to have said that a monkey banging at random on a typewriter would eventually type all the books in the British Museum. (Some of the books suggest that this may have happened, but never mind.) Well, yes. The monkey would. But it could be a wait. The size of the wait is worth pondering.

Let's consider the chance that the chimp would type a particular book. To make the arithmetic easy, let's take a bestseller with 200,000 words. By a common newspaper estimate of five letters per word on average, that's a million letters. What's the chance the monkey will get the book in a given string of a million characters?

For simplicity, assume a keyboard of 100 keys. The monkey has a 1/100 chance of getting the first letter, times 1/100 of getting the second letter, and so on. His chance of getting the book is therefore one in 1 in 100 exp 1,000,000, or 1 in 10 exp 2,000,000. (I don't offhand know log 3 but, thirty being greater than ten, a 30-character keyboard would give well in excess of 10 exp 1,000,000.)

Now, let's be fair to the Bandar Log. Instead of one monkey, let's use 10 exp 100 monkeys. Given that the number of subatomic particles in the universe is supposed to be 10 exp 87 (or something), that seems to be a fair dose of monkeys. (I picture a cowering electron surrounded by 10 exp 13 monkeys.) Let's say they type 10 exp 10 characters per second per each, for 10 exp 100 seconds which, considering that the age of the universe (I read somewhere) is 10 exp 18 seconds, seems more than fair.

Do the arithmetic. For practical purposes, those monkeys have no more chance of getting the book than the single monkey had, which, for practical purposes, was none.

Now, I do not suggest that the foregoing calculation has any direct application to the chance formation of life. (I will get seriously stupid email from people who ignore the foregoing sentence.) But neither do I know that the chance appearance of a cell does not involve paralyzing improbabilities. Without unambiguous numbers arising from unarguable assumptions, invoking time as a substitute for knowledge can be hazardous.

34

Fred to Save Country: Isn't Sure Why

It has become apparent that I am going to have to reform the government of the United States. Frankly I'd rather remove one of my lungs with a ballpoint pen. Still, I'm nothing if not perfervidly public-spirited. I will not stand around like Nehru fiddling while Rome burned. Noblesse oblige, that sort of thing.

To begin, we have much too much democracy. We need to discourage people from voting. In fact, the gravest obstacle to the restoration of civilization in North America is universal suffrage. Letting everybody vote makes no sense. Obviously they are no good at it. The whole idea smacks of the fumble-witted idealism of a high-school Marxist society.

At least eighty percent of the electorate lives in blank medieval darkness regarding any matter of public policy or history. They might as well vote on the incisions needed in cardiac surgery as try to govern themselves. Poll after poll shows that even graduates of America's pathetic Halloween universities (where the young disguised as students are hornswoggled by mountebanks disguised as professors), which means most of the universities, do not know when the Russian Revolution occurred, or within a century when the Civil War took place, or who Galileo was. These are the better informed. The rest barely know what century they live in.

Unalloyed ignorance is not an obvious qualification for governing.

Only two possible reasons exist for universal suffrage, both bad. The first is that if you let idiots vote, the Democrats will sometimes be elected. That is, it is a sort of affirmative action for the Democratic National Committee; this is perhaps slightly more desirable than, say, price supports for mutant cholera. The only good thing that can be said about Democrats is that, when they are in power, the Republicans are not.

The second reason is that, in principle, the idiot vote will keep idiots from being maltreated by the bright. It does not, however, keep the bright from being maltreated by idiots, who are far more numerous. They run the schools, for example, which is why students often can't read after twelve years.

Obviously we need to restore something like the old literacy tests for voting. I'm not suggesting that we ask hard questions like "What German Jew ruled Egypt during the Eighteenth Dynasty?" (Surely you have heard of the Teuton Kamen.) Or "Translate from the Latin: 'Civili si ergo fortibus es in ero; nobili deus trux.'" No. I wouldn't even ask simple questions like when did Reconstruction end, or who was Neville Chamberlain.

However, potential voters would be required to find the United States on an outline map of the world. This would eliminate half the public. Ask them to find Japan and you would be down to ten percent. Then I'd have them read a randomly chosen paragraph from the Constitution and see whether they had the foggiest idea what it meant. Few would. (Think I'm kidding? In 1993 the level of functional illiteracy in Detroit was forty-seven percent.)

Next, nobody under the age of twenty-five should vote. A recent college graduate is a sorry cheese-brained late adolescent. With maturity he may be approximately rational, but at twenty-one maturity he don't got it yet. And he hasn't seen squat of the world. Some will say, "Well, he's old enough to die for his country, so he's old enough to vote," a thought that would embarrass a special-ed termite. A toddler is old enough to die in a car crash, which doesn't establish that he should have a driver's license.

Next, only foreign correspondents should be permitted to run for president.

Reflect how we choose today's candidates. They are either useless gigolos like John Kerry, or pampered drunks inflicted on the polity by Texas in revenge for the Civil War. If they are not unmitigated brats, they have worked their way up in politics. This means that they began as second-rate lawyers, attached themselves like ticks to some party or other, and spent thirty years learning to lie, steal, manipulate, and suck up. Politics is a sieve eliminating the honest. It assures that you get what you don't want. When these moral flatworms are finally nominated for The Big One, they know crooked dealing. It's all they know. How much sense does this make?

Now consider the veteran correspondent. He has spent three years each in, say, Buenos Aires, Teheran, and Singapore, and speaks a couple of the languages. He actually knows something about the world outside of the United States. A reporter spends his time learning about things, not in buying votes or grinning like a mental defective. The reporter's instinct, though seldom that of the publisher, is to find the truth.

He knows the cities and governments of Asia, Africa, and Europe, the bars, villages, and economies. He has seen wars at the level of ruptured abdomens and probably isn't enchanted by them the way some draft-dodging amateur from Houston might be. He knows the people of these countries, and knows that they are people, which seems never quite to penetrate to jejune occupants of the great double-wide on Pennsylvania Avenue.

A foreign correspondent of course has worked as a reporter in America, probably on a large metro daily, which is how you get to the foreign desk. This means that he has covered things like municipal government, that he has ridden with the police and written of the courts and actually knows what goes on and how things work. This sounds like a qualification to me.

Finally I'd set out to promote aristocracy. Though the Floundering Fathers didn't intend it, we now see that representative government quickly turns into the dictatorship of the proletariat. If you doubt this, I congratulate you on not having a television. Today, the worst impose themselves on all, because they can.

We need to encourage the establishment of sharply delineated social classes, to include silly titles and knighthoods and crowns. (I want to be the Duke of Guadalajara.)

Aristocrats are not necessarily brighter or more tasteful than the lower classes. The British royal family is conclusive evidence. Yet aristocrats very much want to *think* that they are superior. To sustain this illusion they will support opera and literature that many of them don't like, so as to distinguish themselves from *hoi polloi*. One thinks of JS Bach at the court of Frederick the Great, or Wagner and Ludvig II. Then one thinks of the White House. Then if one can, one ceases to think.

I cannot imagine that the foregoing recommendations will not be enacted by a grateful country. In anticipation I am going to get a coat of arms from a mail-order company and begin building a castle.

35

Hornets, Brains, and Whales

I've been thinking about hornets. "Why?" you may ask. Because I'm bored with the little voices and can't find my Haldol. Anyway, I claim that hornets show that the human race collectively isn't nearly as smart as it thinks it is. Especially about hornets.

The worrisome thing is that hornets know too much. A hornet has practically no brain, probably a few milligrams or some equally depressing amount. But consider what the dangerous little spike can do.

A hornet can fly, with precisely controlled speed and angle to the ground. It can also hover precisely. This is not easy. Controlling the speed and angle of wings, or whatever the beast controls in (as we say) real time, is not a freshman's project in programming. Boeing couldn't do it.

A hornet can walk over broken ground, effortlessly negotiating obstacles; it can do this hanging upside down. It is no simple thing to control six jointed legs. If you think otherwise, talk to a robotics engineer. A hornet can fly up to a tree branch, adjust its angle in the air, and transition from flight to walking. Easily.

A hornet can see. How well it can see and what it can see, I don't know. I have never been a hornet. Hornets that hunt things can certainly see well enough to find whatever it is that they hunt. This requires integrating the output of the multitudinous ommatidia that constitute its compound eyes into a useful image. Try to figure out how it does it.

Further, it can understand what it is seeing. I'm not sure what I mean by "understand." Probably I mean the same thing you do when you look at something and know what it is. This is a quite different problem from forming an image. It is easy to get a computer to take a picture, much harder to get it to "know" what is in the picture.

How does a hornet with virtually no brain do it?

Today the language and modes of thought of computing dominate the biological sciences. One speaks of behavior as being genetically "programmed" or "hard-wired," and of a brain's "processing power," of "integrating" information in "real time." We are perhaps not always aware that we do this. When you think in terms of a particular scheme, you can begin seeing it where it isn't, begin projecting it onto the world.

When I think of how the control of a hornet's legs must work (except of course that it doesn't have to work the way I believe it must), I think in terms of sensors of angle and force, of procedures to calculate this and that. Do hornets do it this way? Maybe not. Scientists as much as other people struggle to escape their preconceptions or, more usually, don't struggle. Many don't seem to know that they have preconceptions.

A hornet's aggregate behavior is not trivial. It can navigate almost infallibly. In a former rural home in Virginia, I watched them set off across a bean field of a hundred and fifty yards, apparently going to the woods on the other side. They came back. In the jungles of South America, dim under thick canopies, with dense undergrowth, I have seen nests hanging. The insects fly though the growth without getting lost.

Hornets know how to build nests—what to chew, how to find it, when to chew it, and how to paste it together to make (depending on the variety of hornet) a smooth hanging grey gourd full of elaborate cells. This begins to be an awful lot of behavior contained in virtually no brain. (Stray thought: What is the unit of behavior per neuron?)

Hornets know how to mate. Mating with a hornet is not to be undertaken casually, and I do not recommend it to the reader without professional instruction. However, hornets seem to do it. In the default computer-think of the sciences ("default," I say automatically) the explanation might be as follows: The hornet's pheromone receptors send a medium-priority interrupt to the central nervous system which then branches to its mating procedure. Click, click, click, like mechanized tinker toys.

I wonder. I do not know whether hornets mate while flying, as ants do, but it must be beastly difficult to copulate and fly at the same time. Think in terms of airline pilots and you will see what I mean. In terms of computing, mating is an extraordinarily tricky problem. Both bugs have to "want" to do it, recognize each other, know how to align various body parts without error, and produce the needed physiological responses at the right moment.

I know how I would try to write the program to do these things. I do not know how I would make it work. Especially in bare milligrams of brain. Something curious is going on here, methinks, something that we don't understand.

Yet further, hornets know how to protect themselves and their nests. (I have stepped on one barefoot. I can assure you that they know how to protect themselves.) This, like so much of their behavior, is not as simple as it might seem. Stinging in itself may be a reflexive spasm, though hornets that paralyze their prey with stings have to know exactly where to sting. (How do they know?) You generally do not want to miss with a tarantula. Their overall defensive behavior is a tad more complex.

They have to decide that they are being threatened. How? I could come up with some function, probably silly or at least inadequate, of apparent size, nearness to nest, velocity, and so on. ("Function." Back to computers.) That's a lot of calculation in no brain. In any event, being able to simulate a process in a computer doesn't mean that the computer is doing it the same way the hornet is. Computers today clock at several gigahertz. A hornet's barely-brain runs on slow mushy diffusion of chemicals across wet synapses. They are doing something very different.

Further, disturbed hornets look to be angry. They give every indication of being aggressive. Now, it is possible that I am anthropomorphizing. It is also possible that I am not. A thing that appears to be angry may in fact be angry.

Unless I fall into solipsism, I have to assume that if you begin screaming and throwing things at me, you are angry. On equally good evidence, I assume that when my dog behaves playfully or affectionately, she is so. I am not sure why I have to believe that an apparently infuriated hornet isn't.

Now, add up all hornetary behavior, including a lot we haven't touched on—communication between hornets, caring for the young, and so on—and ask how much more complex, if at all, is the behavior of whales, who have brains you could sleep in.

Hornets? I think the little monsters know, within the limits of their world, exactly what they are doing. I am not so sanguine about humans.

36

In Darkest Africa

Letters pour in, or might if some did, saying, "Fred, tell us about the time you were a terribly romantic correspondent in darkest Africa with Jonas Savimbi and bounced around in stolen Soviet trucks and had to drink sumo all the time." All right. Since you ask.

I had just come aboard the *Washington Times* in the early eighties. The editor was Smith Hempstone, an old Africa hand I'd met on a junket to Taipei. Smith had perhaps read too much Hemingway. On the wall behind his desk was a gaudy tribal shield with crossed spears. Anyway, he told me I was going to Angola to run around with Savimbi's guerrillas.

South Africa didn't want reporters running around Angola. Larry Leamer (my photographer) and I landed in Joburg with 200 rolls of film and a line of twaddle about how we were bird photographers. It was all very Terry-and-the-Pirates. We stood under a chandelier in some hotel and gave a password to a guy who put us on a flight to Windhoek and then we got in a high-wing Cessna with some bush pilots and flew to the Caprivi Strip, where I suppose our birds were thought to be, and dropped under South African radar in a blinding thunderstorm about thirty feet above the trees. This was when we weren't ten feet above the trees because of sudden downdrafts. Finally we found an abandoned airstrip and landed and all these very black guys came out of the bushes with AKs. I remember thinking, "These had better be the right very black guys with AKs or this isn't good at all."

Cuando Cubango in southeastern Angola has trees about every thirty feet, so from the air you can't see anything but you can drive the stolen Soviet trucks. See, the Cubans were helping the MPLA, which was the communist government in Luanda, and South Africa was helping Savimbi's group, which was UNITA, and lying about it, and something called SWAPO was active in the south, and the FNLA in the north, and somehow the trucks got to Cuando Cubango and

Savimbi ambushed them. (This is how scrofulous wars always are, mostly Alphabits.)

Anyway we went driving through sand with these heavily armed guys who gave us sumo, which is Portugese for godawful sticky red coolade-like gunch. I came to hate it like poison, which it closely resembled. From time to time we ran into herds of really African-looking animals with funny horns but not much dynamism and had to wait for them to decide to go somewhere else. But it was sunny and peaceful. We felt very manful and adventurous. I mean, why be a reporter if you can't strike poses?

We got to Jamba, which was Savimbi's headquarters in the bush, a large collection of stick huts, which can actually be architecturally elaborate with lintels and things. Blue skies, no clouds, drill-instructor looking guys giving classes in maintaining various machine guns. They had wickerwork things that were supposed to stop napalm if Luanda's MiG found us. I rather hoped it didn't. Lunch was boiled potatoes in a canteen cup with a fried egg on top, and sumo, like really nasty cherry molasses. We both got assigned bearers who carried our camera bags. (I was shooting for *Soldier of Fortune* under the name of Rick Venable to make an extra buck.) All we needed was for Tarzan to come yodeling out of the trees.

We talked to Savimbi at length about his democratic tendencies, which he didn't have any of, but he had graduated from the University of Lausanne and fielded questions agilely in French, Portuguese, English, and Ovumbundu, I believe it was. A very smart guy but I remember thinking that I did not want to be his prisoner. Then we had the boiled potatoes and the fried egg and the sumo. I was reaching my limits.

One day at lunch I finally snapped and came out of my hut, shrieking, "Larry! I think I'm anti-Sumotic!"

"Huh? Why?"

"Because I can't stand the juice!"

He looked at me strangely. The sun is hot in Angola. Maybe he thought I'd forgotten to wear my hat.

We spent a couple of days driving to villages, which made "primitive" seem like one of those Star Warts movies. Savimbi had the villagers trained. They came out in a mob and sang, "Wadawhudda-sah-VEEM-bi! Wadawhudda-sah-VEEM-bi!" and danced hiphop, which didn't exist yet in America but I know what I saw. Once the chief of a village decided to give me a chicken, a vicious beast with death in her eye and a dangerous-looking beak. In a moment of genius I smiled thanks and indicated with a glance that Larry was my hen-bearer, so the chief handed the creature to him. She showed up that night on top of the boiled potatoes.

Savimbi's people had managed to shoot down a Russian Antonov and capture the pilots. I'm not sure just how that happened. Anyway the fragments were on display in a sort of museum made of hut material and the Red Cross was going to fly in and carry off the pilots, who were in good condition. This was to show Savimibi's good will, which he didn't have any of. By this time I was ready to get the hell out, being persuaded that if I even saw another cup of sumo I would develop diabetes on the spot.

We all drove back to the barely existent landing strip to await the Red Cross, who arrived in an ancient DC-3 with a ratpack of reporters. I knew a great moment for posing when I saw one. The Red Cross officials disembarked. Nurses followed to look after the Russians, who didn't need it. Then came the journalists, who seemed to be general-coverage people agog at being in such an exotic and perilous place. They were our prey. Heh heh.

We swaggered out of the bush with the slight cockiness that marks men who have been months in combat in places not even on the maps, men for whom life with guerrilla bands is everyday experience. Yes, we implied, things have been a bit rough, screaming hordes of drugged-up communists coming through the wire almost nightly—though, to be honest, we haven't been shelled for days. Well, not much anyway. Couple of sappers came into my hut last night. Took them out with my knife, you know. The usual. I am a conscienceless fraud.

Off we took and out we went, toward Joburg, very low over the trees to keep SAM-7s from getting a lock, in a plane that first flew I think in 1936. I was happy. I knew for a fact that there was no sumo in South Africa.

37

Go Go Dancer Steals Viagra

A bit back I was in Thailand and doing a pub crawl with my friend Dean Barrett. Dean is a perceptive writer, highly literate, a transplanted New Yorker, and the Kipling of the bar scene in Bangkok. He gave me his book of poetry, *The Go Go Dancer Who Stole My Viagra and Other Poetic Tragedies of Thailand.** Any man who has spent time in Asia will resonate to it.

Dean has been in BKK for a long time. The bar districts are his ambit, or one of his ambits—Patpong, Nana Plaza, Soi Cowboy, Washington Square. They are garish, tinny, exciting, and boring, the girls who work in them willowy, shy, at times feral, and just freaking lovely.

Some of the joints, the ones that seem to be mostly for sex tourists, jump with godawful disco music while a dozen tired and probably drugged-up girls in bikinis circle brass poles. Others, the Takara for example, are more tranquil, popular among the regulars, the expats who have made Thailand their home. The Texas Lone Star Saloon, in Washington Square off Sukhumvit, is a country bar that could be in Texas.

A lot of westerners marry in Thailand and live contented lives. Others have been the marriage route and aren't about to do it again. Others are just happier unattached. Do you want to eat in the same restaurant the rest of your life, they ask? You see the latter two groups in the bars.

The men who patronize these places are easily described as a bunch of drunks guzzling their pensions. Many call them pathetic, hopeless, shiftless, and contemptible. This misses much that is essential. Most I think are not drunks, though they drink. There are men and men. Each has a story to tell. Usually the expats have more stories than the respectable people back in the world. Some are veterans of Vietnam, some worked the oil rigs, or for the big international contractors. Others bailed out after a nasty divorce, or got sick of the tightening laws back home. The older among them often carry Viagra in their pockets. You can call this absurd. I'm not sure it is.

In judging them, if you regard yourself as competent to do so, it helps to ponder their stage of life. Young expats may have businesses or jobs, but many of the older guys are really in Bangkok to die. They might not put it that way, but after sixty-five that's the way to bet. You die young, or you get old and then die. Those are the available options. You have to do it somewhere. Bangkok is somewhere.

Their choice was to age in some boring suburb back home, perhaps with a wife who had grown boring through too-long exposure (though one never, ever says so); or to age in the bars in the company of lovely lasses with cameo skin and glossy black hair and a certain carnal availability, while drinking with their buddies and telling war stories. The decision for many is a no-brainer. Crump we do and crump we will. Might as well do it in a place you enjoy.

It is a mistake to think that such men necessarily lack intelligence, education, or culture. Dean certainly doesn't. They have simply made another choice.

The ambience of the bars is hard to describe to those who haven't known it, which is why Dean appeals. He knows the men, the women, the visiting frauds who moralize and then sneak away from their wives, the young westerners who have looked at what western women are becoming and run like hell.

Depending on your point of view, the expats are exploiting the girls, or the girls are exploiting the expats, or the gals are just providing a service, but it isn't an unfriendly thing. Sometimes it is like the British pub. You have your favorite bars where you know the mama-san and the girls.

I'm not idealizing it, and neither does Dean, who is far too old and wise in the ways of the thing to paint it in roseate hues or to be sniffish. The girls age and have to move on, not always having anywhere to move on to. They have a kid, maybe were working in a fruit-juice stall and decided that they would make more in a bar. It is not always pretty, but then neither are lots of things. The hookers too are people, and they too have their stories. This Dean knows. He knows the scene with all its charm and warts. He knows that some things just are.

And that some things don't change. In his poem "Buffalo Him Die Send Money," he tells of the bar girl who writes her farang boyfriend, now in the States, that her water buffalo has been struck by lightning and she needs money. The boyfriend reflects how curious it is that that this is the third time this year that her buffalo has been struck by lightning. Yep. Old hands will smile at these stories.

It all comes down to the age-old bargain: Women exchange sex for whatever they want. Men exchange whatever they have for sex. Call it prostitution, or call it marriage, which is just prostitution with compulsory brand-loyalty. It's how God made us, probably in a moment of ill humor. Some things just are.

* This and Dean's other books are available at Amazon.

"The Silly Old Man with the Young Thai Girl in the Texas Lone Star Saloon"

He must be twice her age at least
With mottled, wrinkled skin
His hair is dyed a bottle-black
His face is wintry thin
    Blue veins snake down his bony hands
Like roots of ancient trees
He wears a pair of checkered shorts
Above his scrawny knees.
    The girl he's with is beautiful
Her shoulder-length black hair
Surrounds and frames her dark brown face
Her shoulders soft and bare
    He drinks his Mekhong whiskey down
And orders yet again
The girl he's with just sighs and sneaks
A smile at other men.
    They sit in silence, the silly old man
And the girl who stole his heart
Someone should whisper in his ear
"Too many years apart!"
    Someone should whisper in his ear
"Your girl is bored to death!
Your eyelids droop, your shoulders stoop
There's whiskey on your breath!"
    Someone should whisper in his ear
That if he didn't pay
He might just find his lady love
Would soon be on her way.
    He wallows in her loving gaze
So puppy-dog serene
Serenity for her of course
His ATM machine.
    But he might whisper in our ears
"Well, don't you think I know?

I made my choice and so will you
With fewer years to go."
    I'm not so sure what to make of him
There is no guiding rule
I wonder if he could be both
A wise man and a fool.
    He turns his head to pay the bill
And suddenly I see
It's a mirror on the wall
The silly old man is me.

38

Just Rambling

Ajijic, Mexico—

As you start up the hill above the village the going is steep, and loose rock slides beneath your feet, requiring care, but with increasing altitude the trail levels off a bit and runs through scruffy vegetation. The undergrowth isn't majestic but has an appeal of its own. Most wild places do. There is a complexity of life, a dance of many creatures doing many things. Soon you are well above the town, and the lake stretches off yet further toward the horizon.

I have climbed the hill countless times. Usually the path is empty, though occasionally I encounter Mexican boys and girls running up it for exercise. This is not for the weak. There is a place just before a sharp upslope where a large, fast, black insect often hovers threateningly, as if protecting something, but backs off before I get close enough really to see it. Once, much higher, a pudgy brown snake left the trail in front of me. Maybe a rattler. I wanted no truck with it, nor it with me. We both found this to be a workable arrangement.

A while back I saw something small moving on the trail. At first I couldn't resolve it. Pieces of gravel seemed to be going somewhere. On examination, I saw a pair of dung beetles pushing what appeared to be a deer dropping. They stood on their heads and shoved mightily with their hind legs. Somehow they kept it moving in a consistent direction.

My first thought was that I was glad that I made my living by different means, my second that maybe I didn't. Maybe most of us live by shoving dung of one sort or another. I suppose though that few of us do it while standing on our heads. There is progress after all.

On cloudy days an intense stillness hangs over the hills and the leaves darken against a silvery sky. Then I like to sit on the big rock by the little white chapel that sits on a flat spot. Every Easter the townspeople reenact the ordeal of Christ, climbing the hill past the Stations of the Cross, which are marked by white stones, and ending at the chapel. It is hardly more than an open concrete room, and usually deserted.

Sometimes a gringo comes past the chapel with his dogs. These are always friendly and courteous, both owners and animals. People who walk over difficult trails are simply better folk than those who ride dirt bikes or tour buses. I do not know why. I have seen it on many week-long trips along the Appalachian Trail, over the mountainous spine of Taiwan, and deep in the Grand Canyon.

Often, while supervising dry hills in the distance—they explode into green when the rains come—I wonder why people live as they do. In Washington the young go to law school, itself inexplicable, and then work twelve-hour days for many years so as to become partners at the noted firm of Linger, Loiter, and Dawdle. This seems to me a fate greatly to be avoided. They must have a reason for doing it. I just don't know what it is. At the ends of their lives I suppose they can reflect that they saved Lockheed-Martin a great deal in taxes, and won an important suit over a municipal parking lot.

There is in Chile a farming community, Nuevo Braunau I believe, settled long ago by Germans and now a museum of sorts. The region is still undeveloped or, as I would say, unruined. The farm buildings are of wood, large, solid and homey. Germans being Germans, books line the shelves and victrolas gape on tables. In a framed photograph from the 1800s I looked into the eyes of a lovely dark-haired girl of perhaps nineteen, now dust, standing before the farmhouse with her parents and carefully-groomed little brothers. She looked intelligent and faintly amused, as if having a secret that she wasn't going to tell me.

What must their lives have been? Comfortable, certainly. There was nothing of the frontier in the place. Quiet, decent and, I suspect, contented. Intellectually engaged, I further suspect. We have made "farmer" a synonym for empty-headed and foolish, but of course it isn't so. People had fewer books then but knew them better, if I may judge by my grandparents.

I would wager that the small boys in the photograph did well. Children are happier, and turn out better, amid woods and fields than in suburban malls, if I may judge by observation. Family farming is not to be sneezed at. Running a good spread requires greater ability and self-reliance than, say, being Supervisor of Stultifying Business Records for some urban government. Plowing a field is more dignified, actually produces something of value, and you can think while you are doing it. Not so with the stultifying records.

Behind the sitting-rock by the chapel, another trail, little known I think, leads steeply up some hundreds of yards to a pair of erect flat rocks, colored a rich gold by lichens. This is usually as far as I go. Depending on the season, a steady wind blows over them.

I am doubtless mad. For I hear in the wind—I do not know what exactly, but intimations of things beyond the acres of dull green cubicles full of trapped humanity, and underground garages redolent of motor oil, and sirens shrieking the night through. Perhaps it is just me. Still, I wonder whether we haven't built a world that we don't want quite as much as we thought we were going to. Maybe we weren't intended to live on top of each other.

As evidence of this proposition I note how many people in the unvarying suburbs would like to be somewhere else. (See? I do not imagine that I have a unique grasp of the inescapable.) But the economy needs the administrative equivalent of assembly-line workers. The retirement system ties people to the job as tightly as serfdom tied them to the land. And we have been well trained that the purpose of life is the consumption of things produced in factories.

But I ramble. Things are as they are. Coming down I found the black watcher in his, or more likely her, appointed position over the trail. She hovered motionless, just a dark spot in the air. Then she suddenly wasn't there any longer, but a foot to the right. The creature is that fast. Why did she need such speed? Not for growing vegetables, I surmised. But she got out of my way when I walked toward her. That was the important thing.

39

Limestone Days

Yesterday I got back to Mexico after visiting Washington for a week. Returning to the United States at long intervals is like watching a flower wilt in time-lapse photography. As with the slow but inexorable growth of a tumor, the changes leap out if seen infrequently. Though in historical terms the rot goes fast, very fast, it is not easily noticed day to day.

Perhaps the decay is the inevitable destination of mass democracies. One can't be sure. America is the first instance.

In Washington the stage-managed paranoia leaps to one's attention, the tightening embrace of government of all things. Washington's subway illustrates the point. Admonition is constant, typically in a scolding female voice from the loudspeakers. "Children! Do not *run … play …* or *sit* on the escalators. Hold your parents' hand...." Parents are not to care for their offspring. Mother Metro will do it. Or "Stand Back! Doors are closing!" in a calculatedly bossy tone of voice as the train prepares to pull out of the station. Over and over and over, at every stop. Once the doors couldn't close for some reason and for minutes the hostile voice repeated its idiot warning. Is there not somewhere in the country a woman who speaks pleasantly?

The recorded hectoring is very different from a laconic and practical "Doors closing" from the driver. We are now herded by automated nannies. "Please listen carefully because the menu options have changed...." Anything to save a buck.

Between stops come the warnings to watch other passengers, to report any strange behavior immediately to Metro. Oh. Report strange behavior among the multifarious denizens of a big city. Now, that's a good idea. Does this mean the para-schiz arguing with his buzzing demons? The dark brooding men talking in unknown languages? The bag ladies with those suspicious bundles? The Arabs speaking, of all things, Arabic?

The last time I was in the city, Metro had removed trash cans from the stations because someone might put a bomb in one. Now, I'm told, they have special explosion-absorbent trash cans. Presumably this mummery is fear management to drum up support for an unpopular war. The fact is that you could leave a steamer trunk of TNT on the car and no one would notice.

In a restaurant I saw a warning at the bottom of the menu, which I can't reproduce from memory. It said something like, "The consumption of raw or uncooked fish or eggs or whatever can do bad things of some sort." Why is this here, I wondered? Is there anyone on the planet that doesn't know this? Was the implication that the restaurant was likely to serve putrescent food, requiring a warning to the public? Then why not close it? Later I saw the same warning on the menu of The Village Bistro, a classy restaurant in Rosslyn, Virginia, where I have eaten for years. I concluded that it must be governmentally mandated mommyism, presumably from brainless affirmative-action office proles with little to do.

The Sovietizing of America runs apace. It is not imaginary. The Department of Homeland Security? KGB stands for Committee for State Security.

Driving south and then west toward Laredo, we passed through Athens, Alabama, where I lived for a couple of years around 1957. My father was a mathematician working for the Army Ballistic Missile Agency in Huntsville. Athens was then a different America, and to an extent still is. I hadn't seen the town since I was eleven.

After fifty years it had changed remarkably little in its center, though it was surrounded by the usual hideous malls and strip development that blight the country today. The philosophy of unrestricted rapine, whether denominated free enterprise or capitalism or communism, is utterly without esthetic sensitivity. So it was in the Soviet Union. The differences between Russia and America are small, and much fewer than those between France and America.

The town square with its courthouse was much as it had been, though the town itself seemed smaller and more drab than I remembered. The tight segregation of the Fifties had gone. The water fountains on the square were then labeled White and Colored, and gas stations recognized in their bathrooms three sexes: Men, Women, and Colored.

As an unscientific observation the South seems much more genuinely integrated than does the North. In Washington's restaurants frequented by whites, you see the occasional black, but not many. They are sufficiently rare as almost to be objects of curiosity. In restaurants and catfish houses in Louisiana perhaps half of the clientele were black, which seemed to interest nobody. Black waitresses dealt with us with an easy friendliness that contrasted with a certain wariness noticeable in the North. Blacks are easy people to like when they don't carry a chip on their shoulders.

The Limestone Drugstore was still on the square. (Athens is the country seat of Limestone County.) As a Tom Sawyer simulacrum invariably carrying a BB gun, perhaps with my fielder's mitt slung on the barrel, I once passed a slow summery infinity of afternoons there, reading comic books and drinking ice cream floats. The owner at the time, Mr. Chandler (universally called Coochie, perhaps seventy then, with red Harpo-Marx hair) liked little boys, and kept a rack of comic books on the principle of a bird feeder.

Today, liking little boys would be considered prima facie evidence of what would be called a "pederasty problem," and the comic books would doubtless have to carry warnings. In a less admonished age, Coochie just liked little boys. We carried great piles of comic books to the tables, Superman and Batman and the Green Lantern and Archie, and read them ragged. I doubt that the Limestone ever sold a comic book. It wasn't why they were there. Today some green eye-shade at corporate would notice that those books cost twenty bucks a month, and demand that they be kept in a locked glass case. Unrestricted rapine....

But the Limestone wasn't a chain, so Coochie *was* corporate, and ran his store as he pleased. Freedom, you might call it.

The inside of the store had been expanded and looked like most drug stores, but ... lo! ... the soda fountain was as it had been these many years ago! Apparently someone had a fondness for the past. It was empty, no comics were in evidence, and of course no pile of BB guns (mostly the four-dollar Red Ryder kind, though mine was an upscale Daisy Eagle). These, like everything, would today be illegal. It still had the marble bar, the stained glass behind, the black-and-white checkered floor.

I ordered an ice cream float in memory of the splendid, variegated, and free country that I had been born into, and that somehow disappeared, and then we got in the car and headed for Mexico, still free.

40

Manliness, Quiet Desperation, and Paint Ball

A friend recently sent me a story from the *New York Times* about "survival schools" in which men, mostly young and urban, paint themselves in camouflage and pretend to be soldiers or survivors of plane crashes. These games are a pursuit of manliness, avowed to be such by the participants. ("Manliness likes to be unconventional," [an instructor] added. It likes to disobey the law. So now we have reality camps.'")

The woman who wrote the piece made the participants seem fairly ridiculous, which one would expect of a writer both female and an ornament of a volcanic vent of conventionality. They also made themselves sound ridiculous. Being interrupted by one's cell phone in the midst of a firefight is hard not to smile at. I once covered Mitch WerBel's survival school (Cobray) at Powder Springs in Georgia, in which bored podiatrists came to learn "Advanced Sniping Techniques," having learned Basic Sniping Techniques earlier in the morning. ("This little thing is the trigger.")

It was absolutely ridiculous. Ridiculous, until I thought about it. Why were intelligent men (some were engineering students for example) playing like little boys, I wondered? The answer I think is that today there are so very few outlets for manliness. Such is the grip of feminism on the country that the very word sounds faintly silly.

Manliness certainly isn't in demand. The women of today seem to want a metrosexual who loves to shop, helps with the housework, and never does anything that she wouldn't want to do. He may wear an earring. Modern marriage sounds like a sort of heterosexual lesbianism. The man should be as little like a man as possible while having complementary genitals.

This gelding of men, pushed everywhere in the media (note the universal prevalence of girlish male models with waxed chests and slight figures) can easily be seen as the desired consequence of female hostility to men; the corresponding de-feminization of women, as another front in an anti-male war led by hostile feminists. Perhaps. I have assuredly thought so at times. Yet women seem as unhappy in their mannish roles as do men in womanish ones. One thing is sure, which is that women do not understand men—their drives, needs, nature, or inner light.

For example, I would love to set out on horseback across the Great Plains as they were in say, 1825, with a few friends, a good rifle, and a dog or two. Why? A woman would call the idea absurd, and say that I was trying to prove my manhood or regain my youth or something similarly psychotherapeutic. But that's not it at all. It has nothing to do with impressing anyone, and everything to do with a freedom and independence that a man craves, even when he doesn't quite know that he does.

I think of huge skies with the occasional buzzard circling in the updrafts, of towering clouds darkening with distant rain, wind picking up and hissing through the brush, and nobody there, nobody. For a rifle, I'd like the Savage thirty-thirty lever-action that a buddy had for a while, not because it is the best gun for the purpose but just because it was such a sweet weapon.

How do I explain to a woman why I love the wild places of the earth, places where I can be alone with the jungle or the plains or the mountains? Alone, and left alone? Where things are not certain, predetermined, and suffocatingly secure? What meaning can "a sweet rifle" have for her? None. Why would she want to be uncomfortable and insecure? She does cupboards and rugs. I put up with them.

A normal woman, bearing no ill-will but simply puzzled, will lapse into "boys and their toys." A hairy-chested feminist, more poisonous but equally uncomprehending, will run on tediously about machismo and phallic symbolism. Both are clueless.

I have no fantasies about shooting anyone. I have seen enough of that for one lifetime. I don't hunt, having no desire to kill anything I don't have to kill. I don't need to pose with a rifle. Having carried one in the Marine Corps, I do not regard them as exotic. But when you are far from anywhere, you provide your own security. I am comfortable with the idea. So are a lot of men. In today's suburban, mall-ridden world, security is what answers 911.

Somebody said (or if no one did, I will) that women are realists pretending to be romantics, and men, romantics pretending to be realists. Yes. The male desire is to explore, to fly higher and higher, to invent and dare and go and see. The Apollo landings were not inspired by a desire to know the nature of lunar rocks. A man does not get on a rice-burning crotch-rocket on a desert road in Arizona and scream through the hot vastness, *wap-wap-wap* through the gears, 95, 105, 120 … 125 (*go* baby, get it on, do it for me), because it is particularly practical. It is the sheer glory of the thing, the speed and power, controlled but on the edge.

And now he wakes at five-thirty for the two-hour commute from Fredericksburg to Washington in crawling traffic, then to his cubicle at Agriculture where he tracks soybean yields in North Carolina. For his entire life.

It is not what men are wired to do. We just do not domesticate well. While male behavior is perhaps no more inherently absurd than female, it has little application to the suburbs and bureaucratic salt mines.

The world today, the modern parts anyway, is very much a woman's world. It will become more so. The economy values orderliness, routine, and avoidance of waves. It needs patient people who will do the assembly-line work of huge offices whirring with air-conditioning. Women are better at this. I'm not sure they really like it, but they handle it well.

Women want security, comfort, nice houses and nice cars. Men eventually feel cramped by them. Of course there are exceptions. The old social order, in which women were shy and retiring and stayed in the house, was to a considerable extent artificial. You now see women on the long mountain trails, sometimes solo, and diving the deep walls in the Caribbean. But they are exceptions.

And so you get a young engineer who knows that something is wrong but may not know what. He's bright. Engineers are. He is working on some detail of the hot section of a big new high-efficiency turbo-fan. It is interesting work and well paid. After work every day he goes to the local hangout to check out the babes, though somehow they aren't quite what he's looking for, and his buddies come by with their new Lexuses, and they drink beer and talk about the market. Every night. Another birthday rolls around. He asks the overarching question for a lot of young males today in a world that isn't theirs: "Is this all?"

Maybe he gets a motorcycle, or skydives, but it's still the controlled world, artificial adventure. Or, just maybe, he goes to some silly survival school, an answer arguably ridiculous to a question that isn't.

41

A Conversation with Bush

Miracles do happen. I was astonished when President Bush granted my request for an interview. The truth is that I had almost forgotten making the request. As a matter of course in journalism you cover your bases, asking for all sorts of things that you don't expect to get. The theory is that lightning can always strike. So when the current administration came into office I made the usual petitions at State to talk to Condoleezza Rice, at Defense for the SecDef, and so on. It was pro forma.

Then my phone rang in Guadalajara. It was the White House press office telling me that Bush would see me. At first I assumed that it must be a joke. After all, I was semi-retired, no longer with major outlets in Washington. In the news racket we have large egos, but at bottom we know that officials don't care about us, only about our publications. If a chimpanzee worked for the *New York Times*, any president would talk to it. And I had been critical of Bush in my web column. Why ...? It didn't make sense.

Finally it dawned on me. Years back, when Bush was governor in Texas, I had worked as the Washington editor for Richard Cabeza Productions, a now-defunct news service based in Austin. I wrote some puff pieces on Bush, suggesting that he had presidential timber, and we gave him the Richard Cabeza Award. This was a twelve-dollar mahogany plaque that the Press Secretary throws in the trash, but the news service gets a form letter of thanks from the White House to put on the wall.

I surmised that Bush, getting a lot of bad press about the wars, remembered that Richard Cabeza had praised him, and just wanted to hear a kind word about himself. We forget that politicians are human.

Anyway, I flew into Reagan National after changing planes in Atlanta. On final into Reagan, the Potomac shone in the sunlight and I could see wind surfers at the Washington Sailing Marina. I caught a cab to the Old Executive Office Building next to the White House—the Wedding Cake as it is known for all of its ornate columns—and went through security. A Secret Serviceman escorted me to the Oval Office, irreverently called the Oral Office since the Clinton Administration. I didn't know what to expect but, what the hell, presidents were good copy.

President Bush was sitting at his desk with a heavy wool scarf around his neck. He looked—tired I guess is the word. He was a bigger man than I had expected, with an athletic cut to his shoulders, but he looked exhausted.

He said hello and got up to shake my hand. I indicated the scarf and asked whether he was well.

"It's, you know, the windows aren't sealed too well. Sometimes there's a draft. I always try to avoid the draft. I am the Decider. I need to be healthy for the country."

"Yes, Mr. President. I understand. It wouldn't do for the president to have a cold. Your responsibilities are heavy … I don't want to take up too much of your time, sir. If I may, I'd like to touch on the War on Terror. Would you mind answering a few questions for my readers?"

"Certainly, Fred. I think a free press is important for a country that doesn't have terror. That's what America is, a country that doesn't have terror. All those other countries, the bad ones, they do have terror. They hate us because we're free. That's why—when the Decider talks to the press … I have friends in the press you know—when he talks to them, one on one, in a group, that's what keeps us free. The public ought to be informed, except about things it shouldn't know."

"Yes, Mr. President. The polls show that a majority of the American people believe that the war in Iraq is a failure, and want to bring the troops home. Yet you have said that you will not pull out even if Laura and your dog are the only ones who support the war. Is this an accurate statement of your views?"

"Yes. Democracy is what makes us strong, not terror. My job—the people elected me—twice—what people think doesn't matter. Democracy isn't about polls and what people think, it's about freedom. From terror. Americans want to finish the job, even if they don't want to. That's what the public has to understand. What it wants. That's why we have press conferences is this great country of ours."

As the interview continued, I was pleasantly surprised to find that President Bush was more articulate than I had expected.

"Yes sir. Now, some critics have said that America is becoming a police state, that the government is too authoritarian. Would you comment?"

"You can't have freedom unless people do what they're told. Freedom isn't free. I'm a War President. I have to decide. That's why we have to get the job done in Iraq, not cut and run. If we pull out, we won't be there anymore."

"Sir, you have charged that Iran is interfering in Iraq. The Iranians say that the United States is interfering in Iraq. How is the public to know who is telling the truth?"

"America is not interfering in Iraq. America stands for democracy and democracies don't interfere with each other. That's why so many brave American soldiers are there, so nobody interferes in Iraq."

"Some commentators say that victory is not possible. Would you characterize them as too pessimistic?"

"Yes, they are very too pessimistic. We are making progress, not instant—in life you can't get everything at once, except some things, but progress in Iraq and in … that other place."

"Afghanistan, sir?"

"That's it. Dick Cheney tells me the Afghans want nuclear weapons—those can do mass destruction, you know—we can't let Al Quaida destroy our freedom. And Dick says we're starting to have democracy in Iraq too. That's what elections are for, to have democracy. If there's a message I could give to people everywhere, that's what America is about, democracy in Iraq. The Iraqis have to learn that democracy isn't optional."

"Finally, sir, what do you say to those who accuse you of dissimulation?"

"Fred, when I was in the Air Force in Texas, where I learned to keep America free, and not have terror, dissimulation was part of our training. It's what—some other countries are free but—dissimulation is what America stands for. Our dissimulators were just like real airplanes. The buttons worked like real buttons."

I thanked him for his time and left, chastened. The Secret Service quickly passed me on to Pennsylvania Avenue and I walked into Lafayette Park to reflect. The press had led me believe that the President was less impressive, less informed than I had found him to be. As I rode the subway to my hotel on Upper Connecticut, I thought of the tired man in his scarf, and thought that maybe Richard Cabeza Productions, obscure though it had been, had a better grasp of reality than the *New York Times*.

42

Thoughts on War

People ask how we got into our splendid mess in Iraq and why we can't get out. The question is a subset of a larger question: Why, since WWII, have so many first-world armies gotten into drawn-out guerrilla wars in bush-world countries, and lost? Examples abound: France in Vietnam, America in Vietnam, France in Algeria, Russia in Afghanistan, Israel in Lebanon, etc. Why don't they learn?

The answer I think is that militaries are influenced by a kind of man—call him the Warrior—who by nature is unsuited for modern wars. He doesn't understand them, can't adapt to them.

The Warrior is emotionally suited to pitched, Pattonesque battles of moral clarity and simple intent. I don't mean that he is stupid. Among fighter pilots and in the Special Forces for example it is not uncommon to find men with IQs of 145. Yet emotionally the Warrior has the uncomplicated instincts of a pit bull. Intensely loyal to friends and intensely hostile to the enemy, he doesn't want any confusion as to which is which. His tolerance for ambiguity is very low. He wants to close with the enemy and destroy him.

This works in wars like WWII. (Note that the American military is an advanced version of the military that beat Germany and Japan.) It does not work when winning requires the support of the population. The Warrior, unable to see things through the eyes of the enemy, or of the local population, whom he quickly comes to hate, wants to blow hell out of things. He detests all that therapeutic crap, that touchy-feely leftist stuff about respect the population, especially the women. Having the empathy of an engine block, he regards mention of mutilated children as intensely annoying at best, and communist propaganda at worst.

On the net these men sometimes speak approvingly to each other of the massacre at My Lai. Hey, they were all Cong. If they weren't, they knew who the Cong were and didn't tell us. Calley did the right thing, taught them a lesson. There is an admiration of Calley for having avoided bureaucratic rules of engagement probably dreamed up by civilians. War is war. You kill people. Deal with it.

If you point out that collateral damage (dead children, for example) makes the survivors into murderously angry Viet Cong, the Warrior thinks that you are a lefty tree-hugger.

Today, the battlefield *as understood by the enemy*, but seldom by the Warrior, extends far beyond the physical battlefield, and the chief targets are political. In this kind of war, if America can get the local population to support it, the insurgents are out of business; if the insurgents can get the American public to *stop* supporting the war, the American military is out of business. This is what counts. It is what works. The Warrior, all *oooh-rah* and jump wings, doesn't get it. Vo Nguyen Giap got it. Ho Chi Minh got it.

Thus the furious, embittered insistence of Warriors that "We *won* Tet of '68. We slaughtered them! We *won*, dammit! Militarily, we absolutely won!" Swell, but politically they lost. It was a catastrophe on the order of Kursk or Dien Bien Phu. But they can't figure it out. They have never heard of a queen sacrifice.

The warrior doesn't understand what "victory" means because he thinks in terms of firefights, courage, weaponry, and valor. (It means getting the enemy to do what you want him to do. America left Vietnam. QED.) His approach is emotional, not rational. Though not stupid, he is regularly out-thought. Why?

It's not mysterious. An intelligent enemy knows that America cannot be beaten at industrial war. So he thinks, "What then are America's weaknesses?" The first and crucial one is that the American government enters into distant wars in which the public has no stake. Do you want your son to die for—get this—*democracy* in *Iraq*? You diapered him, got him through school-yard fist fights, his first prom, graduation from boot camp, and he comes home in a box—for democracy in Iraq?

The thing to do, then (continues thinking the intelligent enemy) is to make the Americans grow sick of the war. How? Not by winning battles, which is difficult against the Americans. You win otherwise. First, don't give them point targets, since these are easily destroyed by big guns and advanced technology. Second, keep the level of combat high enough to maintain the war in the forefront of American consciousness, and to keep the monetary expense high. (Inflation and gasoline prices are weapons as much as rifles, another idea that the Warrior just doesn't get. Bin Laden does.) Third, keep the body bags flowing. Sooner or later the Americans will weary of losing their sons for something that doesn't really interest them.

However, the Warrior does not grant the public the right to grow weary. For him, America exists to support the military, not the other way around. Are two hundred dead a week coming back from Asia? The Warrior believes that small-town America (which is where the coffins usually go) should grit its teeth, bear down, and make the sacrifice for the country. Sacrifice for what? It doesn't matter. We're at *war*, dammit. Rally 'round. What are you, a commy?

To the Warrior, to doubt the war is treason, aiding and supporting, liberalism, cowardice, back-stabbing, and so on. He uses these phrases unrelentingly. We must fight, and fight, and fight, and never yield, and sacrifice and spend. We must never ask why, or whether, or what for, or do we want to.

The public of course doesn't see it that way. In 1964 I graduated from a rural high school in Virginia with a senior class of, I think, sixty. Doug took a 12.7 through the head, Sonny spent time at Walter Reed with neck wounds, Studley I hear is a paraplegic, another kid got mostly blinded for life, and several, whom I won't name, tough country kids as I knew them, came back as apparently irredeemable drunks. (These were kids I knew, not all in my class.) It was a lot of dead and crippled for a small place. For what?

Cowardice? I was on campus in 1966 on a small, very Republican, very patriotic, very conservative, very Southern campus. The students, and their girlfriends, were all violently against the war. So, I gather, were their parents. Why? Were they the traitors of the Warrior's imagination? No. They didn't want to die for something that they didn't care about.

This eludes the Warrior. Always, he blames The Press for the waning of martial enthusiasm, for his misunderstanding of the kind of war we are fighting. Did the press make Studley a paraplegic? Or kill the guy with all the tubes who died in the stretcher above me on the Medevac 141 back from Danang? Did Walter Cronkite make my buddy Cagle blind when the rifle grenade exploded on the end of his fourteen? Do the Warriors think that people don't notice when their kids come back forever in wheelchairs?

They don't get it.

43

Minorities, Hopelessness, and Trouble

It is possible to derive an ashen satisfaction from watching really stupid people dancing on a tight rope over a den of alligators. At each resounding dental snap one yells "*Yeeeeeeeee*-ha! Told you so!" and reaches for another beer.

It makes a better Saturday night than a six pack and a bug zapper.

From the *Washington Post*: "Nearly half of the nation's children under 5 are racial or ethnic minorities, and the percentage is increasing mainly because the Hispanic population is growing so rapidly, according to a census report released today."

Now in newspaper parlance, "minorities" means "permanently underperforming and inassimilable minorities," which is to say blacks, Latinos and, when anybody remembers, American Indians. It very seldom means successful minorities, such as Chinese, Greeks, white men, Jews, or Anglo-Saxons.

As we look forward to a massive slewing away from the dominance of European whites in America, what may we expect? What will these huge minority populations do? It is instructive to look at what they have done so far.

Some thirteen percent of the country is now black, and thirteen percent Latino: over a quarter in all. Blacks remain intractably far below the white population academically. An astounding proportion can't read, and of those who can, few do. The gap hasn't closed, despite Head Start, integrated schools, segregated schools, more funding, welfare, black teachers, black school boards, black mayors, remedial instruction, or anything else.

The gap appears on every known test of mental capacity or scholarly achievement—SATs, GREs, ACT, LSATs, MedCats, Stanford-Binet, Wechsler, Raven's matrices. Nothing makes a difference. Everything has been tried. Because of this, we got affirmative action or, as kids once said, make believe.

Further, blacks are not assimilating. Despite pushing, shoving, laws, legislation, regulation, and relentless indoctrination, the races are not melding at a rate that will produce results any time soon. The huge black necrotic regions of the cities, that whites never see, are so big and isolated as to be impervious to outside influence. If you have not spent time in police cars in such places, you cannot imagine the hopelessness and hatred that brood there. If you think that "hatred" is too hard a word, go look. I have. Whether the hatred is justified doesn't matter. It exists.

Yes, I will be called a racist for saying these things. I hope so. Today, "racist" means "one who says what everybody else knows." It is a badge of intellectual honor. Nonetheless, it remains that if I could change any of these conditions, I would. I don't enjoy seeing people in lousy circumstances. I just don't know what to do about it. Neither does anyone else.

Now, Latinos. Americans seem to think that the word denotes one kind of people, namely Mexicans, conceived as sitting torpidly under cactuses while wearing sombreros. Actually the variety of Latinos is great, from Argentines who amount to Europeans to Bolivians who are Indians. The Latinos coming into America are heavily Indian and uneducated. Mexican ophthalmologists do not swim the river. Mexicans who can make a decent living in Mexico do not want to live in the United States. Thus the US gets the losers, the second-grade educations, people who on average have neither the intellect nor the urge to study. Yes, there are exceptions. But they *are* exceptions.

Everyone says, "But the Hispanics work hard." They do indeed, in the first generation. Many people in fields such as construction have told me that the Latinos are the backbone of their business, that blacks don't want to work, have attitudes, show up if they feel like it and quit without warning. The Latinos work, now. Their children do terribly in school, however, drop out, and lose the desire to work. Then they join gangs.

Nice white people don't know about gangs. Maybe they think of *West Side Story*. I used to ride in Chicago, with the PD and with the South Side Gang Initiative, a federally funded program in the rotting satellite cities, Markham, Robbins, and Fort Ord. I saw the gangs. There were the Black Gangster Disciples, the Vice Lords, the Latin Kings, the Latin Cobras, the P Stones, the El Ruykins who came out of the old Blackstone Rangers and, earlier, Blackstone Raiders. They aren't the Jets, people. They're killers. And they loathe white America.

I once interviewed a ranking Vice Lord in the Cook Country Jail. Why, I asked, did blacks kill each other so much? "They'd rather kill whites," he answered, "but they know they'd lose." There's a lot of that. When I left Washington four years ago, *Mara Salvatrucha* (look on the web) was appearing in Arlington, Virginia, and now their graffiti are show up in Springfield, Virginia.

Law enforcement in America relies on having a white population that is mostly law-abiding. It has no good way of responding to large numbers of violent criminals, especially when they are backed by politically potent voting blocs. The crucial question, or a crucial question, is what proportion of the new minorities will fall into the permanent underclass? How much permanent underclass can the nation stand?

Another crucial question is this: If half the children today are of minorities, then in no more than eighteen years half the kids of college age will be. Unless they show a sudden scholarly afflatus which has not heretofore been in evidence, this means that soon the US will have to compete with China with the brains of only half the nation. This is not to mention secondary effects, such as enstupidating all schools to hide the failures of the minorities. Do you suppose that the Chinese are doing that?

Now, from the same story in the *Washington Post*, this: "William H. Frey, a demographer with the Brookings Institution, predicted that the United States will have 'a multicultural population that will probably be more tolerant, accommodating to other races and more able to succeed in a global economy.'"

How heart-warming. I suggest that William H. Frey is a thoroughgoing fool, but this is common among academics. The whole touchy-feely multy-culty idea that forcing people together will make them love one another, kum bah yah, is simply wrong. Right now, there is a tremendous repressed hostility between blacks and whites, the lid being held on by federal power, tight control of the press, and rigorous political correctness. Whites, huge numbers of them, detest Latino immigrants and would love to expel them from the country. Serious friction grows between blacks and Latinos as Latinos push blacks out of regions they once controlled. We're not moving toward accommodation. We're moving toward trouble.

What will happen as the economy declines and the minorities continue growing in number? As they continue demanding through political power what they cannot obtain on their merits? As standards of living drop, and the pie isn't creamy enough to give everyone juicy freebies?

It will be nothing if not entertaining. Bring it on. Love them alligators

44

Eighth Grade in Mexico

Just now the furor over illegal immigration from Mexico is most wonderful a'boil, with much billingsgate and vituperation emanating from practically everywhere. Well and good. People should afflict each other as vigorously as they can. I mean, why were we put on earth if not to be disagreeable?

Howsomever, I've received email telling me how poorly educated the Mexicans are. Hmmm. Maybe. You can make a case for it. I know that immigrant kids do terribly in school in the US, which augurs ill indeed. Most kids don't read here either. Still, I found myself wondering just how bad the Mexican schools really are.

My stepdaughter, Natalia, aged fourteen and in the eighth grade, attends a public school in downtown Guadalajara, *La Escuela Estatal Secundaria Manuel M. Dieguez Numero 7 para Senoritas*. I am not an authority on Mexican education and cannot say whether hers is typical of urban Mexican schools. Nor do I know enough about American middle schools in general to make comparisons. The following are scans of pages from her texts of mathematics and biology accompanied by a few observations. I found them interesting. The translations are mine. Please excuse the sloppy scans and slow loads.

From *Mathematicas 2* (ISBN 970-642-210-2)

"Consider two urns, one with 13 balls numbered from 1 to 13, and the other with 4 balls marked with the following figures: a red triangle, a red square, a black circle, or a black rhombus. How many combinations can be obtained by drawing one ball from each urn?

The possibilities can be represented by ordered pairs. For example, if from the first urn is drawn the ball marked with 2, and from the second, the ball with the square, the result is expressed thus: (2, square). The 52 pairs listed in the column to the left represent all possibilities ... The probability of drawing an even number from the first urn is P(even) = 6/13 and the probability of drawing a red shape from the second urn is P(red) = 2/4 = ½. If the two probabilities are multiplied, the following is the result:

P(even) P(red) = (6/13)(1/2) = 6/26"

Not Nobel math, but not too bad, I thought.

From *Biologia 2*, her biology text:

"An important property of phospholipid bilayers is that they behave as liquid crystals; the carbohydrates and proteins can turn, and move laterally...." Note internal hydrophobic tails and external hydrophilic heads. This is not too shabby.

In the next pages is an account of both aerobic and anaerobic respiration, the 36 molecules of adenosine triphosphate resulting from aerobic glycolysis, and so on.

Early in *Biologia 2* is a treatment of the role of RNA, including the substitution of uracil for thymine, transcription as distinct from translation, and the functions of messenger, transfer, and ribosomal RNA. Polypeptides are described and peptide bonds mentioned, but not with the NH3-COOH dehydration synthesis. A typical vocab list: "Endoplasmic reticulum, Golgi apparatus, endocytosis, ribosomes, cellular membrane."

Then, "The synthesis proceeds only in the 5'-3' sense, which means that the chain that is being copied is read...."

Also, (above) "DNA is formed by the union of five atoms: carbon (C), oxygen (O), hydrogen (H), nitrogen (N), and phosphorus (P). The DNA molecule can be decomposed into the monomers that form it. There are called nucleotides, each of which contains three parts: a sugar of five carbons, deoxyribose; the phosphate; and a nitrogenous base, either adenine (A), guanine (G), cytosine (C), or thymine (T). Two of these bases, adenine and guanine, are structures of two rings and are called purines, while the other two, thymine and cytosine, have only one ring and are called pyrimidines."

All of this has a notable resemblance to real if basic molecular biology. I'm not sure that it is anything to be embarrassed about.

Biologia 2 has a 31-page section on human reproduction that is purely scientific as distinct from socially propagandistic. There is no indoctrination about homosexual rights or oppression of the transgendered. (I think this sort of thing is done elsewhere, though.) The coverage is detailed and complete, with cutaway drawings of the genitalia, detailed discussion of meiosis as compared with mitosis, primary meiotic division, secondary meiotic division with prophase, metaphase, anaphase, and telophase nicely laid out; chromatin, centromeres, and centrioles explained, and so on at length. There is an explanation of the menstrual cycle complete with a graph of variations of body temperature; description of embryonic growth; a table of tissues and organs arising from endoderm, ectoderm, and mesoderm; and explanations of various venereal diseases and how to avoid them. The treatment is neither prurient nor prissy. It is just biological: Here is how the lungs work, here is how the heart works, here is how the reproductive organs work.

Consequences however are presented straightforwardly. For example, there is a photograph of a primary syphilitic sore, which doubtless persuades students that they don't want any and, in the section on what we would call "substance abuse," a photo of a badly cirrhotic liver, sectioned. There are no pretty pictures for the sake of having pretty picture. All graphics have a direct bearing on the material being studied.

It may be that all of this is now standard in the eighth-grade in the United States. For all I know, American texts may be more advanced. I can't make comparisons with things I don't know about. But these do not seem to me to be bad books. Certainly when I was an eight-grader we didn't get much of this; when I went on a physiology kick, I had to find a university text.

Still, I have my doubts as to whether the big-city schools in America are greatly ahead of Guadalajara. Detroit recently had, and probably still has, a forty-seven per cent rate of functional illiteracy. Guadalajara doesn't. If someone were inspired to compare the foregoing material with what students, if so they can be called, are learning in downtown schools in, say, Washington, DC, Chicago, and New York, I would be interested to see the results.

It will be said, correctly, that the cities of America are populated by extensive underclasses of blacks and Hispanics. True enough. However, they are still American kids (now or soon to be) who are learning nothing. Natalia would eat them alive. I have some familiarity with the suburban, mostly white schools of Arlington County, Virginia, just outside of Washington, because my daughters went to them. At least one of these schools served populations living in very pricey neighborhoods.

The girls came home with misspelled handouts from affirmative-action science teachers, and they learned about Harriet Tubman and oppression. Of the sciences they learned very little. I knew bright kids who had trouble with the multiplication tables. Yes, there are schools and schools, some better than others, and advanced-placement and such. I do not suggest that Mexico has a great school system, because it doesn't. Yet Natalia, in her particular school, is better off than she would be in Washington, heaven knows, or the Virginia suburbs. Ain't that something?

45

Israel and the Press

Years back, when I was writing a military column for Universal Press Syndicate, I heard of a book on women in the armed services called *The Kinder Gentler Military* (the title as it turned out was ironic) by Stephanie Guttman, a Jewish woman out of Manhattan. It didn't sound like a recommendation. I expected a feminist tirade. However my friend Catharine Aspy spoke well of it. Kate graduated from Harvard and—so help me—enlisted in the army. She had seen what Guttman was writing about. So I read the book.

To my surprise, Guttman got it exactly right. She wasn't political, just reportorial, and described perfectly the fraud and double standards used to make women look successful in the army. Much of it would be hard to credit, except that I had seen it from outside and Kate from inside. In the course of events I met Steph a couple of times, chatted on the phone, and lost contact with her. The book got few and bad reviews because it was not what the media wanted to hear. It was a fine book.

A couple of months ago, I ran across a blurb about another book by her, *The Other War*, described as arguing the Israel**is** take an unfair beating in the press. If Alan Dershowitz had written it, I'd have dismissed it as propaganda—but then, I have read Dershowitz. Instead I ordered the book.

The subject interested me for various reasons, one being an odd contradiction I had noticed. I get considerable mail from the anti-Jewish backchannels on the net telling me that the Jews control the American media. Often these are accompanied by lists, usually accurate enough, of important positions in the media held by Jews. My correspondents often assert that because of this control we hear only good things about Israel.

Well and good—except that for perhaps fifteen years I had never heard anything good about Israel from the media. The country is always deliberately shooting little Palestinian children, bulldozing houses from sheer vindictiveness, reducing Palestinians to poverty, murdering Palestinian leaders, torturing all within reach, and intimidating the press. The Palestinians are noble freedom fighters, just like Davy Crockett, or hapless victims.

Hmmm, I wondered. If Jews control the press and only tell us good things about Israel, how come I never hear anything from the press about Israel except bad things?

I was also interested because I'd had considerable experience in Israel, and indeed cut my journalistic baby-teeth there. In 1967 on recuperative leave from Bethesda Naval Hospital I had gone to Europe with a shot-up squid off of PBRs in Asia, gotten bored, and gone to Israel. We hippied about, had the usual adventured, got mortared in Eilat. (The hippies didn't understand why we were suddenly on the floor. We knew what "ka-*chung*" meant.)

In '73 I went to Israel as a greenhorn war correspondent for the Fredericksburg, Virginia, *Free-Lance Star*. I was pig-ignorant of the news racket, looked like Mehitabel the Cat's degenerate brother, and must have astonished the Israelis, but my credentials checked out and the info people were pretty decent. I got to the Golan, the Sinai, and so on. And I was there for the doings of '82.

Anyway, Stephanie's book arrived. In it she makes a (well documented) case that the mainstream media are relentlessly hostile to Israel. Yes, I know. This is so contrary to what we are told daily that to doubt it feels a bit like doubting gravitation. And don't important papers and networks all agree **with each other**? When you are told something often enough you begin to believe you know it. And since I haven't been to Israel in twenty-five years, I couldn't speak from recent personal experience.

But something stank.

Her description of the behavior of the press in Israel, with which she is intimately familiar, is exactly what I have seen in countless other places—ignorant, herd-like, egomaniacal, clawing over each other to make a name, all snottily agreeing with each other. Of this I know a great deal.

Taking sides instead of reporting is now usual. For example, if whites murder a black for reasons of racial hostility, it is news for weeks, but should the crime go in the other direction, the story will be downplayed and then suppressed. One is as bad as the other—but that is not how it is reported. Should a man suggest that men are better than women at mathematics, the press will not regard it as a question to be investigated but as a crime to be punished. "Political correctness" is nothing but hardwired advocacy journalism.

If they can't get anything else right, I thought, why should I trust them on Israel?

Inaccuracy and untruthfulness really, truly do abound. I was in Phnom Penh for the final siege. The papers in the States spoke of "barrages" of rockets "pounding" the city. Actually, scattered rockets, six or eight a day, and probably not one reporter in fifty knew what "barrage" meant. When Americans were reading about the "starving" city, I was stepping over pigs, fat ones, tied on sidewalks. One of the newsweeklies, I forget which, ran a cover of Cambodians running in terror with the city in flames behind. I was there. No flames. It was a file photo from who knows when.

For years in Washington I covered the military in the company of reporters for allegedly meritorious publications—the *Washington Post*, the *New York Times*, the networks. Everyone has heard about the $400 toilet seat, the $27 dollar bolts bought by the Pentagon. I covered these stories. They were nonsense. The reporters easily could have determined that they were nonsense. In those days the entire press corps (the pack effect) insisted that American weapons didn't work, were too complex, broke constantly. Not even close.

When Guttman writes about reporters hanging around the press bar in Jerusalem and writing I-was-there stories when they weren't, or about photographers looking for the Pulitzer photo without knowing or caring what was going on, or about craftedly dishonest writing to support a political position, she's not kidding.

My objection to the behavior of the press in general, and I think hers to its behavior in Israel, is not to its political positions but to dishonest reporting. The view that, say, Israel should get out of the West Bank is a political one, legitimate in a column. The Palestinians are part of the story too and should be covered fairly. But sloppy reporting according to a double standard is just lousy journalism.

A curious fact, though she doesn't mention it, is that many of the reporters most hostile to Israel are Jewish. For example, Ted Koppel. I assume that Suzanne Goldenberger and Kaplan are Jewish, though I grant that they may be Chinese Protestants with Jewish names. She cites the *New York Times*, Jewish owned, as particularly hostile. Explain it as you will, but I have noticed the same thing.

If you care about the Middle East, I recommend *The Other War*. Judge it as you will. But read it.

46

Possums Come to Harvard

The whole curious story began one evening when Harvard's Conservative Student Union held a mass meeting in a local beer chute. The membership both agreed that the university's practice of affirmative action had gone too far. In particular, it irritated them that the Native Peoples Impressment Office had recruited as students a hundred thirty-seven Tloxyproctyl aborigines from the rain forests of the Amazon Basin. For one thing, the Tloxyprotyls required heated loin cloths in winter, which came out of funds for students' activities. For another, they spoke no language known to philologists and so had been put in the People-of-Color Studies Department, where nobody else did either. The young conservatives, elitist to the core, thought this absurd.

Yet they could have tolerated it. But then the Diversity Enforcement Office declared Casava-Awareness Week, and required students to learn to dig cassava with pointed sticks so as to better understand native cultures. There were no cassavas in Massachusetts. The sociology department, in a spirit of promoting acceptance of downtrodden native peoples, and having nothing to do anyway, canceled classes for a week so that its students could make paper-mache cassavas to bury. The students, now aware of cassavas, could dig them up.

This was too much for the insensitive conservatives. One was studying particle physics and didn't have time to be conscious of tubers. The other, majoring in classical languages, regarded the Tloxyproctyls as barbarous savages. This, being self-evident, could not be mentioned in a university.

Anyway the budding reactionaries spent the afternoon devising a fraudulent manifesto that they emailed to department heads and to the nation's major newspapers. In it they alleged, with much indignation, that Harvard was discriminating in favor of the Tloxyproctyls to the great disadvantage of the Tlacuaches, who were a South American ethnity with claims to unearned preference equal to those of the Tloxyproctyls.

"Not one Tlacuache is even enrolled; there are no Tlacuache professors; and thus there are none on the tenure track. This is clear discrimination against these age-old authentic inhabitants of America." The manifesto was signed by the Gay, Lesbian, Bifocal, Hydrocephalic and Transgendered League, which didn't exist. Probably.

The two boys regarded this as mildly amusing, as perhaps it was in an adolescent fashion. They returned to their studies and forgot about it.

However a junior editor at the *New York Times*, minding the desk for the weekend, saw the manifesto. Having recently graduated from Berkeley, she regarded social remediation as the reason for existence of the *Times*, as well as pretty much everything else.

But we are getting ahead of ourselves. In the Chicana, Lesbian, and Brutalized Aboriginals Department was a girl name Maria Hernandez Maldonado. She was the only daughter of a rich banking family in Guadalajara, Mexico. She had taught herself to read at the age of two and had been discovered by psychologists at the University of Guadalajara to have an IQ of 173. The university had recruited her hard and she had planned to attend.

However, she heard that the Native Peoples Impressment Office, which had lots of money, was going to be interviewing preliterate indigines in the Sierra Madre Mountains. No dummy, she figured a free ride at Harvard was better than paying at U Guad. The education might not be as good, but you made much better contacts.

For two weeks she didn't bathe. Then she donned a beaded dress she made from a duffel bag, strips of rotting leather, and feathers from an old hat of her mother's. Next she went to the Indian village to be interviewed. For a few pesos she gained the cooperation of the Indians, who had no idea why these strange gringos were there. Some said they were related to the sun god. Other Indians from the south said this wasn't a good thing.

Maria babbled to the diversity wardens in broken Spanish mingled with the words of an American rap song that she repeated in Pig Latin. The effect was as she expected. The interviewers assumed that she was speaking an incomprehensible Native Language. She later found that she could achieve the same effect without the Pig Latin.

On the standardized test they gave her she carefully got all of the questions wrong to show that she was academically hopeless and therefore authentic. (She almost overdid it. A note in her file said, "Sometimes forgets to breathe—may need a respirator.")

She settled in at Harvard, going daily to classes in colonialism and discriminatory social constructs. At night she read Kant in the library when her professors were least likely to catch her. This she found to be touchy. There were two other students in the department who could read, and they too did so secretly. Whenever a prof showed up, they began drawing shamanistic stick figures or, in Maria's case, making autistic movements with her head. In this way she maintained her academic qualifications.

Still, she began to worry that she was suspected of elitist scholastic tendencies. If caught reading philosophy, she would lose her authenticity and thus her funding. It was then that the *New York Times* broke the story, "Harvard Discriminating Against Tlacuaches: None on Tenure Track" Maria of course knew that the word was Mexican, or more correctly Nahuatl, for "possum." Harvard didn't. The administration assumed that the school must be discriminating since they had no idea what a Tlacuache was. In any event they couldn't find any on campus. This was prima facie evidence.

Maria saw her chance. Scouring the city, she actually found a pet store with a possum for sale. It seemed that, if hand raised, they made agreeable enough pets. She bought the little beast and began taking it to class. It usually slept in her book bag. Her idea was that if the school was desperate for tlacuaches to prove its commitment to oppressed people, having the only one on campus would keep her on the gravy train.

The problem was that the faculty thought that she *was* the Tlacuache, and the possum some sort of totemic animal of a religious nature. None of them had ever seen a possum or, for that matter, a cow. They were pretty sure that sufferers from discrimination were usually people, if sometimes only barely, and not animals. Further, Maria was brown. She must be some kind of third-world wog and thus a victim of something.

The *Times* hammered away. The networks picked up the story. They didn't know what a Tlacuache was either, but the damning evidence was that none were on the faculty. Officials of the school went into hiding, sensing a career-ending disaster. A reporter for the *Times* managed to push into the office of Larry Summers, former president of Harvard, hoping to get comments. After fifteen minutes of waiting, she discovered that he was hiding behind the door.

There was only one way out. The school announced that Maria, their only Tlacuache, was henceforth on the tenure track. That she was a freshman didn't matter. Fifty million dollars was voted to seek other Tlacuaches. A committee was appointed to discover what one was. Maria went back to Guadalajara, having decided that gringos were crazy. Out of respect for the cultural traditions of the new (and as yet unfound) faculty, who of course would want their totemic ... well, whatever the thing was with the tail ... desks were ordered with comfortable cages and....

To be continued. Practically everywhere.

47

Messicans Their Own Self

I get a lot of email asking me, "What's it really like in Mexico, Fred?" A book would be needed to give a good answer. Since people seem interested, I'll take a few random shots at the topic. Don't expect literature or organization.

The quick answer is that it isn't nearly as bad as many Americans think. Not even close. Sure, it's a screwed up country. (Name one that isn't. Switzerland, maybe?) It has all manner of problems and defects: jobs going to China, corruption, poverty in places, crumbling sidewalks, loud music, poor services, pollution, etc. No paradise here.

But ... but....

Mexico is a democracy, as much as the United States. The government is not repressive. Mexico is not a police state. It is not particularly criminal: Guadalajara is certainly less dangerous than Washington. It is not disease-ridden. I eat in all sorts of restaurants here with no problem. It is not over-regulated and controlled. It is not primitive. It is not a backwater. Mexican big-box stores are indistinguishable from Wal-Mart. The telephones work, cell phones work, broadband is widely available (in my town of 18,000, for example). Guadalajara abounds in book stores and music stores. (Books in Spanish, yes, but everything you've ever heard of, and what do you expect in Mexico? Linear B?)

I think that the Mexico of today is confused with the Mexico of fifty years ago. For example, a clear gradient exists in health between the old and the young. Men of fifty or more often look as if they had spent their lives carrying anvils across the desert with nothing to eat. They are arthritic. They walk painfully. They are just plain wore out, as we say in Alabama. They make for picturesque postcards, but bear little resemblance to today's Mexicans.

The young appear as lithe and healthy as those of their age anywhere, and show no signs of wearing out beyond the normal effects of age. I don't know the average quality or quantity of dental care, but they seem to have their teeth, which appear healthy. (I say "seem to" and "appear" because I don't carry dental picks and a mirror, but when all visible teeth are white and where they ought to be, things can't be but so bad.)

In my experience Mexicans are both hard-working and competent. Recently I wanted a railing put around the (flat, cement) roof of my house. We went to an ordinary shop dealing in such things, in my almost-entirely Mexican town. The resultant railing, made from scratch, was firmly anchored, nicely welded and, to my eye, perfect. When we needed a new water pump, the fellow showed up with it, plumbed it, wired it, installed the level-sensors in the rooftop tanks, perfectly and in a few hours. And he was agreeable. This is par.

Now, you ask with good reason, if this is so, why is Mexico a comparatively poor country? The usual answers are corruption, lack of ambition, and poor schooling.

The corruption is there, and may indeed be the cause. The difference in degree of corruption between Mexico and the US may be somewhat less than is usually thought: American corruption is to an extent institutionalized in such forms as campaign contributions, positions on boards of directors, and affirmative action, all of which are payoffs. But it is a way of life here.

Lack of ambition … perhaps. Mexicans (yes, I'm generalizing) seem to want enough, and to stop there. The focus is on family, friends, and a quiet life. Thus an intelligent and competent mechanic, say, will make a comfortable living from his garage, but will not try to start a chain of garages. Americans are much more driven, and much more materialistic. These qualities pay off economically.

I'm not sure about lack of schooling. Certainly there are schools everywhere I've been, and swarms of kids charging out of them with backpacks full of books, and the books are not bad. I have never knowingly encountered an illiterate Mexican (though there certainly are some, especially among the old). Yet it is not a nation pathologically addicted to study. They don't seem much to care about books. And, as Violeta tells me, even people who graduate from universities often cannot find jobs.

However, I cannot see that they are baffled by technology. When we call TelMex about some technical problem with broadband (configuration of this or that, DNS stuff, POP3, the usual) the techs on the help desk are invariably good and quickly get the job done. The people we have dealt with in computer stores have always known what they were doing. Yet in small towns it can take over a year to get a new telephone line put it. It isn't technical ignorance: TelMex knows perfectly well how to install a line. Somehow it just doesn't get done.

Medical care is interesting. My dentist, Hector Haro, (he's on the web) went through dental school at the University of Guadalajara and did graduate work at

U. Maryland. His partner is a young woman, Patty, who also went to U. Guad. Their equipment is every bit as modern as any I've seen in the US. I've never heard a complaint about their work.

They are high end. If you can pay for good care, you can get it. There are urology clinics in Guad that do things like prostate exams. They have good ultrasound gear, for example, and know it as well as do Americans. (Being an obligate techno-weeny, I always grill them).

But most Mexicans can't afford $400 for a crown. They tend not to see doctors until they have to, and then to use the (free) public health hospitals. These are not as bad as you might think. When my stepdaughter fell through a glass door at a friend's house and severed the tendons in her wrist, a passing taxi took her to a public ER, which sewed her together, and now everything works. But these places do not have the best equipment, nor expensive medicines, nor pricey specialists, and they are badly overworked. How things are in the remote countryside, I don't know, but I can guess. Not great.

Other topic: Mexicans tend to be self-reliant in the sense that Americans were fifty years ago, assuredly including the women. An American friend told me of watching his wife go out to drive somewhere. The car didn't start. She opened the hood and investigated. Then she pulled the stereo out of the dashboard, removed a length of wire, dived back under the hood, put it where she thought it belonged, started the car, and drove away. This is not unusual. Violeta regularly does similar things. Them as can't pay plumbers becomes plumbers. And electricians. And....

Again, I don't mean to idealize the place. It ain't idealizable. Too many things wrong with it. But it isn't as bad as gringos think, and it has many compensating advantages that other places don't. Them's my thoughts.

48

Theater of the Absurd, By the Absurd, For the Absurd

Every time I go to the United States (I have just returned from two weeks in Washington), I am astonished by the antic security, by the proliferation of admonitions and alarms and inchoate fear. Now it is illegal to carry toothpaste on airplanes. I find myself wondering: Is this just another spasm of periodic hysteria, like Prohibition, the Sixties, and a Commie Under Every Bed? Or is it calculated political programming?

Most of it impinges at best lightly upon reality. For example, measures for security at airports are largely useless—if their purpose is to increase security. Think about it. Time and again the public-address system warns that vehicles left unattended in passenger-loading zones "may be ticketed and towed." Why? By the time anyone notices that the truck is unattended, by definition the driver will be somewhere else. He will certainly be able to walk a hundred yards before the tow-truck arrives—and push the button. Boom. In the case of a suicide bomber (which is what we are worried about, no?) it doesn't matter anyway. Boom.

For that matter, at any airport you can drive up, load a hundred pounds of suitcases containing god knows what onto a baggage cart, and go into a crowded waiting area. Boom. You probably couldn't get them onto an airplane. Why would you need to? Terroristically, killing two hundred people in the airport is as good as dropping an airliner.

Most of security is just theater. Over and over, the PA system tells you not to leave baggage unattended or it may be destroyed by security personnel. This doubtless serves to make legitimate passengers watch their luggage. Who cares? A suitcase full of bras and socks isn't perilous. But none of this keeps a terrorist from leaving a baggage cart and walking for two minutes, far enough to be outside the blast radius.

No, I'm not giving ideas to terrorists. Everything in this column is obvious to anyone with a three-digit IQ.

It gets sillier. If you ride Metro, Washington's subway, you will incessantly hear things like, "Passengers! Look up from your papers occasionally. Be alert! Report any suspicious behavior to Metro employees."

Yeah, sure. As a security measure, this is worthless. Why? First, a terrorist would be careful not to look suspicious. Second, what is suspicious behavior on an urban subway? You've got rastas, Goths, spike-haired young in leathers, semi-derelicts, blacks from the slums, people from India, Guatemala, Morocco, drunks, stoners, people talking to Mars through the transmitters the CIA put in their teeth, and swarthy men speaking languages you can't identify. What's suspicious?

So how do report any of this? You could get off the train at the next stop, go up the escalators, and find the Metro kiosk by the exit gates. You find a bored guy inside waiting for his shift to end.

"Hey, I saw this suspicious guy on the train!" you say.

"Yeah? What was he doing?"

"He had a backpack, and he was looking around a lot like he was nervous, and I think he was sweating."

Oh. By now the train you were riding has left. The attendant has two choices. He can call in an emergency, have the train halted at the next stop, tie up the whole system at rush hour, and have police search the train, for a guy who looks like he might be sweating. Now, that's a career-enhancing move. Or he can brush you off. Real world: Which?

Have you ever been on an urban subway at rush hour—which of course is when a terrorist would strike? They are madhouses. People are packed so tight they can hardly move. Everybody is thinking, "Come on, come *on*, get this damned thing moving." Suppose you are aboard, and you see what appears to be a forgotten briefcase. What do you do?

The train is now sailing through the tunnel between Rosslyn Station and the Pentagon. Nobody can move an inch. You could scream, "*Bomb!*" However, the odds are much better than 999 to 1 that it isn't. Years have passed since 9/11, with no terrorism on Metro. People leave things on trains all the time. Let's say that you do scream. Chaos results, people very possibly are crushed to death in the panic, and someone pulls the Emergency Stop handle. You have just shut down Metro in rush hour. Further, you are in mid-tunnel. Oh good. The briefcase turns out to contain two sandwiches and a report from Agriculture on locust infestations in Chad. You probably go to jail.

And of course a terrorist would leave the briefcase on a timer to give himself a few minutes to leave Rosslyn Station and be walking innocently up Wilson Boulevard when the thing went off. Say, five minutes. Real world: What are the chances that anyone will notice the briefcase, take it seriously, and clear the train, in five minutes? Zero.

It's theater. If people actually reported strange behavior however defined, or if Metro cleared trains for forgotten briefcases until the bomb squad arrived, trains would never run.

Are security measures going to keep terrorists out of the US? I just finished reading *De Los Maras a Los Zetas*, by a Mexican crime reporter. (I don't think it is available in English.) He talks mostly about the drug trade, but mentions the smuggling of illegal immigrants. In particular he tells of a tunnel going under the border (estimating that at any one time about forty such tunnels are active) through which, he says, about 150 illegals a day passed. All it takes is $2000 or so any you are in the US. There is no border security, boys and girls. Not against anyone serious. There really isn't.

Now, yes, we may well see more terrorist attacks on the United States. We certainly ask for them. Or they may be prevented by other means. But dramatic announcements on the subway are going to prevent nothing. Nor are color-coded terror alerts that you hear every five minutes in airports. What does anyone do differently when the level is orange instead of green? Cancel reservations? Wear body armor?

On examination, most of the measures purportedly taken to stifle Terror don't. Opening mail without a warrant? It's pointless once the terrorists know you are doing it, but effective in intimidating honest citizens. The same is true of warrantless wiretaps and searches. Does the gutting of habeas corpus make us safer against terrorists? Or merely suppress dissent by citizens?

The whole business looks remarkably like malign vaudeville, like mummery intended to accomplish two things. The first is to persuade the foolish that the nation is At War. Actually only the president is at war. The second, and I would like to be wrong about this, is to train the public to obedience. The formula is simple: Keep'em scared and you can do anything. It works. Americans are rapidly becoming accustomed to Soviet-style surveillance, to the state's power to search and spy without restraint, to being barked at and ordered about by low-level federal employees. People deserve what they tolerate.

49

Conversations With Lanc

Ages ago, for reasons of parental misjudgement, I studied at a small college in rural Virginia, Hampden-Sydney. While surprisingly rigorous, being resolutely Southern and as yet untouched by the foolishness that now degrades schools, H-S was also relentlessly preppy. The studentry tended to be vapid future bankers in small towns and pre-meds who would go to the Medical College of Virginia in Richmond. I loathed them, and they, me. At night, to escape, I walked wooded roads under the stars to smell the honeysuckle and listen to what the insects had to say.

One night I found Lanc's store. Lanc—Lancaster Brown—was an old black man, in his eighties I'd guess. At any rate he had gone to France in a labor battalion in World War I and spoke of the beer gardens and other wonders. He was pretty slow by the time I met him. His had been a long life and not always an easy one.

The store was tiny, old, worn, and unpainted, with battered glass cases of candy and bubble gum, unpainted plank floors and, in the back, a potbellied stove that always had a fire of chilly evenings. The counter had a big jar of pickled sausage, behind it a box of Moon Pies—the credentials of Southern ruralhood. A Camels poster from about 1953 was tacked to the wall. From it a full-lipped and busty honey-blonde in a cowboy hat smiled down at the world.

Lanc was alone that night, sitting on the old church pew across the back wall that served as bench when company came. I asked for a coke. He got it for me. He was not dark-skinned, more earth-colored, being about the shade of the dispirited floppy hat he habitually wore. I think he was embarrassed by being bald as an onion. With a freshman's sense of anthropological exploration I made conversation.

My grandfather, retired then, had been professor of mathematics and dean at the college. It proved a telling credential. As soon as he realized that I was Dean Reed's grandson, I became almost family. Like many people in the region,

Grandpa (as I always called him) didn't like the racial situation, though he didn't know what to do about it. But when a local black woman had needed extensive dental work, Grandpa had quietly paid for it. This was not unknown to local blacks.

Grandpa wasn't at all what would today be called a liberal. He had none of the *amour propre*, too much respect for scholarship, and believed in personal integrity. Worse, he read Latin. He just had a sense of what was right and what wasn't.

I soon got in the habit of dropping in on Lanc during my nocturnal tours of inspection. He usually sat on a broken-down chair, I on the pew. Light, what there was of it, came from a bare bulb hanging on a wire. On bitterly cold winter nights the store was warn and smelled comfortably of wood smoke and I was glad to be there. Lanc liked to roast apples or fry baloney on top of the stove. I ate vinegary sausage.

I was then known as Ricky but, mysteriously, he always called me Mickey. I supposed that oncoming deafness accounted for it. "Hey there, Mickey," he would say when I appeared, "You come on in, sit right down. Yes sir, you sit right down." He extended me credit and depended on me to keep track of the amount. I was Dean Reed's grandson. He knew I would never short him. You can bet I didn't.

We were a strange pair. I was very young, and knew nothing of life other than the small towns of Virginia and Alabama and what I had read in books. Lanc had grown up black in a countryside then more remote than it is now, a world with different rules and different people and utterly another place. And then found himself in Paris.

He would shake his head and smile bemusedly, as though still after so many years trying to understand France. Why, the beer gardens there, why you could go day or night—*day* or *night*—and the lights and how the people were dressed, and the women. In his time a black man didn't talk about white women if he was wise, and Lanc didn't much, even with Dean Reed's grandson. Still it dawned on me that he hadn't always been eighty years old, and that Paris wasn't Atlanta.

I was very young.

I couldn't talk to Lanc about much, I guess. The intricacies of differential equations and ancient victories in the Saronic Gulf were beyond him. I wasn't sure how he had learned to read. None of this seemed to matter. We discussed whatever we could, mostly Paris and the army and local lore. Occasionally blacks within walking distance came in for bread or Spam. One night a high school girl came and asked Lanc where Jimmy was.

"He out coon hunting," said Lanc.

"Two-legged or four-legged kind?" she asked, then saw me and giggled with embarrassment.

Things were not as Uncle Remus-ish as the evenings of fried baloney and Dr. Pepper might make them sound. There was real anger and hostility toward whites, but they knew better than to show it. One year I sublet a room from Ben Hairston, a black teacher at the local school. (I really didn't like preppy snots.) Ben was in his mid-thirties, drove an old hearse he had picked up somewhere, and had slightly screwed-up eyes from having accidentally gotten drunk wood alcohol. He had lived all over the eastern seaboard and definitely qualified as sophisticated.

Which may be why he misjudged things. One night he told me that he was going to a party, and would I like to come? Sure. Shortly afterward we walked into the basement of a house nearby, where a dozen people were dancing. It was instantly obvious that I was not welcome. I think it surprised Ben more than it did me. Five minutes later we were gone.

The years passed. In summer the fields and woods behind the store glowed with fireflies, or lightning bugs as I will always believe they are properly called, and frogs creaked in the marsh. From time to time came the qucksilver fluting of a whippoorwill. Lanc was always on his pew, frying his baloney. For a while he seemed eternal, and the store a place not really in the surrounding world. One year after graduation I went by and the store was closed, Lanc's house nearby locked. Dead, I suppose.

50

When I Was Tom Sawyer

Back before the beginning of time, in the late Fifties when the sun lowered over small-town Alabama like a steaming towel, and it was so humid a tadpole could just about fly, we kids of eleven didn't have many store-bought toys. We didn't need'em, neither. On slow barefoot afternoons with nothing to do, we did things anyhow, most of'em the which you couldn't do now. Some, probably, we shouldn't have done.

Well, maybe it wasn't quite before time began, but it was before it got more than a rolling start. Anyway, I'm going to explain to you how to be a kid. This is going to be a technical manual. A few of you already know it. You can hum along.

To begin with, we all had BB guns. It was a rule. You couldn't be a kid without one. Well, a girl could, and Alabama had some mighty fine girls, but we were four years away from figuring it out. Me and Jimmy Jack 'Callister and Don Berzette and … all of us, had BB guns and lived as small hunter-gatherers.

Today BB guns would be illegal and send mothers screeching and hiding under sofas and calling for federal help. Alabama knew about federal help, and didn't want any. There was a little country store behind our house on Prior Street, really mostly just a shack, that sold Moon Pies, RC Cola, peach soda, and twelve-gauge shotgun shells. Pickled pig's feet too, and Vienna sausage and mayonnaise, which a lot of people ate because it was all they had.

Anyway, the shotgun shells were sold loose, so you get just as many as you needed. I discovered I could stick them in the middle of a roll of toilet paper, then buy the toilet paper and get the shotgun shell. It wasn't honest. It was what I did.

It was a different country then, and the South was a differenter part, warts and all. Nobody much watched us. You could do sensible things, like line shotgun shells up on a board and shoot at the primers from fifty feet away with the BB guns. Contrary to what a Yankee might think, this didn't produce much of a bang because the shell wasn't confined in a barrel, but it was better than nothing.

I guess things were kind of unsupervised. You couldn't do it today. You'd need a Caring Adult to be in charge, meaning some tiresome school marm who didn't think you should make black powder and blow things up. What's black powder *for*, then? Tell me that.

Sometimes we'd cut the front part of the shell off with a pocket knife, which weren't illegal yet. Now they would set off the x-ray machines everywhere and get everybody prosecuted as terrorists, even if they were nine years old. Back then they were just pocketknives. Nobody cared. You could go for years without hearing about a case of pocketknife terrorism.

We'd take the birdshot out of the shell and make spoke guns with it. You got a bicycle spoke with the little sleeve on the end, unscrewed it partway so there was a cavity you could mash a match head into, and then jam a piece of birdshot on top. Then you could hold a lit match under it until, *snap!* it fired like a real live gun. Only not very much like one.

We mostly did this in the back field near the College where this sort of scraggly undergrowth glowed bright green in it when the sun slanted sideways through it late in the afternoon and it looked like fairy castles from a storybook or maybe space-alien invaders that needed shooting with a spoke gun.

Then there were match guns. (We had all manner of guns, and bombs too. I used to fill Nytol bottles, which were some kind of patent medicine, with baking soda and water and snap the tops back on. A minute later, ker-POW the top flew off. Maybe it was violence. Tough.

Anyway, match guns. You got one of those old clothes pins with the two wooden sides and the spring in the middle. There was a way—I could show it to you today—to take it apart, put the sidepieces together backward with a rubber band to make a V, and cock back the spring till it caught in that little half-moon declivity you ought to know about but probably don't. Then you could stick a Lucifer match into it headfirst, though the matches would be illegal today because they might start a fire. When you pulled the spring, it snapped forward, lit the match, and threw it maybe a yard. It was no end satisfying, though not real useful. Maybe not everything has to be useful.

You could buy dynamite fuse at the hardware store on the town square. Contrary to what ninety-eight percent of Washington might think, dynamite fuse doesn't blow up. It goes "Sssssssssssss." However, it will do it underwater too. Fuse had many uses. One was we'd take it to the pond behind the science building at

Athens College, all covered with nasty green slime, and chuck burning fuse in tied to weights. Sulfurous smoke then bubbled up most impressive.

I guess we did this because we were deprived. The times were premodern. There was no crystal meth whatever in the whole town, and nothing called Idiot Barbie for the girls, who also amused themselves perfectly well, and we didn't have a Three Inch Stare from fiddling with video games. It was just like, you know, the Depression, or the Dust Bowl.

Once I got the idea of going out behind the house where apples fell from the tree and rotted with a sticky sweet smell and most of the world's wasps came to eat them. If you needed some dead wasps you could spray them with bug poison. I did. Then I stuck them on an old empty wasp nest with Elmer's Glue and walked around town carrying what looked like a real nest full of active wasps. If you ever wanted to make an impression—I usually did—you sat down in the Limestone Drugstore and started reading comics with a nest of wasps in front of you.

I was going to tell you about how I was a mad scientist and made rockets with zinc and sulfur stolen from the college chemistry lab, or smeared mercury on pennies and made them shiny and slippery like frog eggs. You probably aren't ready for it though so you'll have to wait until another time. Which, come to think of it, this sure is.

51

A Modest Proposal to Abolish Universities

I think it is time to close the universities, and perhaps prosecute the professoriat under the RICO act as a corrupt and racketeering-influenced organization. Universities these days have the moral character of electronic churches, and as little educational value. They are an embarrassment to civilization.

I know this because I am sitting in my office in Jocotepec, consorting with a bottle of Padre Kino red—channeling the good Padre if you will. It is insight cheap at the price. A few bucks a liter.

To begin with, sending a child to a university is irresponsible. These days it costs something like a quarter of a million dollars, depending on your choice of frauds. The more notorious of these intellectual brothels, as for example Yale, can cost more. This money, left in the stock market for forty hears, or thirty, would yield enough to keep the possessor in comfort, with sufficient left over for his vices. If the market took a downturn, he could settle for just the vices. In the intervening years, he (or, most assuredly, she) could work in a dive shop.

See? By sending our young to college, we are impoverishing them, and ourselves, and sentencing them to a life of slavery in some grim cubicle painted federal-wall green. Personally, I'd rather be chained in a trireme.

Besides, the effect of a university education can be gotten more easily by other means. If it is thought desirable to expose the young to low propaganda, any second-hand bookstore can provide copies of Trotsky, Marcuse, Gloria Steinem, and the *Washington Post*. These and a supply of Dramamine, in the space of a week, would provide eighty percent of the content of a college education. A beer truck would finish the job. The student would save four years which could more profitably be spent in selling drugs, or in frantic cohabitation or—wild thought—in reading, traveling, and otherwise cultivating himself.

This has been known to happen, though documentation is hard to find.

To the extent that universities actually try to teach anything, which is to say to a very limited extent, they do little more than inhibit intelligent students of inquiring mind. And they are unnecessary: The professor's role is purely disciplinary: By threats of issuing failing grades, he ensures that the student comes to class and reads certain things. But a student who has to be forced to learn should not be in school in the first place. By making a chore of what would otherwise be a pleasure, the professor instills a lifelong loathing of study.

The truth is that universities positively discourage learning. Think about it. Suppose you wanted to learn Twain. A fruitful approach might be to read Twain. The man wrote to be read, not analyzed tediously and inaccurately by begowned twits. It might help to read a life of Twain. All of this the student could do, happily, even joyously, sitting under a tree of an afternoon. This, I promise, is what Twain had in mind.

But no. The student must go to a class in American Literature, and be asked by some pompous drone, "Now, what is Twain trying to tell us in paragraph four?" This presumes that Twain knew less well than the professor what he was trying to say, and that he couldn't say it by himself. Not being much of a writer, the poor man needs the help of a semiliterate drab who couldn't sell a pancake recipe to *Boy's Life*. As bad, the approach suggests that the student is too dim to see the obvious or think for himself. He can't read a book without a middleman. He probably ends by hating Twain.

When I am dictator, anyone convicted of literary criticism will be drawn and quartered, dragged through the streets as a salutary lesson to the wise, and dropped in the public drains.

Why is the ceiling spinning? Maybe the earth is off balance and wobbling in its orbit.

The truth is that anyone who wants to learn anything can do it better on his own. If you want to learn to write, for example, lock yourself in a room with copies of Strunk and White, and Fowler, and a supply of Padre Kino, and a loaded shotgun. The books will provide technique, the good Padre the inspiration, and you can use the shotgun on any tenured intrusion who offers advice. They tend to be spindly. A twenty-gauge should be sufficient.

Worse, these alleged academies, these dark nights of the soul encourage moral depravity. This is not just my opinion. It can be shown statistically. Virtually all practitioners of I-banking, advertising, and law began by going to some university. Go to Manhattan and visit any prestigious nest of foul attorneys engaged in circumventing the law. Most will have attended schools in the Ivy League. The better the school, the worse the outcome. Any trace of principle, of contemplative wonder, will have been squeezed out of them as if they were grapes.

Perhaps once universities had something to do with the mind, the arts, with reflection, with grasping or grasping at man's place in a curious universe. No longer. Now they are a complex scam of interlocking directorates. They employ professors, usually mediocre, to sell diplomas, usually meaningless, needed to get jobs nobody should want, for the benefit of corporations who want the equivalent of docile assembly-line workers.

See, first you learn that you have to finish twelve years of grade school and high school. The point is not to teach you anything; if it were, they would give you a diploma when you passed a comprehensive test, which you might do in the fifth grade. The point is to accustom you to doing things you detest. Then they tell you that you need four more years in college or you won't be quite human and anyway starve from not getting a job. For those of this downtrodden bunch who are utterly lacking in independence, there is graduate school.

The result is twenty years wasted when you should have been out in the world, having a life worth talking about in bars—riding motorcycles, sacking cities, lolling on Pacific beaches or hiking in the Northwest. You learn that structure trumps performance, that existence is *supposed* to be dull. It prepares you to spend years on lawsuits over somebody else's trademarks or simply going *buzzbuzzbuzz* in a wretched federal office. Only two weeks a year do you get to do what you want to do. This we pay for?

What if you sent your beloved daughter to a university and they sent you back an advertising executive?

I think we're having an earthquake. When the floor stops heaving, I'm going to send out for more Padre Kino.

52

The Boy Crisis

One hears often now that boys flounder in school, drop out, generally perform less well academically than girls, and don't go to college. A considerable amount of this commentary comes from women who seem quietly to enjoy the spectacle. Given that women control the schools, this might suggest that, if they are not actually causing the problem, neither are they in a hurry to do anything about it. Other people worry that the comparative superabundance of female college graduates will have no one to marry: While men will marry down, women won't. Regarding all of which:

The cause is not that boys are stupid. Boys have higher average scores than do girls on standardized tests, for example, and at the high end are far ahead of the girls. Putting it straightforwardly, the very smart are predominantly male, particularly in mathematics, and the exceedingly smart, almost entirely so. You don't have to like it. You don't have to think it fair. But it is a fact, and everybody in the field knows it.

Consider. The maximum score on each half of the SATs, both verbal and mathematical, is 800. You have to be, or had to be until the tests were recently dumbed down ("recentered," I meant to say, "recentered."), quite bright to score an 800. In 1999, when I checked because I was writing a column, 1611 girls in the country scored 800 on the math section; 4815 boys did. Verbal? Girls, 2828; boys, 3087. The male average on the math SATs was 531. The female was 495. That's not a trivial difference. Verbal scores? Males 509, females 502. The latter difference is slight and probably attributable the larger numbers of girls taking the test. The difference in math scores isn't.

This embarrassing disparity has been widely known at least since the publication of Camilla Benbow's paper in 1980 from Johns Hopkins. It remains despite alteration of tests (for example, National Merit) specifically to improve the scores of females, despite "recentering" of the SATs to make women and minorities look better at the high end. So what is the problem?

Whatever it is, it is new. I graduated in 1964 from a mediocre high school in rural Virginia. Demographically it was a bit of a curiosity. Many of the students were children of scientists and navy officers from Dahlgren Naval Weapons Laboratory, and the rest rough country kids. There was no discrimination by sex in the curriculum, incidentally: All in the college track took two years of algebra, a year of plane geometry, and a year of solid and trig, for example. If your parents had gone to college, you went to college, regardless of sex. All the kids of educated parents graduated, and almost all of the others. The exceptions were a few truly witless boys (boys predominate at the low end of intelligence too).

There was no "boy crisis." The girls made better grades, the boys better scores on standardized tests. There was no yawning gap.

In short, girls haven't come up. They have always done well in school. Boys have gone down. Why?

I can guess. Boys are churning wads of energy. They are physical and competitive. They want to climb things, test themselves, jump off of things, explore, drive fast, fight, behave like damn fools, and besiege cities. In later years this energy may serve them well, but not yet. School is hellish for them, with its year after year of sitting, bored out of their skulls, while some drone babbles. It is worse for the bright, verging on child abuse. They hate it. I did.

Girls are more orderly, patient, accept rules with less resistance, and do their homework. They have better handwriting and cut pictures from magazines to paste into projects. They finish assignments on time. In general girls are easier to deal with, certainly for the female teachers who now are almost the only teachers.

Now, 1964 was very different from today. Families were intact. I do not remember a single kid whose parents had been divorced. There was therefore a man in the house. Adolescent boys are wild men. A man can control them. A divorced woman often has a hard time controlling daughters.

There were men in the schools. We had a hard-eyed male principal, Larry Roller or, as we called him, Chrome Dome. You did not screw with Roller. He could, and would, expel on the spot any boy who seriously transgressed. (Girls just didn't commit expellable offenses.) This of course meant that he almost never expelled anyone: We were teenagers, not suicides.

Discipline was not harsh. The boys clowned in class and engaged in pranks (I may know somewhat of this), but we knew where the limits were. There were a goodly number of male teachers, who helped us know the limits.

Further, parents would back up the teachers without question. If I had said, "Fuck you" to a teacher, the French Foreign Legion would have been my only choice. Facing my father would have been—how shall I put it?—unproductive.

Boys need someone who can control them until, in a few years, the internal controls are in place. Women can't do it. Therefore we have police in the schools, and we drug boys into somnolence with stimulant drugs otherwise illegal. Parents, instead of even trying to control their kids, will litigate.

Boys cease to be students and become problems, so teachers don't like them.

Further, in the schools today we have feminization, feminization, feminization. Instead of treating girls like girls, and boys like boys, all are expected to be girls. It doesn't work. Boys by their very nature *like* to roughhouse. They *like* contact sports. You don't have to force them to play football. They are competitive. Women don't understand this, and what they don't understand, they outlaw. Today estrogenated school after estrogenated school bans dodge ball as too dangerous, outlaws tag ("They get too rough," meaning too rough for Mrs. Teacher), and insists on "groups games led by a caring adult."

It is hideous for boys. Everything they are, it isn't. "*Ohhhhh*, let's have a caring non-competitive game...." If he is really bright, with an IQ north of 150, he will decide that his teachers are idiots, which most of them are, and withdraw. There will be a price for this one day.

You want to end the "boy crisis"? Easy. Give boys male teachers who understand boys and care about them. Women do neither. Let them compete. It's how they are. Encourage them to burn off energy in the gym. Reward achievement, not pretty projects. Turn them into men, not transvestites.

Nahhh, never happen.

53

Curmudgeing Through Paradise

A year ago Violeta and I sat in a sidewalk cafe in Rome, a city of blowing exhaust, wretched traffic, and illegible graffiti spray-painted left and right. Talking was difficult above the blatt of trucks too big for narrow streets. Around the city ancient monuments slowly dissolved in dilute carbonic acid and turned gray from drifting soot. Italians, not particularly agreeable people, passed by in the international jeans-and-sweatshirt scruff that is less a style than an absence of thought.

We had reached the fag end of a couple of weeks of wandering around the country, mostly from Naples south to Sicily. Vi had not been out of Mexico before. I was pleased to find that she was a born traveler, relentlessly practical and unfazed by anything. It was a blessing. Being on the road with a hysteric quickly palls.

I think she had expected Italy to be sophisticated and stylish. Hadn't Hemingway said so? Didn't the movies show such things? Instead she concluded, correctly, that Naples and Rome were barely distinguishable from her native Guadalajara: noisy, dirty, ugly, walls defaced by punks in need of a horsewhipping. I was less surprised, having seen the symptoms in many places. A rule of near universal application is that anything lovely is old, and anything new like everything else new.

It is curious. Ancient Rome had little disposable income, and ancient Greece less. Building a Parthenon required great effort, as did the Gothic cathedrals. Yet they were built, and statues carved, and fountains made to play in the downtowns. Emperors built these things to glorify themselves, rich men to impress. Whatever the motive, they were built and adorned their times.

Today, with resources thousands of times greater, with bulldozers, steel, and unlimited money, we build little but square boxes and freeways. Our civilization is become a sprawling eyesore.

I had made the mistake of contracting a group tour, thinking that Vi might find it less stressful than my normal get-there-and-figure-it-out approach. As it turned out she detested the contrived jollity and brainless lectures as much as I did. In Naples we broke away and just wandered. It is a grimy nasty city, but speckled with anomalous churches from other times.

I remember one in particular. The interior was dark and hushed. The walls, of thick stone, excluded the noise of traffic. It was empty except for us. The vaulting, stained glass, and frescoes were exquisite and, as always, unlike any others I had seen. These things were not designed at corporate, one size fits all. Vi, being Catholic, felt herself to be in something that she was part of. We went our different ways to ponder in the gloom. Some things you do not do with others.

I wondered what life had been many centuries back when the church would have loomed larger and humanity, smaller. Any church diminishes against the scale of monumental office buildings. Eventually they become little more than tourist attractions except to dwindling numbers of believers. It must have been different when humanity was still a minor occurrence against the landscape. The tenor of existence has to change when you walk or ride horseback through wild forests and mountain passes, seldom seeing others.

Capri was hideous. Mobs of tourists covered every inch of the place that wasn't occupied by trinket shops selling commemorative baseball caps. The island itself was startling in its clouded peaks and sharp declivities against the Mediterranean. Tiberius' taste was perhaps not limited to small boys (if that wasn't slander). But how do you enjoy such splendor with fat people from Rhode Island squalling at each other, "But Charlie, the *guide* said…."?

There are too damned many people in the world, and they have too much money. They also have very little taste. The United States has fully achieved dictatorship of the proletariat, and other countries follow. Karl would be proud. Further, the unworthy have credit cards and so rush off in droves to have a European Experience as they might to Disneyland or Sea World. They may not know just where in Europe they are, or who the Normans were, or what or when the Reformation was, but that isn't the point. Just what is, I don't know.

The age of Mass Man is at last upon us. Globalization, with its attendant homogenizing, runs apace. Beijing begins to have traffic problems, like those of everywhere else. It also looks like anywhere else. An urban shopping mall in Guilin differs little from one in Tokyo or Georgetown or Nong Khai. Like supermarkets, they provide things people want at prices they will pay, and cannot be called evil. Yet they are uniform, drab, and somehow disheartening. Square ugly office blocks and square ugly apartment buildings appear overnight around the globe. They are built so because they are cheap and efficient. These seem to be the only considerations today.

A Claudius or a Trajan might have built imposing buildings with the help of the best artistic talent to be found. Corporations have no interest in such things. Neither does the United States, which is as esthetically impoverished as it is industrially fecund. Nor, as far as I can tell, does any other country, though many show more respect for what they have.

In America today, if there is public statuary at all, it will be bought by a committee of bureaucrats who, knowing nothing of the matter, will be gulled into buying some atrocity approved by an Art Consultant. A new library, if there are new libraries now, will be a brick box. The symphonies die, the arts metamorphose into "entertainment," and careful writing is regarded as a gas-station attendant might regard Sophocles in the original. The final triumph of the unwashed has occurred.

I think it sad. The distinctiveness and eccentricity of things lent flavor to life. When Bourbon Street turns into a Bourbon Street Theme Park, which it has, when Virginia's horse country gives way to identical subdivisions named Willow Run Vistas and Buena Vista Estates, and the Vatican is so jammed with people from Ohio that you can't move, we lose something.

I sometimes think that the chief difference between cockroaches and people is an insufficiency of legs. But I am a curmudgeon.

54

Conservation of Parody: Pondering the President

I'm wondering. Help me wonder. Either Georgie Bush is the minor, depressing, witless ferret I think he is, or I am. It has to be one or the other. If things don't start looking up pretty soon internationally, I'm going to be pretty sure which.

As best as I can tell, what the Maximum Cipher lacks, among an inexhaustible list of other things, is a hop-toad's understanding of how people work. Here we have the explanation of just about everything he does. He's dealing with a world full of people, but has no idea what people are. He probably couldn't recognize one. So he doesn't take their predictable behavior into account.

Think about it. When he went braying into Iraq like a learning-disabled jackass, he thought people would roll over, throw flowers, and have a democratic revolution. This would start a domino effect that would make all the other Moslem countries want to be democracies too. They would climb over each other to be democracies. They would love us because democracies love each other. He just knew it.

This makes perfect sense if you have no freaking idea how human beings work.

Of course, if you have read any history, which Bush hasn't, you will have noticed that people do not like being occupied by force. They don't like having their cities bombed. It galls them. It can, under certain circumstances (such as any circumstances) make them hostile.

If you think in terms of abstractions too simple for *Reader's Digest*, you might reflect as follows: "Democracy good. Iraqi people, love'm democracy, so love'm us. *Urrrg.*" Then you might be real surprised when their gratitude was exiguous after you remorselessly wrecked their cities, killed their army (which consisted of other people's husbands, brothers, and sons: ever think of that?), groped their women when you didn't have time to rape them, and left them without water and electricity.

I'm not saying the Iraqis *ought* to dislike these things, only that pretty reliably they *will* dislike them. The Afghans too, or either. It's how people are. Ungrateful.

Bush has no idea how people are.

This crackpot Boyscouterine outlook runs through everything the little man does, or more correctly tries to do. He really believes it, I think: The world is just waiting for us to bring it our favorite abstractions. They hate us for our freedoms, and yearn to be bombed into having them.

People don't work that way. Bush doesn't know it.

Remember when he had Kind-of-Twofer Rice publicly offer help to the Syrian opposition so they would overthrow their evil dictator and become wildly democratic? Same problem. Nobody told her, the poor bat-brained thing, that people don't like being messed with by outsiders. Nor, being Secretary of State, did she know how intensely the United States is detested by most of the world. How would she know? It's a secret known only to eight billion select people.

Bush wouldn't have a clue if you gave him another one.

Remember when Baffled Boy wanted all the Moslem countries to have elections and be democracies? And was all surprised when it worked, and he got Hamas and all? Let's ponder this. The analysis will be difficult, but I have faith in my readers.

What happens when you have elections in a country in which most of the people hate you? We'll do this by multiple choice, to give everyone an even chance. Answer: they elect a government that (a) loves you, loves Israel, and wants desperately to do everything you tell it to, or (b) hates your guts. If you went for (a), you are a Republican and have no idea how people actually work. And you probably listen to ooom-pa music

Nowadays our Keystone President, ever impervious to reason, experience, or the obvious, leers at Iran like a deviate in a nudie bar. (He probably wears a raincoat when thinking about policy.) He figures that the Iranians too want to be attacked in the name of unasked-for virtue. It didn't work in Iraq, or in Afghanistan, so it will work in Iran. He wants to encourage Iranian dissidents so that they will overthrow the evil mullahs and set up a ... yes ... Democracy, and love us, and be our drinking buddies and sit the dog while we go on vacation.

How is he going to cause them to rise up in love for us? By massively bombing several hundred places in Iran, killing many thousands of its people, and humiliating them in the eyes of the world. Why, what could make more sense? Sense anyway if you don't know enough about people to grasp that nationalism trumps internal divisions. They will of course rally 'round the flag, because people don't like being messed with by outsiders.

Bush doesn't understand this. He doesn't know about people.

Let us suppose that you don't like Bush. If the Chinese bombed your home, and killed your sister, would that make you join the Chinese and want a puppet government?

It is not how people work.

As we speak, the Israelis have pretty much destroyed Lebanon. Bush keeps the UN from doing anything to interfere, and sends advanced bombs to the Israelis so they can blow up anything that's left. He thought—get this—that since Hezbollah is Shiite, the Sunnis would join with (yes! Yes!) Israel to fight them. Was there ever such a fruitcake? (I like to think of a fruitcake in a raincoat.)

He had no idea how people work.

It's breathtaking. He has occupied and made rubble of two Moslem countries, and heavily supports Israel, hated by all Moslem countries, in turning Lebanon, a third Moslem country into rubble, and is threatening Syria and Iran, two more Moslem countries, with attack, possibly nuclear. By doing this he is going to inspire Moslems with a passion for American democracy, change the Mid-East into Fifth Century Athens, and make them love us.

God Almighty, what a fool. What a bus-station clown. It isn't how people work.

The same fertile stupidity shows in his relations with Latin America. The first thing to recognize about the world below Laredo is that the countries there deeply, deeply resent American meddling. Whether you think the resentment justified, or the meddling for that matter, is irrelevant. Rule One of diplomacy here is "don't get into Latin faces unless you really need to."

So what does Befuddlement do? Some Cuban officials came to Mexico City and checked into a Sheraton. He had the Sheraton eject them. It was utterly childish, and utterly pointless (you don't suppose there might be another hotel in Mexico City, do you?) and infuriated Mexico. People are still angry. And sympathetic to Cuba.

But Cuba does not practice democracy, and to Dudley Do-Right, or the Do-Right Dud, the abstraction is what counts. Cuba bad, democracy good, *urg.* Bow-wow.

He has no faint idea of how people work. The man is an idiot.

An old reporter's saying holds that a "burro" is an ass, and a "burrow" is a hole in the ground. A newsman, it is said, should know the difference. Maybe presidents too.

55

Fred: A Drug Dealer's Memoirs

I'm going to tell you how I entered the underworld, and became a money launderer, and international drug wallah, and remorseless criminal, just like Carlo Gambino or Bin Laden or Condoleezza Rice. Yes. I am now of one blood with Pablo Escobar. It is a service of the Anglo-Irish Bank. I imagine that my picture can be seen on wanted posters in European post offices.

How did I come to this frightful pass? I decided a while back to get such money as I have out of dollars. In the White House the Maximum Ferret was playing promiscuously at being Sergeant Rock around the planet, which he seemed to regard as his private litter box, and would one day inflate the currency to pay for it. He doesn't pay for my hobbies, I thought. Why should I pay for his? Anyway, I didn't want to kill Moslems. Various other people, yes, but not Mohammedans.

Where to put my minute shriveled pittance, all that is left to me of a misspent life? (I live in a swell house in Mexico with a lovely wife, a splendid if occasionally insupportable stepdaughter, a disturbed dog, a rabbit, and lots of ribs and beer. I don't have many excuses for feeling sorry for myself. I make the most of them.)

Europe appealed, redolent as it is of stability, solemnity, and stuffy reliability. A couple of years before a shill from the Anglo-Irish Bank of Dublin had come through my Mexican town, which is full of expatriate money. Ireland, I thought. Just the thing. The Irish are a delightful race, a tad crazy, sometimes drunken, and literarily gifted, all of which recommended them to me.

Ireland, I was sure, had few Calvinist Texans with beady eyes like windows opening onto a wall, and impenetrable English you could armor a tank with. I thought of broad green lands and leprechauns and bosomy barmaids with twinkling eyes and countless magnificent authors and Roland the Headless Thompson Gunner.

I duly, and foolishly, sent the bank a deposit, along with copies of my passport, Mexican residency papers, driver's license, dog's paw prints, grandmother's

DNA, and all the other dry foliage of my life that the bank required. This was enough, I thought, to identify several people. But no. The bank was darkly suspicious. It suspected me of Laundering Money. (I wish it suspected me of having money.) The multitudinous requirements sprang, I presumed, from international law intended to discourage honest people from putting money in banks. Crooks have ways around these requirements, and also have more money.

Now, any bank's protestations that it wants to avoid the laundering of money constitute pious fraud. Such assertions would embarrass an electronic church promoting your grandaunt's social security check. Criminal enterprise reaps immense sums, being unhampered by governmental regulation. Do you think any bank whatever doesn't get weak-kneed at the thought of billions in poppy lucre? The drug trade is a valued part of the world's economy.

But all right. I sent this stuff off to Dublin, FedEx and forty-five dollars. I emphasized, please communicate with me by email, as the Mexican mails are casual about things like arrival. Please, email.

Many weeks later, my check to AIB having cleared, I assumed that I had a properly constituted account. Then Violeta discovered a sodden envelope in a muddy spot in the road near our house. This missive turned out to be from AIB. Perhaps the bank had an eccentric conception of email. Usually I find it in my inbox and not in a hole in the street.

In it I discovered that the bank, in the person of a Mr. David Milne, was not happy with the documentation from my bank here, Lloyd. He didn't much like the bank. From the peremptory nature of his eruptions ("I shall require …") I realized that Mr. Milne must be at least a duke, or maybe a dauphin, or perhaps a king. No doubt his car was escorted by pikemen. As a barefoot West Virginia boy I was awed by dealing with royalty but happy to be climbing in the world.

I cannot lie. His dark suspicions were not entirely without foundation. I had links with the opium trade.

Violeta recently found a poppy growing in the back yard, next to the goldfish pond. I don't know how it got there. We weren't even sure whether it was an opium poppy, though I fervently hoped so. By this time I rather wanted to belong to the criminal element. Out of sheer vengefulness I decided to sell that poppy and launder the money through AIB. I would have, too, except that the rabbit ate it. I thought she looked very calm for the rest of the afternoon.

Since this column is read by expatriates around the world, suggesting that they have too much time on their hands, I explained to the earl that I was a journalist, and asked what would have happened had I not found his email in the mud hole in front of my house. Would my money have been confiscated by some august governmental body given to thievery? What was AIB's objection to Mexican banks? Did his majesty know something I didn't? He declined to answer. I suppose that archbishops are quite busy.

The rub was that he wanted some document from my Mexican bank imprinted with the bank's stamp. But Lloyd's doesn't have a stamp. It isn't how things are done here. I guess that if you live in a castle surrounded by a moat, and spend your time calking drafty cracks, you don't have time to learn about banking practices. Anyway Veronica, my patient account manager at Lloyd's, composed a letter testifying that I existed and so on, had it translated into English, and sent it to the His Excellency. Forty-five bucks more for FedEx, which began setting up a branch office to handle my correspondence.

This didn't work either. Nothing does. I wondered why the good baron didn't simply email Lloyd's, which would remove all doubt about whatever it was that he doubted. I then realized that Lloyd's parking lot was paved, and that it didn't have a muddy spot in which to receive email. Technology arrives slowly in Latin America.

With this much trouble getting money into the bank, I assumed that there could be no earthly hope of getting it out. In fact AIB seemed to regard depositors with resentment, as annoyances having nothing to do with its line of work. Perhaps before the bank was born, its mother was frightened by a client, engendering lifelong gollywoggles whenever approached by one.

On and on it went, and goes. I don't know whether I will live long enough to see my funds, orphaned and sorrowing in some cold account. They probably won't even recognize me.

56

A Civil Feminist

I found myself some time ago under social circumstances in a group that included an angry radical feminist, which is to say a radical feminist. Out of nowhere that I remember, she announced, "Men are sexist pigs." Such assertions are par for the species.

It was not easy to know how to respond. She was clearly attacking. You don't insult a group some of whose members are present unless you mean to offend. While I may have doubts about, say, the legitimacy of psychotherapy, I do not say while dining with a practitioner, "Therapists are swinish frauds." While "sexist" might be regarded with sufficient straining as a political category, "pig" is a schoolyard insult. The comment was simply ill-bred. So are feminists.

I could have responded, "Women are useless bitches." The problem is that I don't think that women are either useless or bitches. A few are, yes. A few men are sexist pigs, and I don't like them either. True, I don't care for some of the attitudes that seem to characterize a lot of American women. This is far from thinking that women are pigs or bitches.

Why do feminists go out of their way to be disagreeable? Much of human behavior is templated. Certain kinds of personality do certain things. They can't help it. Common templates are the True Believer, the Hater, and the Victim. The salient point is that the template comes first, the content second and sometimes almost as an afterthought. They are like empty forms waiting to be filled in.

The True Believer needs to believe in something truly and, really, doesn't much care what: Christianity, evolution, Islam, Marxism or market forces. He needs the certitude. He doesn't need to hate anyone, however. For example, evolutionists do not.

The Hater does need to hate something. Sometimes the choice is obvious, as when a black in the slums comes to hate Whitey. Sometimes the choice is less explicable, as when a man who has suffered no direct or clear damage at the hands of Jews becomes virulently anti-Semitic. A defining characteristic of the

Hater is that maintaining the grounds of his (or, most assuredly, her) hatred is far more important than truth, reason, or kindness. The hatred is an end in itself, an identity, the core of his (or her) being. All thought and balance vanish in the insistence on painting the hated in as bad a light as possible.

The Victim believes that all of his miseries and failures are the fault of others. Victims are often Haters as well. Feminists combine the two.

The need to hate is different from the possession of an opinion. A reasonable person might believe, for example, that Jews exert too much influence over American foreign policy and various domestic policies, but also grant without demur that Jews had contributed much to the economy, the sciences, and the arts. The details could be debated, but the position is not that of a Hater. The Hater in anti-Semitic form cannot go for ten minutes in private conversation without adverting with hostility to various crimes and conspiracies which he attributes to Jews, and can never concede that Jews ever, however inadvertently, have done anything good. He is obsessive about it.

So are feminists.

A feminist sees men exactly as anti-Semites see Jews. This is because she *is* an anti-Semite—the same template, the same bottle but with different wine. She has a more hair-trigger anger ("Men are sexist pigs") because she can get away with it, a more bellicose incivility for the same reason, but the same (watch, and see whether I am right) lack of humor, obsessiveness, and the characteristic basing of her personality on the hatred.

Haters seldom know much about those they hate. It doesn't matter to them, and just gets in the way. As anti-Semites are clueless about Jews, so feminists are clueless about men. Anti-Semites know that Jews rub their hands and say "heheheh" and want to destroy Western civilization. Feminists know that men don't have feelings and want to oppress women, and hurt them, and degrade them. Yet they (both) think they know the hated enemy. They both pour forth half-truths, thudding clichés, carefully selected facts, and abject foolishness, and both are blankly unable to see the other side's point of view or to concede it any virtue at all.

I have known only a few such feminists well, though I have read many. They have struck me, without exception that comes to mind, as fitting a peculiar mold: bright, very hostile and combative, but physically timid and pampered, hothouse flowers really, usually from fairly moneyed families and often Ivy or semi-Ivy schools. Often they have done little outside of feminism and would be helpless out of an urban setting. They have no idea how anything around them works—what a cam lobe is, how a refrigerator makes things cold, or how a file-allocation table might be arranged. Their degrees run to ideologizable pseudosubjects such as sociology, psychology, or Women's Studies. They seem isolated from most of life.

None of this is characteristic of women in general. I used to belong to a group called Capitol Divers, of Washington, DC. About a third of the members I'll guess were women. We dove the deep wrecks off North Carolina, chartered the Belize Aggressor for a week near Central America, and so on. It wasn't lightweight diving. Sometimes we were in the open Atlantic in seas a lot higher than recommended, or ninety feet down at night on a wreck or, I remember, at 135 in the Blue Hole of Belize. (Cap Divers was a bit of a cowboy outfit.)

The women were fine divers, treated as equals by the men because they in fact were equals. Nobody thought about it. In a lot of aggregate time with them over the years, I never heard a single, "Men are sexist pigs." The pattern is one that I've noticed anecdotally but widely. Women who are good at things that men respect are respected by men, and they tend to like men because they have things in common. They are not templated neurotics. Feminists are.

If you do not believe that haters are all the same people, wrestling with internal demons rather than trying to solve real problems, make a point of talking to them or, failing that, reading them. Remember though that a hater is not someone who recognizes an unpleasant truth about a particular group. A woman who says that men are much more given to violence is stating an obvious fact. So is a white who recognizes that low academic achievement among blacks is a problem. Neither is necessarily a hater.

No. You want the ones with the grinding all-encompassing hostility. "The kikes are destroying America." "The niggers are destroying America." "Men are sexist pigs." These people are fascinating. Talk to them. Care is needed, particularly with feminists, to keep them from exploding before you can conduct an examination. But do it. Note that many are well educated. They can be polished. But the fundamental difference between a radical feminist and a Jew baiter is … is….

Wait. I'm thinking.

57

The Greezy Wheels—Dispatches From A Parallel Universe

Damn! Cain't believe it! Hoo-yeeha-wow! And all.

Let me try to get this to make sense, though the odds are long. I was tending the computer in the bedroom of my house in Jocotopec in darkest Mexico, maybe ten in the morning. The Mamas and the Papas roared from the speakers, third Negra Modelo gettin' low in the can, big brown-ass hills indolent and shiftless out the window just like mankind was meant to be but ain't got enough sense, and I'm thinking about how the vandals stole the handle and remembering twisted times in the High Desert back in the Sixties when Jimmy and I nearly fell down the mine shaft ... ah, but the world I isn't ready for that.

On a vagrant impulse I fed *The Greezy Wheels* into Google's maw.

Not a chance, I figured. What did Google know about high art? Or low dives? It probably doesn't inhale. The *Wheels* were a great band, even if you were straight. Or so I've heard. That was maybe 1973 in Austin which was the exact temporal point of the Big Bang or more likely the Great Mushroom, viewed through Window Pane, but anyway the start of anything that mattered or, I sometimes think, still does.

Google eructated, gurp. Hunh? The *Wheels* got a freaking web site! Better living through chem—I mean, electronics. How come they're still out there? How come I am? Holy fruitcake, Batman.

You gotta understand. Austin in the Seventies was the great symbiotic corn-fed Texas-plus-hippy evolutionary musical weirdness center, with these blond strong kids from the fields who came in from the farm and hit the freak years, ker-blunch. Young America, the part that mattered anyway, was wobbling around the continent like carmine particles in some sort of macroscopic Brownian-motion. I'd drifted in from—either it was NYC or it wasn't: I'm sure of it—to see a friend who lived in a cardboard shack mostly up on Montopolis on Crumley Lane, I think. Or somewhere else. It was not a factually fastidious time.

Anyway, *The Wheels* were a country band. I mean real country and they felt the music because it was what they were, but they had perhaps some slight acquaintance with smokable enlightenment. Maybe not that slight. I don't know. A kilo here, a kilo there, and it adds up to drugs. Who can tell? Hey, it's how things were. Our childhoods made us do it.

The head fiddlist for them (this is all from lengthening memory, but you will have to deal with it) was Mary Egan who (we understood, anyway) had started life as a classical violinist and realized her error and took up the fiddle. Apparently she found it redemptive.

God plays the fiddle. Everybody knows it. In fact, he only created four instruments, the soprano recorder, the country fiddle, the mouth harp, and the clarinet. All the rest are unfortunate derivatives.

Now, Armadillo World Headquarters—this is getting difficult. You probably didn't know that armadillos had a headquarters. Well, they did. They're more organized than you think. It was an open-air music-and-lotsa-beer joint where wild bands played seditious music for dirty rotten anarchistic hippies, like me, and all these Texas gals, the which there ain't no better on this or any other earth, except maybe in Arkansas, (well, or Alabama, or....) wandered around in tight cut-offs and the music soared and flew and flapped and you hollered "LSD!" at the waitress, who brought you a whole mug of it. (It meant Lone Star Draft. At least during working hours.)

They had this crazy dog, and you'd roll a piece of spongy volcanic rock and he'd run fetch it. I worry about that dog. He may still think lava is what dogs eat.

Actually, the 'Dillo wasn't alone. There was Soap Creek Saloon where you'd get pitchers of beer and listen in thumping dark to some really good band, which Austin crawled with like ticks on a backwoods dog, and girls would jump on the tables and dance to the twang-and-whoop—we're talking banjos here, five strings and twelve fingers—because in those days it was still America.

You can't play a banjo right with less than a dozen fingers. It's a scientific fact. That's why so many banjoists come from West Virginia.

Sometimes the Soap would have a beer-drinking contest. You'd chug a styrofoam cup and throw it to show that you'd finished. It looked like a snowstorm. All they needed was penguins. After five rounds they picked a winner somehow and the prize was ... a pitcher of beer. Which the winner drank on the spot.

Then the *Wheels* would get it on. Mary would wail into Orange Blossom Special on the fiddle and the crowd would yoop and holler and go wild. It was, after all, Texas.

Anyway, I remember Mary and Cleve, and Lissa who sang Whatever Happened to Romance, in the swirling murk of lots of joints and occasional tobacco and I was in love with her because, well, nothing else made sense. Women are wonderful creatures when they aren't vicious Yankee dykes, and when they play in bands the wonderfulness goes exponential. The Wheels would play Okie from Muskogee and it was exactly right, maybe better'n Merle, 'cause they were Texans but it was a joke too given the pharmacological background, or foreground, of the audience and the times. (White Lightning may have been the greatest trip but it sure wasn't the only one.)

Then, we heard, they put Cleve in jail because he was in the airport coming back from Mexico and his suitcase accidentally fell open, the police said (uh-huh) and all this Margie Weenie fell out. It wasn't fair. I'm sure he didn't know it was there. I mean, you can't tell what people will put in your suitcase if you don't watch it. Anyway it didn't help the band at all, or anyone's spirits. Given that the entire city of Houston with more than a million dollars in its pocket, which was pretty much the entire city of Houston, was flying on corruption and cocaine, it didn't seem right. I guess we'd all be better off if the government just kept its long sticky fingers to itself. Or curled up and died.

Then I went away. I must have, because I'm not still there. Cleve must have gotten out, because he isn't still in. The years rolled on, senselessly. It's what they do. I figured the *Wheels* had gone extincter than seven mastodons in a tar pit, but no, they're still there. Maybe there's a little bit of justice in the world after all, but I doubt it

58

Terror and Deckheads

Oh help. I am still getting nutcake email from the deranged telling me about various conspiracies involving those wretched buildings in New York. Stop sending them. My hard drive is not an asylum. I don't know how to email Haldol. Try taking rat poison.

Two of these plots in particular might be exterminated to my inexpressible happiness. The first was that no Jews were in the towers when they were hit, the implication being that the attack was an Israeli plot and doubtless mediated by Mossad. The story enjoyed a brief vogue and still shows up occasionally, like tularemia.

Now, if you told me that Mossad, Bush, the CIA or the Republican National Committee blew up those buildings, I might wonder. Intelligence agencies are dirt. To judge by the current infestation of the White House, Republicans are too stupid to be dirt, but may be proto-dirt, and advance to true dirt-hood with careful coaching. Democracy is ever fascinating.

But … how many Jews do you suppose worked in the towers? New York being New York, and the towers being full of lawyers and commercial people, the answer has to be A Whole Bunch. Let's think about this.

I picture Rachel Goldstein, a tower slave, in her apartment at night when the phone rings.

Rachel: "Hello."

Voice: "Rachel. This is Mossad."

Rachel: "Oh, hi! I'm Mahatma Gandhi."

Voice: "No, Rachel. This really is Mossad."

Rachel: "This really is Mahat…."

Voice: "Honest. Really, *really*. Cross my heart and hope…."

Rachel: "Take your medication." Click.

It is hard enough to get a Jew to agree with himself, much less with several thousand others. To buy this theory, you have to believe (a) that Jews are interconnected by a surgically implanted wireless network and respond robotically to beamed instructions from a secret satellite beyond the orbit of Saturn, or (b) that they were all willing to stay home, knowing that their friends and colleagues were about to be killed. If you think either of these ideas makes the slightest sense, take your medication.

Here is a point I've noticed about most of the conspiracy theories: They either involve preposterously large numbers of conspirators, or just don't make sense.

Another theory, very much alive, holds that the Pentagon was hit not by an airliner, but by (a) a fighter aircraft, or (b) a missile fired by a fighter aircraft, or (c) a cruise missile.

I was in Washington at the time and could have simply walked over to the Pentagon to see what had happened. I didn't for several days. I figured a smoking hole was a smoking hole. So what? Maybe I'm jaded.

Anyway, my little contribution to the story:

Washington is an insider's town. There are layers of insiderness, which is constructed on the plan of an artichoke: The closer to the center, the softer the brains get. (I don't mean that artichokes have....) (Though maybe.) Anyway, there is the Washington that the press writes about. There is the Washington the press knows about. Then you have the Pentagon war room and, higher yet, the conclaves of the highest White House staff. These are all the outer rings, for hoi polloi. A far more secret and closed group, esoteric, more powerful than Superman, and unknown even o the National Security Agency, is the Plastic and Foam Only Club.

If you turned right coming out of my condo at the time in Colonial Village, just across the river from Washington in Virginia, and followed down Wilson Boulevard and to the left, you came to the Virginia terminus of Key Bridge. Here the bike path picked up, running parallel to the GW Parkway, often in sight of the Potomac. It's a pretty ride. You passed the Pentagon, and then National Airport, and finally came to the Washington Sailing Marina. It is perhaps a seven-mile ride each way. For years I did it several times a week in good weather.

Behind the restaurant of the Marina was a wooden deck with a snack bar that sold beer. A highly motley group of people foregathered there of an afternoon to ingest the elixir. We called ourselves the PFO Club (Plastic and Foam Only, which was written on the trashcans) or more casually, the Deckheads. There were Paul the Carpenter, a couple of working-stiff journalists, a retired general, a possibly legal Mexican, Hot Ticket Lisa the Blonde Bombshell, occasionally a Korean woman we called Ninja, some federal bureaucrats, a pathological liar who believed he held a major position in the stock market, an airline pilot, and so on.

We chatted and had a hell of a good time. Every minute or so we stopped talking because an airliner taking off from National drowned out conversation.

In summer, from quitting time for office maggots until at least nine at night, revolving shifts of these kaleidoscopic reprobates showed up, got sozzled, argued about wildly variegated subjects, and left. You could hear Paul the Carpenter and a German employee of the government argue alternately about the price of nails and the future of the Deutschmark. There was even a resident schizophrenic. (Not me.)

One of the journalists (I was the other) we called Broadcast Dave, to distinguish him from other Daves among the Deckheads. He was Dave Winslow, then the voice of UPI Radio's World Edition, or whatever it was called. He had worked somehow in the airplane business, maybe in air freight, knew all the airliners at a glance, and had an apartment near the Pentagon.

I knew Dave for at least a couple of years before 9/11. He was a good-humored cynic, as reporters are when they are not ill-tempered cynics. In Washington you are either an ideologue, and believe passionately in some reprehensible and improbable system of error, or you don't believe anything. The latter has been the usual position of working-stiff newsmen, when sober. (At other times they believe they'll have another drink.) Reporters these days tipple less than they once did, I grant. Broadcast Dave was never drunk that I saw him, but he didn't believe in things easily either. I like that kind of folk.

A few days after Nine-Eleven, I got back to the deck after an absence. Broadcast was there. He told me that he was in his apartment at the time of the strike and heard an airplane coming in, way too low. Something wasn't right. Looking out his window, he said, he saw the tail of an airliner pass by and then, *kerwhoom!* Being a reporter, he sprinted to the phone, and believed that he was the first journalist to report it. If he wasn't, the other guy got it in less than ten seconds, I figure. These things matter to reporters.

Now, boys and girls, either Broadcast Dave was planted years in advance by The Conspiracy to mislead the Plastic and Foam Only Club (an entity I grant to be of high priority for penetration by international terrorists) or there was an airplane.

59

Essaying Cultural Psychiatry

Letters pour in from desperate readers (or may at any moment) saying, "Fred, explain America today. Say something tendentious and irritating about what is going on in this curious country. Why do we do what we do? Sock it to us."

All right.

The United States is an uneasy, frightened country, yet aggressive, truculent, and looking for trouble—which it finds. Fear: Terrorists are everywhere, like cockroaches and governmental cameras. Citizens should watch each other on the subway and rat out suspicious behavior. People need to go through metal detectors in county courthouses, because the government is scared of them, and get spied on by the government to protect them against the ever-present danger of ... of, well, the unspeakable and unspoken angst of existence. And so, in the customary manner of large scared bullies, the country lashes out, at Iraq, Iran, Syria, North Korea, Afghanistan, Venezuela, wherever.

A friend says, "Fred, gringos *want* to be controlled. They *love* this police-state stuff. It gives them meaning. They lead miserable lives in boring suburbs. The husband is a mouth-breathing oaf with his retinas sewed to the football machine. His wife is a pucker-faced shrew with cellulite like the dark side of the Moon and his kids are whining dopers who gawp at the box and gurgle over stupid video games. The guy has no control over anything in his life. He's scared of the boss and the pissed-off middle-aged man-hating divorcee with thick ankles in Human Resources who would love to outsource his job to Mumbai. He knows he'll get raped if he splits from the wife. So he wants to kill something. He doesn't care what, and anyway finding out might require reading a book, which god knows he isn't going to do."

This may be harsh. It also may be true of more people than one would like. The United States does not look real happy just now. It is a lower-middle-class country with an upper-middle-class income, except the credit cards are maxed out and people are in debt up to their gills. They don't read much. The cultural center of gravity is the black ghetto with its irremediable anger. Americans tend to equate social class with income, but Archie Bunker in a call-me-Arnold SUV is still Archie Bunker. And his job, no matter how air-conditioned the office, is probably as rewarding as screwing lug-nuts on cars passing on the assembly line.

It is a purely consumer society. There is not much to life out there except buying things. Granted, a medieval serf would have regarded this as a problem much to be desired, but it leads to a certain bleakness today. You don't buy a house because you love it, because of the lush vegetation thereabout and ancient trees and an enchanting air of calm and antiquity. No. You buy a "starter house" with the intention of unloading it when you make partner. Then you buy a shoddy McMansion, exactly like three hundred others surrounding it. Then it's home theater and granite counter-tops and more-complex iPods and, just maybe, one day, a Hummer, that most thunderous of motorized codpieces. A suspicion dawns that something somehow isn't right. Yep.

Other uneases brood over the landscape. Women dominate domestic politics and so we have the Fear State. With them security security security trumps liberty or taking chances of any sort, and so we must ban pocket knives. They are afraid of guns, want kids to wear helmets on bikes, and think tag is a violent and dangerous game. Yes, there are exceptions, but fewer day by day. We must fill in the deep ends of swimming pools and fear second-hand smoke and things that go bump in the night. I suspect a lot of this vague anxiety stems from the lack of a settled and satisfying place in society.

Men run foreign policy, and do it with the ardor and brainless territoriality of retarded pit bulls. We must confront The Threat—this threat, that threat, any threat in a storm. After the Soviets punked out on us, we adopted Terr, Terrace, and Tersm as interim threats until China comes online. We must Fight, we must Show Them, we must Draw the Line. All across America men with grade-school minds and beachball paunches growl that we gotta gettem before they get us, if we don't stoppem there, they'll land on the beaches of Peoria.

Women are limited creatures. They couldn't be this stupid if you wired the entire sex in series.

Anyhow, this division of irresponsibility leads to contradictions. In school, low-IQ teachers try to make little boys into girls and expel them if they play soldier and say Bang. Then the Pentagon recruits these transvestite artifacts and sends them off to shoot people they've barely heard of. What a plan. What clarity of vision. What consistency.

A thing about society now is that nobody knows the rules any longer, if there are rules. In the past, from about the lower middle class and up, women behaved as ladies and men as gentlemen, concepts now identified with oppression. Even the lower classes were usually courteous after their fashion. The arrangement had its uses. When general agreement enforces consideration of others, life is better. You can go for days without wanting to strangle anybody.

Today, many people are civil, but many aren't. You don't know what to expect. Do you respond to abuse by being abusive in return? Or get walked over? That is the question. We now have Road Rage. In the streets you find people pushing onto the subway like piglets looking to suckle, and throwing the finger. Women are worse, apparently confusing ill-bred pugnacity with virility. (Men are careful how they treat each other, as there are consequences. Women do not suffer consequences. It must be nice.)

Further, the ghetto rules everywhere, seeps in, or threatens. Americans are not social climbers, but social descenders, rappelling deliberately into the grubby depths. On the radio one hears regularly such lyrical confections as "Muthah-fucka, muthafucka, she a ho, shit." Ah, but the chief rule of discourse today is that one must never offend the offensive. You must never suggest that they straighten up and mind their manners, mouth, grammar, and work ethic.

The pervasive overregulation adds to the national edginess. The government decides what and whether your children will learn in school, and makes it nearly impossible to flee. Getting on an airplane requires a strip-search by federal dimwits. You can't hire people without proving that you have enough of this race and that sex and don't discriminate against left-handed Pomeranian sadomasochists with Hispanic grandmothers. Rules, laws, regulations, paperwork. A sense arises of being trapped. Many hate it.

Add it up. A frightened people over-controlled, having no communal roots, blocked by government from raising their children as they see fit, parlously indebted, sexually confused, and lacking a sense of permanence or of a connection with the natural world, both of which have since time immemorial mitigated a certain emptiness in human affairs. Like a dog tormented by evil children, the country is ready to bite. And it does.

I hope that was adequately irritating. I can do no worse.

60

White House without a Bouncer

I miss the days of smoke-filled rooms when crooked pols chose corrupt presidential candidates who were approximately sane. Today we have a sort of presidential bus-station lottery. We choose as ruler any beer-hall putz who can shake hands and grin his way successfully through New Hampshire. This, plus the deep rot of the American political framework, is allowing the rapid conversion of the United States into something that previous Americans would hardly recognize.

Permit me a foray of a paragraph into psychojournalism. It fascinates me to know that George Bush was a male cheerleader at Andover. Yes, it could have been worse. He might have been a table-dancer. But most of us who were in high school when he was recognize that you either came to watch football, or you came to watch the girl cheerleaders. There was something odd about a boy who wanted to be one.

("Ricky, Ricky he's our man. If he can't do it, nobody can. *Goooooooooooo* Plesiosaurs!")

We are ruled by a male cheerleader who favors torture. I wonder what things twist in the inner fog.

Given a president who seems chiefly concerned to display his indomitable manhood, the question arises: What restraints keep him from absolute control of a formidably armed nation of three hundred million? The Constitution, noblest of fables, was designed to do just this. But absent the will to enforce them, checks and balances do not exist, and laws, principles, and constitutions mean nothing. If no one says "no," the president simply behaves as he wants. The genius of the strange little man on Pennsylvania Avenue has been to recognize this, to divine the weakness of the American political order.

When he wanted to attack Iraq, he simply lied, and lied again, and shifted his ground and lied again. It worked. When he didn't want to follow the Geneva Conventions in his treatment of captured Iraqis, he just declared his prisoners of war not to be prisoners of war. Torture? He just did it and faced down the country and the world. Disregard of civil rights? Spying? He just did as he chose.

Here is the great discovery of the man who doesn't read. America is not the land of the free, nor of the brave, nor of the politically sentient. Nor is it a country of laws or of principles. It is a country of those who just do as they want. A president can do anything he chooses. Who will tell him no? Nobody has.

Today there is speculation as to whether he will make war, perhaps nuclear war, on Iran. The universal assumption seems to be that if he wants to, he will just do it. The legislature, already having given up its authority to declare war, seems to regard the military as the private guard of the president. Is it not interesting that one dim, pugnacious, ignorant little man can bring on nuclear war all by himself?

When Mr. Bush gets caught lying or breaking the law, he shows no embarrassment, contrition, or sense of having done anything wrong. He seems to have no conception of right and wrong, of principle. He is not accustomed to being told "no," and accepts no constraints on his power. All that matters to him is that he get his way. He gets it.

Where will this lead? Obviously, to vastly increased police powers. But I wonder. If, down the pike, Bush announced that to protect us from terrorism he would have to postpone the presidential elections and remain in office—what would happen? Suppose he came up with a bit of supportive theater. If just before the elections something blew up, and were attributed not to the CIA but to Terrace, what then? The Reichstag has burned before. The public, the congress, the judiciary are so very, very easily manipulated. All it takes is the will to do it.

And that the little man has.

A tribal rite in the column racket is the discovery of darkness in the hearts of presidents, or witlessness, and we discover away industriously. I have done my share. I thought Clinton a bright, libidinous lout, Jimmy Carter a moralizing cipher, Reagan a sort of Grandfather Barbie and, by contrast, Eisenhower a wise man hiding behind remarkable syntax. None was evil, or mad. Bush is something new in presidential politics, genuinely dangerous and genuinely out of control. The time is ripe for him. America no longer has the institutional defenses to say "no."

What would happen if a president just refused to go? To remove him, someone would have to act. Who? Little would be necessary to stop a coup, granted. A couple of helicopters of Marines landing across the street from the White House would be enough. The various federal police bully civilians well (ask Steve Hat-fill), but would find fighting real men another thing. But who in the military would have the courage to do it?

Would the public do anything? I doubt it. The Born Agains would support him, the suburban Christians suck their thumbs and wait, blacks ignore the matter, conservatives see it as necessary to stop Tersm, and most people would watch football on television. The necessary strength is not in the country. The timbers are rotten.

A popular uprising I cannot imagine. Who would rise? Overweight people with Volvos do not become urban guerrillas. Again, conservatives, who tend to be armed, rank among the most ardent supporters of Mr. Bush. In any event, how does one rise? Would upset semi-heterosexual professors at Cornell hold a Take Back the Night march? Oh joy. After three days the vigilists would become bored. Back to the television set.

The Supreme Court certainly would, and could, do nothing. The court consists of insular antiquities who so far have shown no disposition to stand up to Bush. The termites have hollowed the judicial woodpile.

Congress? It does what is paid to do, by anyone. What could it do? Some might say that it could shut off funding. With the threat of imprisonment at its collective head? It would huff, fumble, and hold committee hearings. But a coup would have to be squelched immediately or not at all.

My impression is that much of the public wants authoritarian rule, or would be perfectly content with it if it even noticed its arrival. No, I can't prove it. But what do most people care about beyond television on screens that grow ever larger, beyond porn, beer, and the competitive purchase of grander SUVs? I ask this not as a lifelong curmudgeon being tiresome (though doubtless I am both) but seriously. Who in a sprawling TV-besotted country cares about the Constitution? A comfortable police state is after all comfortable.

I do not predict that the reigning curiosity will stage a coup (which should it occur would not be a coup but "an emergency measure," necessary to protect us from Terrace). I do say that what is happening today is unlike anything that has happened before, and that people do not always see what is coming. If you read books from the Germany of the 1930s, you will find that people were uneasy, divided, unsure of things, but had no idea just what the squatty little man with the voice had in mind for them. He just did it. The unimaginable does sometime occur. We notice only afterward.

61

A Laudable Insurrection

When, one wonders, will mutiny begin among the troops in Iraq?

Recently I talked by email about the war with Jim Coyne, an airborne-infantry friend who served two tours as a gunship door-gunner in Viet Nam and then made a career in journalism. I asked, "Do they [I meant the officer corps, the official military] actually believe the optimistic twaddle this time around? Do they really not know what is happening?"

Jim's response: "In my opinion, they really *don't* know; they may not even want to know on some level. You know as well as I, these are mission-oriented folks; *can do* folks; failure and its introspective handmaidens are not options to them. And in a tactical mission-oriented world our military doesn't really fail very often; in a strategic military/political world such as the Mideast and Iraq, however, we simply cannot win.

"Again, as in Viet Nam, the career officer corps salutes and marches toward the sound of battle. Eventually however (and it won't be long now) it's the *grunts* who will begin to revolt, first in small ways (as in the 101st in late 1968, "No sir. We are *not* going up that hill again.") and then, quickly thereafter (As in 1973, "Fuck you, asshole.") By that time the media may get wind of things and spin it exponentially out of control. That's what I think."

So do I.

We have two sharply differing versions of Iraq. One comes from the professional officers. It holds that the military is making progress and the insurgents losing ground. The Iraqi people love us and want the benefits that we will bring them. The increasing attacks by insurgents are signs of desperation. Things seem bad only because the media emphasize the negative. The officers see light at the end of the tunnel. The body counts are great; the bad guys can't much longer take the pounding we are giving them. Onward and upward.

The other view comes from enlisted men (and from a lot of reporters before being edited to say whatever the publisher believes). These assert that the Iraqis hate us and we, them; that the insurgency is growing in strength, that we are not making progress but going backward, that our tactics don't work and we can't win.

The pattern is so common in recent wars as to be routine. The enlisted men know that the US is losing. The officers do not know it, or refuse to know it. This will eventually have consequences.

When men die pointlessly in a war they know cannot be won and that means nothing to them, when they realize that they are dying for the egos of draft-dodging politicians safe in Washington—they will revolt. It happened before. It will happen again. But when? Next year, I'd guess.

It is important to understand that officers and enlisted men are *very* different animals. For example, enlisted men do things (drive the tank, repair the helicopter) whereas officers are chiefly administrators. But the important difference is psychological. Enlisted men are blue-collar guys or technicians. They carry little ideological overburden. They want to fix the tank or finish the field exercise and then go drink beer and get laid.

Above all, they are realists. If the new radio doesn't work, or Baghdad turns out to be a tactically irresolvable nightmare, the enlisted guys feel very little urge to pretend otherwise. This is why officers do not like reporters to be alone with the troops. And they seriously don't.

The standard response of the officer corps is that the troops cannot see the Big Picture. (Unless of course the enlisteds say what the officers want to hear, in which case their experience on the ground lends irresistible authority). But the Big Picture rests on the Little Picture. If a soldier sees slow disaster where he is, and hears the same thing from guys he meets from everywhere else in the country, his conclusions will not be without weight. Sooner or later, on his third tour with a pregnant wife at home and seven friends killed by bombs, he will say, in the crude but expressive language of soldiers, "Fuck this shit."

By contrast, officers can't conclude anything but the positive. There are several reasons. Career officers, first, are politicians. You don't get promoted by saying that the higher-ups are otherworldly incompetents. An officer's loyalty is to his career, and to the officer corps, not to the country or to his troops. If this sounds harsh, note how seldom an active-duty officer will criticize policy, yet when he retires he may suddenly discover that said policy resulted in unnecessary deaths among the troops. Oh? Then why didn't he say so when it would have saved lives?

There is a curious moral cowardice among officers. They will fly dangerous missions over Baghdad, but they won't say that things aren't going well. They don't go against their herd.

Further, and I want to say this carefully, officers often are not quite adults. They can be (and usually are) smart, competent, dedicated, and physically brave, and some are exceedingly hard men. But there is a simple-mindedness about them, an aversion to the handmaidens of introspection, a certain boyishness as in kids playing soldier. A lot of make-believe goes into an officer's world. Enlisted men, grown up, see things as they are. Officers are issued a world by the command and then live in it.

Note the heavy emphasis of the military, meaning the officer corps, on ritual and pageantry. It is adult kid-stuff. Three thousand men building a skyscraper just show up, do their jobs, and go home. The military wants its men standing in squares, precisely at attention, thumbs along the seams, with brass perfectly polished. It wants stirring music, snappy salutes, and the haunting tones of taps, "Yes sir, yes *sir*, three bags full, *sir*." This is justified as necessary for discipline. It isn't. A gunny sergeant has no difficulty maintaining his authority without the hoop-la.

Officers remind me of armed Moonies. There is the same earnestness, the same deliberate optimism-by-policy. Things are going well because doctrine says they are. An officer is as ideologically upbeat as Reader's Digest, and as unreflective. This is the why they don't learn, why the US is again flailing about, trying to use elephant guns to fight hornets. "Yessir, can do, sir." Well, sometimes, and sometimes not. It is not arrogance, more like a belief in gravitation.

And so we hear phrases that embody the eternal precedence of *oo-rah!* over realism: "There is no substitute for victory," or "The difficult we do immediately; the impossible takes a little longer," or "Defeat is not an option." But sometimes it is an inevitability.

I think Jim is right. Sooner or later, a unit won't go up the hill again. Then it will be over.

62

Sex Discrimination

An industry exists today in the writing of pieces proclaiming the weakness of men and the superiority of women, a favorite word in the description of men being "fragile." I weary of it. Women of course engage in this, as do some heterosexual males. Much is made, and should be, over the rising majority of women over men in the universities and some professions. What is this about?

It is not about reality. Fragile men hold nearly every Olympic record in sports in which men compete. In professional sports the sexes compete separately because otherwise there would be no women's sports. On test after test of mental ability, men regularly outscore women: SATs, GREs, National Merit, and so on. In psychometry, it is settled knowledge that at the high end of the scale of intelligence, men outnumber women, and that the higher you go, the more the male preponderance; the disparity in mathematical talent is stark. Even an avowedly liberal psychologist, Paul Irwing of the University of Manchester, writing in *The Independent*, unhappily confessed that there are twice as many men as women with IQs about 120 and 30 times as many over 170. On the other hand, women live longer.

Why, then, the relative decline of men in so many professions?

Some of it is probably that women better tolerate the routine (men would say "boredon") that characterizes most jobs today. Some of it is simply that women are finally competing. On their merits, a lot of women are better than a lot of men at a lot of things, so that, even if we decided things by ability, they would rise. This would be as it should be. But we don't decide things primarily by merit. We decide them by race, creed, color, sex, and national origin.

There is today an enormous amount of affirmative action in favor of women and against men. Much of it is hidden. For example, when boys outperformed girls badly on the National Merit test, a fairly high-end test of scholastic ability, it was modified to reduce the disparity. Few know this.

Much affirmative action, though absurd, occurs openly. When Larry Summers, then president of Harvard, noted that men are better at mathematics, about which there is no doubt, feminists cowed Harvard into promising fifty million dollars to recruit female professors. This is nothing more than extortion.

The SATs were recently slanted ("recentered," I meant to say) to make bright members of the affirmative-action classes (chiefly women and blacks) indistinguishable from Asian and Caucasian males of much higher ability. Universities can then accept the bright girls over the brighter boys without an appearance of discrimination.

School, always unpleasant for rambunctious boys, which is almost to say boys, has been made almost unbearable for them. To be blunt, the schools have been feminized to the point of being hostile to boys, and particularly to bright boys. The sports and roughhousing that boys love have been outlawed as too violent; boys who point fingers and say "bang" are expelled; boys who are not adequately somnolent are drugged by the schools. Competition, upon which boys thrive, is now verboten. When boys reach college, they are likely to be subjected to anti-sexism training which amounts to little more than sanctioned hazing. This seems to spring from sheer female hostility.

But it is working.

In jobs, there is unending pressure to put women (and blacks) into jobs regardless of qualifications; the price for questioning this policy is high. The practice is packaged as pursuit of equality, but it isn't: If eighty percent of students in a medical school are female, this is a triumph for women, but if eighty percent are male, it is sexism and results in recruitment of women by any means.

Special privilege for women is pervasive and enforced by the full weight of government. The federal government has special set-asides and sweetheart deals for businesses owned by women (and blacks). In the military, physical standards as well as the rigorousness of training were greatly diminished so that women could pass. Big Sister watches carefully. A friend of mine moonlights as a one-man shop in graphic design. Periodically he gets a federal form asking how many blacks, women, and so on he employs. Heavy fines attach to failure to respond or false answers.

Further, much policy aims at preventing women from having to compete with men, while making it look as if they were. For example, a company that doesn't hire enough women (or blacks) is subject to federal persecution and private lawsuits; if it then fails to promote them in statistically correct numbers, a company will again pay a heavy price. So it hires them. It is then reported that women (and blacks) are making great strides. Objective measures of merit are discouraged or forbidden. Try giving IQ tests to prospective employees.

A conspicuous example of the illusion of competitiveness was the television show Eco-Challenge in which teams raced each other over courses that required mountain biking, rappelling, swimming, and other physically demanding chores. The rules stated that each team of women had to include at least one man, and each team of men, at least one woman. This produced an appearance of sexual equality. But of course, since the teams had to stay together, each moved only as fast as its slowest member. The women were superb athletes and have my admiration. Yet the question, which this arrangement was designed to avoid answering, is what would have happened if all-male teams had been allowed to compete.

Then there is compulsory togetherness. Great governmental and political emphasis falls, thump, on keeping men from doing anything by themselves. If men want a bar or club of their own where they can enjoy masculine company, women will fight furiously to quash it. Logically they could as well start a bar for women only, to which no man would object. All-male colleges must be integrated (though not all-female ones). There is in all of this a tacit admission of inadequacy: Those who genuinely believe that they can compete don't need federally enforced social access.

Historically of course merit has mattered less than membership in the right group. In particular, men maintained their dominance for thousands of years without regard to the merits of females. In 1900 there were women qualified to serve in congress, or for that matter to do almost anything, but were not allowed to, and there were many men who weren't qualified but did serve. Still, it is annoying to those whites and males who opposed special privilege by race and sex to find that that blacks and women do not want equal opportunity, but special privilege.

But perhaps the math department at Harvard doesn't matter. If no further scientific discovery were ever made, we would be well fed, comfortable, and replete with with video iPods. The modern part of the world, no longer wild and impoverished, has become a vast bureaucracy. Offices require stability and predictability, not great talent, and efficiency seldom matters. What the hell.

63

Ivy Blindness

It occurs to me that a surfeit of money, and the associated life within an invisible plastic bubble that seems to accompany it, may explain many of our curious political lunges. I have nothing against money (you can test this by sending me a lot) or people who have it. But it has side effects.

Two incidents come to mind, of no shattering import but serving as windsocks. First, a politician I barely know, but of import in the making of national policy, told me recently that he had never been in Washington's subway, though he lives in Washington. Second, there was the astonishment of the senior Bush on observing the technology of a checkout line in a supermarket, into none of which had he apparently been. He didn't know how to buy groceries.

I wondered: How much of the dysfunction of national policy can be explained by our rulers' never having been in the subway? Never having encountered the world in which the rest of us, here and abroad, live? Sure, things other than insular innocence play a part: ambition, greed, idealism, vanity, good intentions, bad intentions. But ... how do you manage a world you haven't seen?

I grew up mostly in the South in small towns surrounded by woods. In such places you learn about school-yard fights, in particular that you need either to avoid them or win them, and about hunting rats at the dump with a .410, and working late shift at an Esso station on a lonely highway, and that country boys from poor families don't think like nice suburban people. You still have to deal with them.

Most of us have learned these things, though in different ways and places. A high school in Brooklyn or Casper is different from mine in Virginia, yet very much the same. The young find themselves with a slice of humanity, not all of it agreeable, and have to figure it out on their own. When you learn a high school in Brooklyn, in a sense you learn the United States. I wonder what you learn going to Andover with your chauffeur.

There are experiences, of which few have had all but most have had some, by which people learn how life works. The very rich do not seem to have these. I wonder whether they really know where they live.

During the sixties, I spent time on the big roads, thumbing from coast to coast and from wherever to wherever else. So did countless other kids. (This isn't a column about how special I am, but about how special I'm not.) We learned much about truck stops at three in the morning, about taking care of ourselves on a deserted road at dusk with rain coming on, about the wild variety of people that make up a country and, particularly, about people without a lot of money.

We also learned that there are men who will beat you senseless with a pool cue just because they don't like your looks, and no, they won't listen to reason. Life is not an embassy party.

Do the delicate flowers of *National Review* know these things? Has George Bush even been on the road? Have they seen America from a dying coal camp in West Virginia? A great deal of money is a good thing, or at least one I would like to try. But I suspect it isolates you from the world beyond Yale.

The military is another such adventure, common among the generation which now manages the country. Literally millions passed through the armed services, many of them through the war of their time. In the enlisted military you come to know … many things. You learn how armies work and think, meet black kids from the slums of Chicago and white kids from shadowed valleys of Tennessee, learn what it is to be hungry and exhausted and never able to sleep. You see what a war really is, and what people look like who have been badly hit.

In the White House they don't know these things, or at the slick policy-shop magazines manned by bright Fauntleroys. I am not sure what they do know, other than board rooms and good hotels.

There is the simple matter of working for a living other in an ermine-lined sinecure. Tending bar, for example, driving an eighteen-wheeler, working summers in a saw mill, or doing construction. Starting your own business without daddy's millions. When you know the woman pushing seventy who is waitressing long hours with swollen ankles—"I'm too tired to work, and too poor to quit"—you might change your ideas about, well, lots of things. Some folk don't have silver tea services.

Who in the White House understands any of this?

There is travel of the sort that shows you the planet as it is. If you look in the back streets of Asia and South America, or of Europe for that matter, you will find people, mostly from their late teens to early thirties, who are traveling on a low budget. Sometimes they stay in one place for six months or a year and work on the language. Sometimes they keep moving, backpacking it, grabbing the tramp freighters or rattletrap goat-and-chicken buses. Many are well educated. Not infrequently they are professionals who don't want the Hilton.

On third-class buses in Michoacan, in the ramshackle motor launches in the pampas of Bolivia, they learn … it's hard to say exactly what. A sense of humanity, perhaps, that people in other countries are not dinks, slopes, sand-niggers, zipperheads, spics, dot-niggers, or gooks. They learn, however strange it may seem from Crawford, Texas, that the Laos, Thais, Mexicans and Colombians actually like their countries and cultures, and fiercely resent meddling. This latter has consequences. Consult your newspaper.

They don't know these things in the White House, or at the rattling little policy magazines. I watch as if contemplating idiot children as the current administration consistently and needlessly infuriates other countries by its moral lectures to sovereign states, as it miscalculates over and over the reactions of other nations, as it publicly announces that it is seeking "regime change" here and there. The effect of course is to make people rally around the regime. But in the White House they have no idea.

How could they? They have never been in the real world. How many speak—I'll be kind and say "another language" instead of "any language"?

In that strange real world where most of us live, there are the street trades—police, fire, and ambulance. Granted, these are accessible only to their practitioners and to the occasional reporter. Here you see another United States, that of the huge hermetic slums, and how they work and their intractable misery. You see the ghastly car wrecks and the paramedics who try desperately to get to shock-trauma with something other than a corpse. Have those who set policy for society seen this? Have they seen anything?

A rich friend once invited me to his house in the West End of Richmond, Virginia. At supper when you wanted the mashed potatoes, you didn't say, "Pass the potatoes, please." No. You rang a little bell and a black guy came out and held the bowl while you scooped potatoes. It was hugely embarrassing. I suspect that he felt like a fool. I know I did. I wanted to scream, "What's wrong with these people?" and go have a beer with the black guy.

It doesn't matter whether an investment banker has seen a barracks or a pair of work gloves. Making policy is different. It bothers me to have policy made, and wars started, by those who have never seen the country they rule, or the world they play with, who have never had to make a living, to carry a rifle or worry about snipers, who have never run the back alleys of Taipei or anywhere else and, god help us, can't serve their own potatoes.

64

Turning Fifteen in Messico

A girl only turns fifteen once, so we figured we would do it up right. We did, too. Violeta rushed around for two weeks negotiating for music and food and I invited everybody who needed to be invited and wrote lists of things everywhere and lost them, and Natalia, in the final throes of her fourteenth year, looked nervous. She had never had a monster party thrown in her honor. I guess it would weigh on anyone.

A quinceaños is something like a debutante shindig in the States. Among the over-moneyed they can cost $15,000 without effort, though we spent a tenth of that and Natalia seemed to be just as fifteen when we got through. There's a lot of ceremony involved, or supposed to be. The quinceañera—ie, Natalia—is supposed to begin the evening in flat shoes and then the father, for practical purposes me, replaces them with high heels to signify that she is now a woman. It seemed too complicated, so we dispensed with it. Besides, you can't dance on grass in heels. Unless you want to stay in one place.

Instead we put up a pavilion in the back yard for the kids. The music people came in with huge speakers and two hundred CDs and a deejay. The adults got another pavilion on the mirador, the rooftop patio. The beer company supplied tables and chairs. Vi bought a long ton of shrimp which in the heat of battle we forgot and so we ate shrimp for three days afterwards.

Natalia looked nervous some more and went off to Elisa's to get gussied up. It's what girls do, and a good thing too. It's especially important when they are about to be fifteen. Elisa is the Mexican wife of my friend Larry. She could organize the Normandy landing with the left side of her brain, run IBM with the right, and apply makeup to a quinceañera with the interstices. If you want a complicated party, you need to talk to Elisa. Or if you want the UN actually to work.

People began to trickle in at five. Vi was in a mild frenzy. I surveyed the proceedings with what I hoped was serene masculine confidence. Actually I was sure

an unseasonable rainstorm would break out, the temperature drop into the thirties, and the roof collapse from the weight of the guests.

In Mexico "five o'clock" is another way of saying, "six-thirty." This works well
if you know about it. Not everybody does, so parties get front-loaded with gringos. Tom the Robot came in from Chapala, down the lake a ways, and John, who
was in the Pacific in WWII and has turned himself into a superb photographer,
and Jim Coyne from the wild old days at *Soldier of Fortune* and, well, so on. We
went up on the roof and drank good things while the mountains turned dark and
the lake turned silver and the Mexican kids drifted in and Natalia came back.

Hoo-ah!

To say that she looked nice would be like saying that Godzilla was, like, big.
I'm not sure she quite understood that at these things the adults arrive with pre-
sents for the central young lady. She was delighted to find a mound of books and
blouses and things, and then headed for the yard, now full of kids. The music
started and she looked deliriously happy.

It's working, I thought.

I tried to imagine what it must be like to be a young Mexican girl, and
couldn't. It didn't matter, since she was the one doing it, and seemed to have it
under control. It was hard enough remembering what it was like to be an American boy of fifteen in the countryside of Virginia. I recalled a desperately
unwanted innocence, and a lot of adventures, some of them lawful. But it was
hard to remember not knowing the vast number of things I didn't know then.
You had better be sure when getting rid of innocence, because you can't get it
back. (That's like, you know, profound.)

Adriana Perez Flores, my immigrations attorney, arrived with her husband
Kevin and their two small boys, Marshall and Dillon. (Honest.) Or perhaps
Dylan, now that I think about it. They ended up in the yard watching the adoles-
cents dance. The latter were nice kids. The boys presumably were libidinous hor-
mone-wads, of course, but wholesome libidinous hormone wads. To the extent
possible. Kids have to figure out this sex stuff, which they usually think their generation invented, but some ways of approaching it are more civilized than others.

It's funny. Kids are kids, but these seemed less—"jaded" may be the
word—than American kids of the same age. Less used up, less unhappy even. I'm
not suggesting any sort of moral superiority. Kids here get pregnant at a pretty
good clip, though not, I suspect, Natalia's friends. But they seem to be kids,
doing kid things, whereas Americans look tired.

I could say something facile, such as that the American young seem to learn
too much too fast, but the kids here know where babies come from. They get

detailed sex-ed classes. Drugs are available here, mostly marijuana, but they seem less a problem. On the other hand, American kids are more independent, readier to set out into the world, to backpack to Tibet or go to college on the other end of the continent. Mexicans are homebodies. You pays your money and takes your choice.

By eleven, things were winding down. Several kids and Natalia were still dancing, which Mexicans do naturally. They're Latins. (It's a scientific fact that Protestants don't have hips. It says so in Gray's Anatomy.) A fair few empty beer bottles suggested that some tippling had taken place, but what the hell. In Joco, you walk home. If the occasional Dos Equis is presented as not greatly forbidden, then kids have less desire to get blotto to defy their parents.

By midnight we had shut the music down. We have to live with the neighbors. Vi and I chatted with Ron the Mechanic, the last of the guests. He is a tall lanky Canadian who bailed out many years back and now fixes cars for expats. Then Ron too left. Natalia was still glowing. Fifteen.

65

Fred: A True Son of Tzu.
Guderian was the Mother

Being a military thinker of the profoundest sort, I offer the following manual of martial affairs for nations yearning to copy the American way of war. Read it carefully. Great clarity will result. The steps limned below will facilitate disaster without imposing the burden of reinventing it. The Pentagon has my permission to print copies for distribution.

(1) Underestimate the enemy. Fortunately this is easy when a technologically advanced power prepares to attack an underdeveloped nation. Its enemy's citizens will readily be seen as gadgetless, primitive, probably genetically stupid, and hardly worth the attention of a real military.

(2) Avoid learning anything about the enemy—his culture, religion, language, history, or response to past invasions. These things don't matter since the enemy is gadgetless, primitive, and probably genetically stupid. Anyway, knowledge would only make the enlisted ranks restive, and confuse the officer corps.

Blank ignorance of the language is especially desirable (as well as virtually guaranteed). For one thing, it will allow your troops to be seen as brutal invaders having nothing in common with the population; this helps in winning hearts and minds. For another, it will allow English-speaking officials of the puppet government to vet such information about the country as they permit you to have.

(3) Explain the invasion to the American public in simple moral terms suitable for middle-school children at an evangelical summer camp: We are bombing cities to bring the gift of democracy and American values, or to defeat some vague but frightening evil, perhaps lurking under the bed, or to get rid of a bad dictator no longer of service to us, or to bring freedom and prosperity to any survivors. (This doesn't work in Europe, which is honestly imperialistic.) The public can then feel a sense of unappreciated virtue when the primitives resist. Sententious moralism should always trump reason.

(4) A misunderstanding of military reality helps. Besides, comprehension would only lead to depression. As Napoleon said, or may have, in war the moral is to the material as three is to one, which implies that unpleasant facts should be played down in favor of cultivating a cheerful attitude. Most especially, it should not be noted that a few tens of thousands of determined, probably genetically-stupid primitives with small arms can tie down a large cheerful force however gaudily armed.

Pay no attention to tactics, which are boring. It should never enter your mind that in this sort of war, if you don't win, you lose; if the enemy doesn't lose, he wins. Think about something else. Above all, do not understand that the enemy's target is not you, but public opinion at home. You don't need to remember this, as the enemy will remember it for you.

(5) Do not forget that a military's reason for existence is to close with the enemy and destroy him. An army is not in the social-services business. Do not let the mission be impeded by touchy-feely considerations. If you have to kill seventeen children to get a sniper, so be it. The enemy must realize that you mean business. Ignore cultural traits, which are of concern only to idealistic civilians. Grope the enemy's women. High-profile rapes are a good idea as they teach respect. It is better to be feared than loved. Be sure the embassy has a helipad.

(6) Intellectual insularity should be a primary goal, as it avoids distraction. This salubrious condition can be achieved by having officers read Tom Clancy instead of history. In military discourse it also helps to encourage the use of phrases like "force multiplier" and "multi-dimensional warfare," as these increase confidence without meaning anything.

Remember that doctrine and optimism should always outweigh history and common sense. Discourage colonels and above from reading about similar campaigns fought by other armies, as this might lead to nagging doubts, conceivably even to thought. Encourage the belief that other countries have lost wars by being inferior to the United States. "The French lost in Viet Nam? What else would you expect from the French? Never happen to us."

Some military philosophers favor actually removing from military libraries books on what happened to the French in Viet Nam, the Americans in Viet Nam, the Russians in Afghanistan, the Americans in Afghanistan (a work in progress), the French in Algeria, the Americans in Iraq (also in progress), the Israelis in Lebanon the first time, the Israelis in Lebanon the last time, the Americans in Lebanon 1983, the Americans in Somalia the first time, and so on. However, the best thinkers hold that it doesn't matter what books are in military libraries, as only those on stirring victories will be checked out.

(7) Keep up to date with the latest nostrums and silver bullets. Organize your military as a lean, mean, high-tech force characterized by lightning mobility, enormous firepower, and extraordinary unsuitability for the kind of wars it will actually have to fight. Flacks from the PR department of Lockheed will help in this. Recognize that an advanced fighter plane costing two hundred million dollars, invisible to radar, employing dazzling electronic countermeasures, and able to cruise at supersonic speed, is exactly the thing for fighting a rifleman in a basement in Baghdad. Such aircraft are crucial force multipliers in multi-dimensional warfare. Anyway, Al Quaeda might field an advanced air force at any moment. It pays to be ready.

(8) It is a good idea to bracket your exposure. Be ready for wars past and future, but not present. The Pentagon does this well. Note that the current military, an advanced version of the WWII force, is ready should the Imperial Japanese Navy return. It also has phenomenally advanced weaponry in the pipeline to take on a space-age enemy, perhaps from Mars, should one appear. It is only the present for which the US is not prepared.

(9) View things in a large context. People who have little comprehension of the military tend to focus exclusively on winning wars, missing the greater importance of the Pentagon as an economic flywheel. Jobs are more important than wars fought in bush-world countries. An American military ought to think of Americans first. This is simple patriotism. It is essential to spend as much money as possible on advanced weapons that have no current use, and none in sight, but produce jobs in congressional districts. Good examples are the F-22 fighter, the F-35, the Airborne Laser, the V-22, and the ABM.

(10) Insist that the US military never loses wars. Instead, it is betrayed, stabbed in the back, and brought low by treason. For example, argue furiously that the US didn't lose in Viet Nam, but won gloriously; the withdrawal was due to the treachery of Democrats, Jews, hippies, the press, most of the military, and a majority of the general population, all of whom were traitors. This avoids the unpleasantness of learning anything from defeat. Further, it facilitates a focus on controlling the press, who are the real enemy, along with the Democrats and the general population.

(11) Avoid institutional memory. Not having lost of course means that there is nothing to remember. Instead, read stirring novels and cultivate a cheerful, can-do attitude unintimidated by primitives in sand-lot countries, who are probably genetically stupid.

(12) Do it all again next time.

66

Peeing on Hydrants: Thought on the Human Male

I sometimes think that the defects of men, and the virtues of women, are equally understated. An unreconstructed male will say that men have invented most of civilization and built this and that, which is true. Feminists measure themselves by the extent to which they manage to resemble men, which is a mistake. Both largely overlook the gravest plague to afflict humanity: the infernal and irremediable aggressiveness of males.

When one speaks of being uneasy at having wandered into a bad neighborhood, it is solely from fear of attack by the males, is it not? If a woman's car breaks down on a lonely road at night, she will be frightened of attack not by women or wild animals, but only by men. People do not avoid bar districts in the neighborhoods of the lower classes from wise concern about drunken pugnacious women. Men attack. Women don't.

Physical incapacity has little to do with it. While the average woman cannot beat up the average man, three could, if accustomed to fighting. Women are neither accustomed to fighting nor interested in doing it. It is not by mere extended coincidence that nine of ten people in prison are men. The cause is their inherent aggressiveness. Theirs is the behavior of ownerless dogs living in the street.

"Hey, muthuh*fuckuh*, who you lookin' at?"

Men, like street dogs, are both territorial and creatures of the pack. It starts early because it is instinctive. A boy of eleven showing up at a new school will be eyed by the other boys, tested, regarded with initial suspicion—but only by the boys. He earns his place in the pack. The girls are far more likely to say, "Hi, I'm Sally. What's your name?" The little boys in a neighborhood form gangs, perfectly harmless in suburbs of the middle classes but gangs nevertheless, and guard their territory against intruders. They are playing, as puppies play. They are practicing for more serious times.

Come puberty and, in bad neighborhoods, things become ominous. The young males are now propelled by adult muscle and impelled by combative hormones. The Crips and Bloods in California, the Jets and Sharks of light opera, the Vice Lords, El Ruykns, Latin Kings, Black Gangster Disciples and so on of Chicago, the Hells Angels and the Confederate Angels and the Sons of Silence of motorcycledom: They are now dangerous.

They still closely resemble both street dogs and eleven-year-olds in fundamental motivation. They are intensely territorial. Members of one gang are very aware of the unwisdom of going into the neighborhoods of another. They have elaborate means of indicating membership in the pack: gang signs made with the hands, hats worn at specific orientations, jackets of particular colors, tattoos. The Hells Angels will beat you to death if you wear their paraphernalia. The graffiti sprayed everywhere nowadays in cities are precisely the territorial markings engaged in by male dogs, though the means differ. Despite the occasional stories asserting that girls are now forming violent gangs, they don't. The appeal of hostile bands works its sordid magic only on males.

The instinctive (and sexual) foundations of all of this are obvious in other things. A young American male in, say, Asia, will find the local women willing to date him for all the usual reasons that cause women to date men. (Note the theme of *West Side Story*, which in this respect is perfectly accurate.) The local men will watch with hostility, however disguised. Males try to prevent access by outsiders to the women of their group. Thus they are less concerned about intrusion into their regions by white-haired men. These pose no sexual threat.

Within a society, the aggressiveness of the males can be moderated by rigorous enforcement of civility. In particular, the unshirted sexual forwardness of the male can be abated: A man in a suit seldom says, "Nice tits, baby," or grabs a handful, though both thoughts occur to him. This is why feminists are fools to deride the twin concepts, Lady and Gentleman. But even among the socially elevated, such street-doggery as dueling has often existed. The elaborate ritual of throwing down the gauntlet is nothing more than an elegant form of the gangbanger's strut-and-holler. Hey, muthuh*fuckuh*....

The aggressiveness of males has wreaked unremitting havoc throughout history in the form of war. Women don't do war, don't like war, don't fantasize about war. They put up with it. *Lysistrata*, though written by a man, captures the distaff mind well.

These days every war is said to have some justification of the most solemn import, but it's just Crips and Bloods. Among primitive peoples a young man becomes a warrior through some curious rite, and then goes on raids to steal horses and women. With us it's boot camp, jump wings, Ranger patch, and raids to impose democracy. The essential difference is as follows:

What we call statesmanship is, emotionally and morally, indistinguishable from gang war in South Chicago. The scale is more imposing and, under some administrations, the grammar better. Aggressive males rise to power in heavily armed countries of many millions. Then they push and shove, bark and bow-wow at others like themselves in other countries. The tribal trappings remain, particularly among the warriors: Baubles and medals and patches and different hats, talk of honor and duty and valor. Nah. Male dogs in an alley.

Women have very little use for it, though there is precious little they can do to change things. Their focus is different. In three decades of covering the military, I noticed that women thought in terms of people. To a male, a firestorm in Hamburg ignited by bombing constitutes a great victory. To a woman, it is tens of thousands of people burned alive. She is likely to ask, "Are we sure this is a good idea?" The aggressive male doesn't want to hear about children being roasted to death and (I've been through this with them countless times) gets angry if you bring it up. He uses phrases like "collateral damage," or says, "In war, shit happens. Deal with it." Among men, "Anti-war" is likely to be an insult; among women, a compliment.

Male aggressiveness pervades human life. It fuels the unending drive to found empires. A woman might say, "Look, Alex, you've got a perfectly good palace in Macedon, plenty to eat, a bar on the corner, nice women. Are you quite sure you need to conquer India? What are you going to do with it?" Men are more likely than women to favor capitalism (or "free enterprise" or "unrestricted rapine," according to your politics) than women because it sanctifies commercial combat. Fifty billion isn't enough, I must destroy the competition and eradicate Linux....

What to do about it? Nothing, at least any time soon.

67

Can Israel Last?

I wonder what is going to happen to Israel. Its existence depends entirely on its only ally, the United States. American support depends on the Israeli Lobby. Independent of the Lobby, a lot of Americans support Israel for many reasons, yes: Varieties of Christians for reasons of religion, people who see the Moslem world as a national enemy, those who think that Israel should be left alone to live in peace, and those who don't precisely support Israel but don't want to see what would happen if it were overrun. Together, these are not a contemptible constituency.

But most of this is soft support. As long as the price of backing Israel is a few billions a year, the supply of weaponry, and vetoes in the United Nations, few will object. But the world is changing. America appears to be on the verge of becoming a greatly reduced power. Where will that leave Israel?

Even now, neither the Israeli nor the US military is convincingly dominant. The American forces are enormous but designed for wars they are not going to fight. Carrier task forces, armored divisions, and nuclear submarines would excel against the Imperial Japanese Navy or the Red Army in the Fulda Gap. They lose to ragtag guerrillas. The ragtag guerrillas have noticed this. America hasn't won a war since 1945.

The Israeli military is similar, relying on aircraft and tanks. Israel cannot successfully invade Lebanon against the wishes of irregulars, nor the United States defeat a small force of insurgents. As long as Israel is supported by the US, no Arab power will have any hope of invading it, but Israel's capacity to intimidate neighboring powers has diminished. Times have changed.

Which brings us to nuclear weapons. These, as long as Israel has them and her enemies do not, serve as a trump card. Should Syria attack and begin to win, it would simply disappear, and knows it. But if Moslem nations have the Bomb, then Israel risks nuclear retaliation if it uses its own. This (I suspect), not the dan-

214

ger of an unprovoked attack by Iran, is the importance of a Moslem Bomb. Perhaps Iran can be prevented from building nuclear weapons, but it hasn't been yet.

Mr. Bush seems to be losing his wars. If I'm wrong, I'm wrong, which would probably be a good thing. But if I'm right, when the United States is forced out of Iraq, American influence in the region will decline precipitately. For at least a decade, and perhaps forever, the US will not send troops to the region. The Moslem world will regard itself, correctly, as having defeated the Great Satan, and will no longer fear Washington. American control of Pakistan will probably vanish and, bingo, there's the Islamic Bomb. Presumably the American puppets, such as Saudi Arabia, will blow with the prevailing winds.

The rub is that the industrial world lives on oil. Much of it lies in nations that now detest the United States or, as in the case of Russia, see themselves as being in competition with the United States. Mr. Bush has also made a policy of antagonizing, well, everybody, but in particular Venezuela, which is visibly looking to change markets eastward. Crucially, the emerging Asian giants offer the oil producers other buyers for their oil.

If those with oil loathe America, no longer fear it, and have other markets, they are likely to say, "Choose: Israel or oil." Then what? In the long run there are solar power, oil shale, and so on. But we live in the short run.

How does American domestic politics play into this? If the consequences of declining American power are slight, if the price of gasoline goes up a bit and the shift of economic dominance to China runs gradually, little will happen domestically. Let us hope. But if the effects are more drastic, people will look for someone to blame. Israel is an obvious designated villain and, by extension, Jews. There is a lot of this, sotto voce, on the web.

It isn't particularly rational. Of the chief advocates of the Moslem wars, who could stop them tomorrow—Bush, Cheney, Rice and Rumsfeld—none is Jewish. Bush and his faithful dog Blair are clinical Christians. Many non-Jewish interests favor the war: the Religious Right, military industry (after all, when you spend hundreds of billions on a war it goes into somebody's pockets), Big Oil, barking patriots, and those multitudinous Americans who like the idea of empire but won't quite say so.

However, a vaguely Christian country isn't going to blame its disasters on Christianity. The military industry will cover itself in patriotism and say, "We were only filling orders." Big Oil is awfully abstract, and anyway we all like gasoline. The imperialists will say they weren't really. Etc. Who does that leave?

I don't suggest that some deep well of Polish-style anti-Semitism exists in the US waiting to erupt. It doesn't. Serious hostility to Jews, if not dead, is at least on a respirator in America. Yet there is enough suspicion that The Lobby had something to do with getting the US into war that, should the affright in the Mid-East lead to serious domestic hardship, blaming Israel will be tempting. A high proportion of the neoconservatives who push the wars are Jewish, as is widely noted on the internet, and the wars can easily be packaged as being fought in the service of Israel. Whether this is true matters little. (I argue that the wars, threatening to drive America out of the Mideast, will prove catastrophic for Israel.) Lobbying for the country would then become politically more difficult.

Bear in mind that Israel is susceptible to all manner of emotionally appealing criticism for such things as brutality toward the Palestinians. Actually of course Israel has done nothing to Palestinians that the US isn't doing to Iraqis, or didn't do to the Vietnamese, on a far larger scale and with far less justification. But this won't matter. Countries seldom look at their own defects. Always one sees warts on those one wishes to have warts, while ignoring one's own. (Observe that Mr. Bush, operating a Latin Lubyanka in Guantanamo, criticizes Cuba for violations of human rights.)

The foregoing contains a lot of ifs. Bush hasn't withdrawn from Iraq, Iran doesn't have the Bomb, and no American domestic consequences have occurred. They may not. If Bush wins, Israel will be safe for the foreseeable future. Otherwise, we will have a small, nuclear-armed country that won't roll over and die, has nowhere to go, and at this point probably can't make peace with its enemies. The latter will regard themselves as being on the march and see no reason to compromise. The Moslems will control their own oil, and America will have to suck up to them. Where will that leave Israel? What resolution would be possible?

By way of PS: An internet columnist has more of a window than most people, though a skewed window, on such things as anti-Semitism. Over the years, I've written several columns suggesting that Jews aren't terrible people, or at least no more terrible than the rest of humanity, which I grant to be faint praise. The response, while not a statistically valid sample, has always been markedly more favorable than hostile. However, I do get a regular smattering of anti-Jewish mail, as for example the following, from one who signs himself only Hengist73@aol.com

"Fred,

You are a whore.

A jew-media whore, charlatan and race traitor.

To hell with you Fred, and to hell you are undoubtedly bound.

Enjoy!"

Actually I am a Presbyterian media whore, though probably hell-bound, where I expect to meet Calvin. I confess myself intimidated by the crystalline clarity of Mr. Hengist73's intellect, by his weighty erudition and sparkling logic, all embedded in the lucent amber of elevated thought. But such people are out there.

68

Rotting Away Down South

For most gringos, Mexico is a place to retire. The Mexicans say, "The Americans come here to die." Not exactly. It isn't why they come, but it is what they do, there being eventually no choice. Everybody has to croak somewhere, so why not in the sunshine with little brown kids running back and forth and the street dogs lounging contentedly about? It beats, for some anyway, a wretched sanitarium and lots of tubes.

In the hills on the north side of town, where the nice houses are, you see aging couples like couples anywhere. It could be Lauderdale. They have each other and insurance and pensions and savings. In the bars you see the old single guys. They have close to nothing.

At nine in the morning they sit on green iron benches and wait for the cantinas to open. Little beyond white hair unites them in appearance. Some are thin, others fat, others whatever you can think of except moneyed. "Drunks" is not quite the right word for them. They are just old guys whose lives are spent. They sit around and drink beer and wait. It's what they have. They seldom fall off stools or get into fights. They are anything but dangerous. They are just old guys with nothing, waiting.

Some would find them reprehensible. Why don't they do something improving, learn to knit, or take up square dancing? This is harsh. What does a man do when he is seventy years old, his wife died eight years ago in Louisiana, and the trucking firm no longer wants him as a driver? Social Security and a small pension don't go far in America. He comes to Ajijic and moves into the residential hotel, Italo's, a block from the plaza and easy walking distance to the bars. It's cheap and decent and the rooms come with kitchenette and the maids clean them. I've stayed there.

He's seventy and tired, too old to learn a language and probably not of that bent anyway. He doesn't want to learn to square dance. He is not looking for a cultural experience, not looking for much of anything. Women no longer interest him except as nice people, and anyway the diabetes doesn't help in that depart-ment. So he talks to his friends. And he drinks. It takes the curse off. Besides, if he bothers no one else, it is the business of no one else—n'est-ce pas?

It is a mistake to think these men to be of no account because they are ending their days on a bar stool. They have had lives, traveled, drifted, worked, loved, had families or not, seen things and done things. Often they are intelligent and thoughtful. They are just through.

We live in a censorious age in America, an age of "Gotcha!" in which drinking looms loathsome, smoking is a crime to be punished, second-hand smoke a fear-ful threat to children and plants and wallpaper. Oh dear. We all must be vigilant for racism, sexism, and the rest. Psychologists call it "passive aggressiveness," though I think that "the Higher Priss" does nicely. Well, I say, each to his or her or its own. Still, I have always found people who smoke and drink and do the occasional doob to be more interesting than those who don't—certainly than the drab Comstocks of the current Carryan Nation.

So I'll cut these guys some slack. You choose an exit door, or fall through one. They have. So will you.

Not all stay in one place. In Italo's when I was there I met a guy well into his seventies who was about to get on a third-class bus to Guatemala, I think it was. He didn't walk too well and moved as if he had sand in his joints. He seemed sad but was keeping his chin up. He knew a hotel in a nice town outside Guatemala City where the food was cheap and the young girls just so pretty. He meant noth-ing sexual. They were just pretty, like pictures. He liked watching them and the kids and Guatemala.

Now that's rough, I thought. To be at the end of his days and bouncing around bad roads on a Guatemalan bus, alone, going where he probably knew nobody—that's not the feather-bed route out the door. But he didn't want to spend the winter in Ajijic. At least he was free. I wished him well.

Some drunks have other stories. There was a fellow, in his thirties I'd guess, who always wore a white cowboy hat and lied compulsively about what daring things he had done. This is common. It's called "border promotion." You know: "I was a SEAL team leader before I was an astronaut, between being a fighter pilot and president of IBM." Sometimes it seems like half the gringo population used to be in the CIA.

Anyway, the guy with the white cowboy hat said he used to be a dead-end drunk, and had the tremor to prove it. But he was over it, he said, and in fact seemed to be. Then one night he got a ride home with somebody, pulled a pistol from somewhere, put it under his chin and blew the top of his head off. AIDS, or at least HIV. We make our choices. The consensus was that he should have done it somewhere else, where it wouldn't have put a hole in the roof of the car and generally made a mess.

Sometimes one of the old guys will take up with a poor Mexican gal of twenty-five with four kids. They move in together. You could say that it was absurd, that neither knew the other's language and he was a dirty old man and she a gold-digger. You could also try to exercise a little decency. Not everybody has choices. Usually he treats her well, puts food on the table, maybe gets her some dental work or insists that the kids go to school. It's better than nothing. She cooks and keeps house and has a few years of security, and he leaves her whatever he can. I've seen such couples who seemed happy together. You play the hand you draw.

Things are different for those of intellectual resources, who take up photography seriously, fly ultralights, read, or keep on at whatever they did for a living at a reduced level. I'm not sure just how different things are, though. They too are waiting. So are we all. But there were drunks before there were moralists, and I hope there will be drunks after, as they are so much less tedious, and closer to the human condition.

69

Suckering the Troops

It's all but official: The war in Iraq is lost. Report after leaked report says so. Everybody in Washington knows it except that draft-dodging ferret in the White House. Politicians scurry to avoid the blame. One day soon people will ask aloud: How did we let several thousand GIs die for the weak ego of a pampered liar and his desperate need to prove he's half the man his father was?

The troops from now on will die for a war that they already know is over. They are dying for politicians. They are dying for nothing. By now they must know it. It happened to us, too, long ago.

The talk among pols now is about finding an "exit strategy." This means a way of pulling out without risking too many seats in Congress. Screw the troops. We must look to the elections. Do we really want an exit strategy? A friend of mine, with two tours in heavy combat in another war, has devised a splendid exit strategy. It consists of five words: "OK. On the plane. Now." Bring your toothbrush. Everything else stays. We're outa here.

It is a workable exit strategy, one with teeth, and comprehensible to all. But we won't use it. We will continue killing our men, calculatedly, cynically, for the benefit of politicians. The important thing, you see, is the place in history of Bush Puppy. Screw the troops.

Face it. The soldiers are being used. They are being suckered. This isn't new. It happened to my generation. Long after we knew that the war in Vietnam was lost, Lyndon Johnson kept it going to fertilize his vanity, and then Nixon spoke of the need to "save face"—at two hundred dead GIs a week. But of course Johnson and Nixon weren't among the dead, or among the GIs.

I saw an interview on television long ago in which the reporter asked an infantryman near Danang, I think, what he thought of Nixon's plan to save face. The reply was, "His face, our ass." Just so, then, and just so now. Screw the troops. What the hell, they breed fast in Kansas anyway.

Soldiers are succinct and do not mince words. This makes them dangerous. We must keep them off-camera to the extent possible. A GI telling the truth could set recruiting back by years.

The truth is that the government doesn't care about its soldiers, and never has. If you think I am being unduly harsh, read the *Washington Post*. You will find story after story saying that the Democrats don't want to do anything drastic about the war. They fear seeming "soft on national security." In other words, they care more about their electoral prospects in 2008 than they do about the lives of GIs. It's no secret. For them it is a matter of tuning the spin, of covering tracks, of calculating the vector sum of the growing unrest and the ardent-patriot vote, which may be cooling, deciding which way the liberal wind blows, and staying poised to seem to have supported whoever wins. Screw the troops. Their fathers probably work in factories anyway.

Soldiers do not realize, until too late, the contempt in which they are held by their betters. Here is the psychological foundation of the hobbyist wars of bus-station presidents. If you are, say, a Lance Corporal in some miserable region of Iraq, I have a question for you: Would your commanding general let you date his daughter? I spent my high-school years on a naval base, Dahlgren Naval Proving Ground as it was then called. Dahlgren was heavy with officers, scientists, and engineers. Their daughters, my classmates, were not allowed to associate with sailors. Oh yes, we honor our fighting men. We hold them in endless respect. Yes we do.

For that matter, Lance Corporal, ask how many members of Congress have even served, much less been in combat. Ask how many have children in the armed services. Look around you. Do you see many (any) guys from Harvard? Yale? MIT? Cornell? Exactly. The smart, the well-off, the powerful are not about to risk their irreplaceable sit-parts in combat. Nor are they going to mix with mere high-school graduates, with kids from small towns in Tennessee, with blue-collar riffraff who bowl and drink Bud at places with names like Lenny's Rib Room. One simply doesn't. One has standards.

You are being suckered, gang, just as we were.

It is a science. The government hires slick PR firms and ad agencies in New York. These study what things make a young stud want to be A Soldier: a desire to prove himself, to get laid in foreign places, a craving for adventure, a desire to feel part of something big and powerful and respected, what have you. They know exactly what they are doing. They craft phrases, "Be a Man Among Men," or "A Few Good Men," or, since girls don't like those two, "The Few, The Proud." Join up and be Superman.

Then comes the calculated psychological conditioning. There is for example the sense of power and unity that comes of running to cadence with a platoon of other guys, thump, thump, thump, all shouting to the heady rhythm of boots, "If I die on the Russian front, bury me with a Russian cunt, *Lef*-rye-lef-rye-lef-rye-*lef*...." That was Parris Island, August of '66, and doubtless they say something else now, but the principle is the same.

And so you come out in splendid physical shape and feeling no end manly and they tell you how noble it is to Fight for Your Country. This might be true if anyone were invading the country. But since Washington always invades somebody else, you are actually fighting for Big Oil, or Israel, or the defense industry, or the sexual ambiguities who staff *National Review*, or the vanity of that moral dwarf on Pennsylvania Avenue. You will figure this out years later.

Once you are in the war, you can't get out. We couldn't either. While your commander in chief eats steak in the White House and talks tough, just like a real president, you kill people you have no reason to kill, about whom you know next to nothing—which one day may weigh on your conscience. It does with a lot of guys, but that comes later.

You are being suckered, and so are the social classes that supply the military. Note that the Pentagon cracks down hard on troops who say the wrong things online, that the White House won't allow coffins to be photographed, that the networks never give soldiers a chance to talk unedited about what is happening. Oh no. It is crucial to keep morale up among the rubes. You are the rubes. So, once, were we.

70

Hangmen of the Arts

The arts, I say, constitute a brazen fraud—the arts at least as peddled in boutiques, sanctified in galleries, and rattled-on about by professors who ought to find productive jobs.

To begin with, the poseurs who have awarded themselves charge of the arts wouldn't recognize an art if they found it swimming in their soup. It is true. Start with literature. I have read several times over the years of wags who copied out three chapters of some classic—*The Reavers*, or *Moby Dick* ("Call me Fishmeal")—and sent them, perhaps with the names changed, to publishing houses in New York. Invariably they were rejected. The professional judges of manuscripts recognized neither the books nor good writing. You would get better results having literature judged by a committee of taxi-drivers.

I ask you this: Suppose I went pub-crawling in London and stumbled on an unknown play by Shakespeare, the equal of *Lear* and unquestionably genuine. Maybe Shakespeare had left his driver's license with it. Suppose further that I sent it to New York, and to the English department at Harvard (which these days might or might not have heard of Shakespeare) and told them that it was my senior essay in creative writing at Texas A&M.

Are you sufficiently hallucinatory to expect an explosion of appreciation? "My god, we've found genius in the outback!" or maybe, "Geez, this kid writes like he'd actually been there!"

No. There would be condescension and polite silence. The perfessors don't think old Bill is good because he is good, which they are not capable of ascertaining, but because he is Bill. You could show them a pizza order signed "Willybill S.," on decayed parchment, tell them that it was found at Stratford, and they would wet themselves with emotion. Double cheese, anchovies.

Fact is, most art isn't. Let some cultural executioner hang anybody in a museum, and he becomes Art, sort of by appointment. The critics will then make a career of sitting around appreciating themselves for appreciating him. Criticism is about critics; the art is barely necessary.

Or again, take The Bard, as we say more pompously than absolutely necessary—good phrase-maker, tired plots, low plausibility, but suitable for a quick buck with a mob audience. Twelve thousand PhD theses later and he has had all manner of dreadful significance read into him that would never have occurred to the man.

On television I saw the story of a rich woman in New York who had, she thought, and so did others, a genuine Somebody. You know, Renoir or Gauguin or what have you. She was no end proud, kept it in a thermally controlled room, and fed it nothing but exotic cheeses and designer water. Critics came to visit it. They said, "Ah! The light …" and "Oh! The masterly play of …" and "Only He could have…." Then it turned out that the paint had been made in 1947. The value dropped by several million dollars, the critics vanished, and the woman probably didn't commit suicide but it would have been a good end to the story.

Which shows that painting has nothing to do with beauty but only with sniffishness and social predation among the cerebrally understated with too much money. A Degas on the Upper West Side (I think that's a good address) is the equivalent of, in a sports bar, a baseball signed by Willy Mays. (If the ball were signed "Claude Monet," it would be in a temperature-controlled case on the Upper West Side.) Should a painting be adjudged of value for what it looked like, then you wouldn't care who did it. But when the point of the game is name-dropping, then the only reliable art critic is a mass spectrometer.

But if we rashly assume that art has something to do with beauty (it doesn't), think about copies. In Italy a girlfriend and I once went to see Michelangelo's David ("Old Marble Dick," she called him. Women have no respect.) Now, David's a pretty good statue. I won't deny it. He could hold a lantern on *my* lawn any day, though he might need pants. What if you took a laser scanner and made a copy of Dave accurate to within the radius of a marble atom (we'll assume here that marble is atomic) and colored it perfectly? Let's say that no critic yet born could tell it from the original. So why wouldn't it be worth as much?

Because art isn't about Beauth or Trudy. It's about staying ahead of the Hirschorns. It's a scam. It's a racket.

You may now want to say, "Fred, you obviously think that there is no art. How can you be such a cultural Philippine? Can centuries of art critics all be wrong?" Sure. And, yes, I could think that there was no art. I am professionally perverse enough. Anyway, you can see the evidence in any museum.

But in fact I don't think it. Actually there is lots of art. Thing is, unless you build a museum around it, it doesn't count.

Look, there are three hundred million people in the United States, let alone everywhere else. Artistically this is probably equivalent to ten billion Frenchmen in 1890 because almost all Americans have the time and minor disposable income to paint or play the saxophone in a chamber group. Most don't. But they could. Yes, the truth is that lots of those Impressionistic frogs were really damned good. But can you possibly imagine that America, or France for that matter, couldn't find twenty times as many people as good today if we looked?

It wouldn't take much looking. In Washington D of C, there is the Corcoran Gallery, which annually has a contest in which (I think I have this right) every state sends paintings by a couple of its best high-school artists. This is an extraordinarily good idea, but they do it anyway. I know about this because my daughter Macon was in it for Virginia and ended up getting her stuff sent to New York somewhere to be hung for a while, like John Brown. (Talent skips generations. That's why.)

Anyway, I propose the following for any who are interested in art: Go to Washington when the Corcoran has the show. Start by spending several days at the National Gallery on the Mall. The collection is pretty good. In addition to the usual there are paintings by Thomas Cole, Cropsey, Durand, Church and suchlike that you don't hear about because they aren't European. (More fraud. See?) Of course there is the tiresome Early Christian stuff, all gold foil and grotesque misshapen babies, and overdone post-card painters like Redon. Never mind. A fair bit of it is tolerable.

Don't go in the usual state of intimidation expected of hayseeds in galleries: "Gee, I'm just a lowly pedestrian slug, and in the presence of genius, and don't understand Art, and if it looks like this turkey can't draw, there must be something wrong with me...." More likely, the turkey can't draw.

Then go to the Corcoran to see what the kids have done. You will find freshness, imagination, and unabashed talent. You can't call it that, though, without showing yourself to be a rube. If you told the critics it had been found in Cezanne's basement, or a tomb in Egypt, they would run for their swooning couches like a herd of enraptured bison, so great would be their appreciation. But if it's signed by Sally Tugwinkle of Broken Needle, Arkansas ... naah, doesn't count.

Ages ago when my younger daughter Emily, now a blues singer in San Francisco, was eight or nine, we went to the Hirschorn in DC. There we encountered a white canvas, about the size of a ping-pong table, blank except for a red circle, as large as a healthy orange, in one corner. It was Art. The museum said so. We dutifully appreciated at it. Later I asked her what she thought.

The scorn would have curdled motor oil.

"Big deal. A *red dot*. Gag me."

Sound judgement, clarity of expression, no frou-frous. Now that's criticism.

About the Author

Fred Reed is an ex-Marine keyboard mercenary and part-time sociopath with thirty years as a police reporter and military correspondent. He lives in Mexico near Guadalajara, and detests almost everything. When he isn't writing scurrilous commentary, he is usually drinking Padre Kino red and smoking Cuban cigars.

978-0-595-44374-1
0-595-44374-5

45891607R00146

Made in the USA
Middletown, DE
16 July 2017